# Egypt

*Civilization in the Sands*

To all those close to us, young
and old, who share our passions
and insatiable curiosity.



Original Title: *L'Egypte des sables. Une civilisation du désert*



Translation from French: Tim Jones, Rösrath
Denise Barstow-Girel, LeMans
Isobel Kerr, Bonn
Editing: Bessie Blum, Cambridge, MA
Proofreading: Lizzie Frege, Cologne
Typesetting: Agents - Producers - Editors, Overath
Project Management: Tammi Reichel for A - P - E, Overath
Project Coordination: Nadja Bremse-Koob
Production: Ursula Schümer
Printing and Binding: Stige, San Mauro

Printed in Italy

ISBN 3-8290-5441-6

10 9 8 7 6 5 4 3 2 1

Pauline and Philippe de Flers

# Egypt
*Civilization in the Sands*

KÖNEMANN

*Let us search like those who must*
*find, and let us find as those who*
*must continue to search.*

**Saint Augustine**

*That leaves much to be desired ... Who could ask*
*for more?*

**Roger Munier**
*Proverbes*

*The travelers, errant poets,*
*follow the traces of the wind*
*into the abysses of infinity*
*guided by the flashes of the night*
*Only these traces*
*that impress the language of the wind*
*on the back of the dunes*
*contain the sighs*
*and the emotions of this earth...*

**Hawad**
*Caravanes de la soif*
*(Caravans of Thirst)*

# *Preface*

## Professor Jean Leclant

*Permanent Secretary
L'Académie des Inscriptions
et Belles Lettres*

The word "Egypt" immediately evokes images of palm trees reflected in the waters of a wide, life-giving river—a long oasis extending along the Nile. But there is another, completely different Egypt, the Egypt of the desert, fascinating in its isolation. This enchanting region is where Pauline and Philippe de Flers take us.

The authors themselves have undertaken many expeditions into the Sahara, a paradoxical region of impressive monotony and abundant variety: Here are dunes and sandy plateaus, depressions and mountain ranges, oases and springs. This book was written by people who have actually witnessed the desert's glorious dawns and sumptuous sunsets, drawing directly from their own experience. At the same time, they have also assembled reflections of the desert by such diverse authors as Herodotus and the Arabian historians, as well as the writings of many of the great European explorers, including such legendary names as Almasy, Bagnold, Barth, Rohlfs, and Monod. All together, they convey a wealth of information that is not readily available elsewhere.

Part One introduces us to the oases, rare centers of life in the heart of the vast, solitary expanses of the western part of Egypt. Strabo likened this desert to a leopard's coat, speckled with inhabited spots surrounded by a "forlorn region without water." The term *oasis*, now in common use among geographers and always an evocative word in the imagination of tourists, has been used for about 4,000 years, since the 6th Pharaonic dynasty, around 2300 BC. It can be found at Aswan in the tomb of Herkhuf, a bold trapper, who tells the story of how he reached the river basin of Dongola, above the third cataract of the Nile.

The main oases are introduced sequentially proceeding from north to south. First is Siwa, made famous by the pilgrimage of Alexander the Great in 331 BC to the Oracle of Ammon, his divine father, to receive the latter's acknowledgment of his world dominion. The next oasis is Bahariya, with large necropolises from the Ptolemaic and Roman eras where vividly colored, mummy-shaped sarcophagi, some with gilded masks, are found. Farafra follows, well irrigated at the heart of its White Desert; then Dahkla, where French excavations have recently uncovered the mastabas of the governors of the Pharaonic Old Kingdom (Balat, Ayn Asil). And finally, Kharga, with its great temple of Hibis dating from the time of Persian domination, an extremely original system of underground canals (the qanats), fortified Ptolemaic and Roman temples, its Christianization and connection with St. Athanasius and Nestorius, and the Bagawat necropolis containing well-preserved paintings.

The Great Desert itself, the Sahara, is the focus of Part Two. The authors interpret the work of geologists and geomorphologists for us, giving detailed descriptions of the many types of sand dune, the huge sandy plateau of Gilf-Kebir in the southern part of the Great Sea of Sand, the "living sand" with its mysterious "songs," and the terrible storms in this perilous dry ocean. Following in the footsteps of intrepid explorers and scientists, we are introduced to the flora and fauna whose incredible capacity to adapt allows them to survive in a harsh environment including scorching sun, lack of water, and savage winds. We meet the eremiaphile, a sort of cannibalistic praying mantis, shy venomous animals (snakes and scorpions) and lively, quick jerboas. As for the camel or, to be more precise, the dromedary, we explore the conundrum of its history, as its presence has only been recorded since relatively recent times.

Mysteries of all sorts abound: the Djara cave with its stalactites and stalagmites, the jar fields of Abu Ballas, so-called Libyan glass (believed to be impactites from cosmic bombardments).

At the edge of the better-known Egypt of pyramids, magnificent temples, and splendid tombs, we have here an Egypt of sandy expanses, one that exerts its own mysterious attraction. In the Pharaonic era, it was the western home of the dead, the place where the sun went to rest in the evening at the end of its divine course. Unlike the valley, a fertile and well-ordered region, it was a place of peril: strange, and inhabited by strangers. This territory of hybrid monsters was regarded with terror. With the advent of Christianity, the desert remained a place of trial, but was sanctified as the domain of anchorites.

For people today, subjected to all the mad speed, noise, and vexations of the modern world, the desert is an ideal place for contemplation. Its sublime, magnificently pure landscapes, beautifully brought to life in this book, still bear witness to an unparalleled splendor.

# Contents

# Introduction

Magical as it is, the very word "Egypt" evokes images of the Nile Valley lined with temples from the Sudan to the Mediterranean. Here lay the cradle of Egyptian civilization for 3,000 years before our era. The monarch of rivers runs through the country like a narrow, green ribbon cut into the desert, nourishing the land along its banks. While the rich and overpopulated river valley provides its inhabitants with all the necessities of life, its course between two of the driest deserts in the world is not always smooth. Between the Nile and the Red Sea lies the Eastern Desert, which, owing to the short distances involved, could be crossed without difficulty even in ancient times and has thus lost much of its mystery. The Western Desert, on the other hand, is more extensive and still poses an ostensibly impassable barrier. Travelers are still wary of intruding into its formidable expanse, which remains the territory of legends and mysteries: the kingdom of the dead, a secret and sacred landscape reserved for the initiated. This desert shows us a different Egypt, the kingdom of the setting sun, Théodore Monod's "desert of extremes."

The Libyan Desert to the west of the Nile is the eastern part of the Sahara. This geographic area has been shaped by eons of widely varying, and sometimes violent, climatic conditions. The theories of continental drift and plate tectonics that try to explain the formation of the earth's land masses suggest that 200 million years ago there was a single supercontinent encompassing all the land masses of the southern hemisphere, called "Gondwanaland."

The theories also propose that 180 million years ago, during the Mesozoic Era, Gondwanaland broke apart. The regions that had been joined in the Paleozoic Era were separated and began to "drift," until they gradually took the positions we know today: South America and Africa, India, Australia, and the Antarctic. It is difficult to imagine the violence with which the land masses must have been torn apart, leading to the birth of North Africa and probably the creation of the Mediterranean. Of course, these geologic changes must have been accompanied by major climatic changes. The scope of such change can only be hinted at when we consider the sudden disappearance of the dinosaurs 65 million years ago as the result of another enormous, and probably violent, cataclysm, most likely the fall of a meteorite.

The Eastern Sahara was formed in gradual steps. Its contours and rocks were formed in the Cenozoic Era, while the sea advanced and retreated in turns and the climate underwent several changes. Once the sea receded for good, granite massifs dominated the sandstone plains along with masses of sand deposited by fluvial and marine erosion. Then began the volcanic activity.

In the Quaternary Era, glaciers advanced, which leveled off the rocks as they retreated from the region. The effects of heat and wind on the rocks over time led to the formation of sand and sand dunes. Humans appeared on the scene as well, settling in various places in the desert.

Prehistoric human habitats were widely scattered. Favored regions were the "playas" situated around depressions in the land where there were lakes created by the receding sea or fed by rain and abundant springs. These were fertile areas where all sorts of vegetation could thrive.

Oases have proliferated in those basins with their fertile soil deposits. They form a chain that has always supplied the inhabitants with food, given them a permanent abode, and allowed them to carry on their traditions. Between the Nile and the Great Sea of Sand, Siwa the Remote, Bahariya the Black, Farafra the White, and Dakhla and Kharga, gates to the Sahara, are still the heirs and guardians of desert civilization.

Although these regions are rather inhospitable, humans have always lived in them. We know from rock drawings that animals were hunted in the Sahelian zones before they turned to desert.

Wildlife found enough water to evolve in what must have been savanna. But the increasingly dry climate drove the hunters toward the large river basins. In both the east and the west, the basins provided them with a more favorable living environment and offered possibilities unimaginable in their native territories.

The large depressions in the Western Desert formed a zone where the wildlife on which hunting peoples depended could flourish, and where semi-nomadic peoples found sources of water as they approached the Nile Valley. Here were rich deposits of clay thanks to the natural artesian springs that have sustained human settlement since the earliest times. The drainage bed buried under the Nubian sandstone provided a plentiful water supply for the still-rudimentary agricultural practices, geared mainly toward supplementing a hunting and gathering economy.

According to known evidence, human settlement took place in the early third millennium BC. But the region was probably settled much earlier—so long ago and in such a way that no traces remain of a social organization as advanced as those uncovered by archaeological excavations.

The desert depressions attracted people, for here an environment comparable to that of the Nile Valley could be re-created. The name the Egyptians gave the depressions, *wahat*, in present-day usage means a deep vessel, a sort of cauldron, which gives a clear idea of the difference in level between the Libyan plateau and the oases. To reach the oases in the *wahat*, one has to descend along steep, vertiginous slopes between rock and sand dunes. The name *wahat* is still used in Arabic today and is related to the Greek *oasis*.

The soil in these "cauldrons" made it possible to use the agricultural techniques developed in the Nile Valley, and the settlers brought with them their culture, beliefs, and their sense of community, of belonging to a world constantly nourished by the Nile, even though they lived at a distance from it. Thus, a society developed in these remote regions similar to that of any province situated at a distance from the capital city, led by governors representing the royal authority and a local administration that was subordinate to that of the capital, and marked by towns, temples, necropolises, and people bearing the same names as their contemporaries in Middle Egypt.

Even today, if you walk through the more important oasis towns, you are likely to have the strange sensation of being in Egypt and yet of being in a very different world as well. The farmers flood their fields just as they would in the Nile Valley, but today the water gushes out of man-made wells often more than 3,000 feet deep. The overuse of the wells for irrigation today exhausts the artesian supply, exposing the crops to excess salinity. In earlier times, the principle was the same, but the water supply was husbanded more rationally: The long *qanats* excavated by the French Institute of Oriental Archaeology (IFAO) south of the Kharga oasis show how cleverly this resource was distributed from the Persian era to the Roman. There is also a modern example in Farafra that demonstrates the enduring effectiveness of this farming technique.

The inhabitants of these oases never considered themselves independent of the great civilizations on whose peripheries they lived. Siwa may be an exception, situated between two worlds, the African and the Mediterranean, the Maghreb and the Middle East. Although Siwa was isolated from the outside world, it has always been a highly prized target of conquest. For Alexander the Great, Siwa's subjugation had symbolic value. It has served as a strategic vantage point for warlords desiring to control the desert and was a place of refuge and mystic power for Islam.

The oases are not a world unto themselves. As places of permanent settlement, they also form a chain of communication. They have always provided stopping places for hunters and rich fertile soil for farmers from the banks of the Nile. They will forever remain both dwelling places, reflecting the culture of their inhabitants, and indispensable gateways to the desert for all sorts of commerce. They still play this role today, reminding us that contemporary political borders do not always reflect history. They form a part of this world in which human settlement is permanent—but only a part. What would the verdant expanse of Siwa, the ochre fields of Dakhla, or the vast orchards of Farafra be without the immense and varied desert that surrounds and protects them? Let us hope that the large development projects underway to cultivate these regions will not upset the equilibrium that we can still admire.

# The Origins of the Oasis Depressions
by Professor Rushdi Saïd

*The oases of the Western Desert of Egypt form depressions excavated in the great limestone plateau of that desert. Because the regional dip of the strata is toward the north, the southernmost oases of Kharga and Dakhla lie along the formational boundary of the oldest exposed strata. Both oases are situated in the shadow of that boundary, which forms an escarpment made up of hard limestone beds covering loose sand and easily denuded shale. The floor of these two oases rises gradually on the other side to the general level of the desert. The more northerly oasis of Farafra is excavated into slightly younger rocks and assumes a triangular shape that is bound by steep cliffs on the east, west, and north sides. The northern cliff, although not as high, is conspicuous owing to its dazzling whiteness. The most northerly oasis of this series is the Bahariya oasis, which is bordered on all sides by precipitous cliffs surrounded by younger strata. The Bahariya oasis differs from all the other oases, which are open on one or more sides, by being closely surrounded by escarpments and by having a large number of isolated hills within the depression.*

*The origin of the oases of the Western Desert of Egypt has been the subject of controversy. Because they are closed inland basins with no access to the sea, many people believe that they were formed by the action of wind. Although it is certain that wind played an important role in giving the oases their present shape, it is also certain that their excavation was accelerated by the water action of the pluvial periods experienced by the Western Desert in the past. The oases have been forming since their elevation from the bottom of the sea some 40 million years ago. The rocks that surround and make up the floor of the oases were created at the bottom of this ancient, retreating sea.*

*After its elevation, the entire Western Desert formed a great flat plateau covered by limestone beds. During the long years that have passed since it rose to become land, it has been exposed to the elements. It has seen many pluvial periods and many drainage systems, of which at least one was older than the excavation of the oases. The rains sank into the limestone rocks of the elevated plateau, widening their joints by solution, forming caves and underground channels, and filling the groundwater reservoirs. In the case of Bahariya and Farafra, which lie in depressions within the plateau and are encircled by escarpments, it is possible that their origin was due to the action of this gushing groundwater, which dissolved the limestone beds covering their escarpments. Once these hard layers were removed, the wind was able to deepen the depression by acting on the floor of the two oases, which consisted of layers of friable sandstone and shale. Both Farafra and Bahariya lie in tectonic zones allowing vigorous spring activity.*

*It is possible that the Kharga and Dakhla oases, situated in the shadow of the great plateau of the Western Desert, were excavated in much the same manner. They also lie along tectonic limes where there is much spring activity. Some authors, however, trace the formation of these two oases back to an old drainage line that presumably shaped the flat surface of the southern part of the Western Desert. This surface was probably formed some six million years ago when the Mediterranean was at a low level. The two oases could thus represent the remnants of this ancient drainage system.*

# Part One

# The Oases

*The Island of the Blessed:
the islands of the sea; inhabited
regions surrounded by great deserts.*

**Herodotus**

ROYAUME DE TUNIS
Kaireuan · Sousa · Tabarca · Pâtalarée · Passara
Tebesse · Esfakes · Lampedouse · la Valette · I. DE MALTE
DE · Mesda · Tourga · Tabia · Meerata
Beladulgerid · Golfe de Gabes · I. de Zerbi
TUNIS

MER MEDITERRANÉE

I. DE CANDIE · Candie · Scarpanto · C. de Gata · I. DE CHYPRE · Nicosita · Baffo
C. Matapan · Cerigo · Milo · Santorin · Rhodes · I. du Chau Roux

SYRIE · LE DIARBEK
Alex andrete · le Bir · Merdin · Ourfa · CURDIS · Mosul
Alep · Hama · Kepha · Scher · Nesbin · Iribil

ROYAUME DE TRIPOLY
Viex Tripoly · Tripoly · Turhona · Sukna
Desert d'Ezzab Haicha · Desert de Serte · Mont d'Ilseemat · Desert de Barca

Bouches du Nil · Golfe des Arabes · le Begum · TERRE SAINTE
Damiete · Alexandrie · Rosette · I. de Cavallis

ARABIE PETRÉE dependante de l'Égypte · M. Sinai
Jerusalem · Gaza · Corondel · Aila · Thadmor ou Palmyre ruinee
Maan Chateau et Village ou il y a de bonne eau · Grand Palais ruinee · Desert de l'I

BARBARIE ou PAYS DU FAISAN
ROYAUME
Gadamis · Gadams · Taourga · Chate ou Faisan · M. Guibet ou Mont Atlas

Desert d'ouguela · Ouguela ou Augela · Si-ouah ou Sant rie relevant de Tripoly
Thab Pays desert · EGYPTE · LES TROIS ELOUAH

ARABIE DES
Montagnes de l'Hyaz · Taulabie
Almohadan chau inhabité · Karzoka
MER ROUGE

LES BREBERES
Pays Zala ou il y a Zouada les foires et des marchez celebres
Arabes · Zaouila ville située comme une Isle au milieu du Desert

LES LEVATA ou LEBETES · Ain Cais Desert

LES LEMTA OU LUMPTUNES dou sont sortis les Merabitins nommée Almoravides par les Historiens
Roudan Majalat · Arcan · Medheram Isa · Pays de Berdoa ou il y a 5 ou 6 villages et 5 Chateaux

Puits dont les habitans de Zaouila se servent n'ayant pas d'autre eau

Kucu ville assez peuplée

Deserts de Sable

les Kenus espece de Barberins

DESERT DE BARBARIE · LES BERDOA
Pays de Caour · Hembrun Arabs · les Yayahe Arabes
Desert de Berdoa d'une grande Secheresse ou il n'y a pas de sureté pour les marchands a cause des voleurs

Pays de Kovar · Tombec d'un Fakir · Montagnes de pierre noire

les Mahases espece de Barberins dependans du Turc
d'Artmire · LES BUGIENS nation errante

Desert de Lumptunes habité par une Nation superbe et brutale
Canum ou Alkanem · M. de Tanton ou il y a de bones mines de fer
Desert de Bournou · Semegoula

ROYAU. DE GAOGA OU DE KAUGHA
Kaugha ou Gaoga · Lac de Gaoga

les Barabra ou Barberins PAYS de Nubie
Mocho · Arco · Dongola · Dafar

ROYAUME DE SENNAR OU DE NUBIE
Desert de Bahuada les Chanedi · Berkan ou Dequin
les Takaki · Taka

ROYAUME DE CANUM d'ALKANEM
Deserts et passages dangereux et pleins de voleurs

ROYAUME DE BOURNOU · Nebrina

NIGRITIE

R. DE ZANFARA · Tasava · Zanfara
ROYAUME DE ZEGZEG · Germa · OU DE PHARAN
Sagra · Sama · Amazen · Pays de Zaghara
Bournou seule ville du Royme de Bournou

R. d'OUANGARA ou de Ghanara d'OUANGARA dou l'on tire de l'or du Sené et des Esclaves
Tirca · Niger

ROYAUME DE TEMIAN dont les habitans sont a ce qu'on dit Antropophages
Lac de Bournou · M. de Tibesten

ROYAUME DE DAUMA
Desert de Zeu

Royau. DE GABOU d'ou vient du Jaspe et des Esclaves
DE BENIN

ROYAUME DE MEDRA
Desert de Seth · Median · Gambarou ou Comadou R. · Syre
Quelquesuns croyent que le Niger est un bras du Nil et l'appellent a cause de cela le Nil des Negres

ROYAUME DE GORHAN dont les habitans ont une langue particuliere et demeurent continuellement dans ces deserts

Montagnes ou il y a dit on beaucoup d'Emeraudes

Roy. DES CHANGALA ou Ethiopiens errans
Falasjan ou les exilez Juifs fugitifs
ROY. de AGAUS
CAFRES ou nasranis du Roi d'Eliopt
BERTUMA ou Galles

ROY. DE DAMBEA · R. de DAMBEA
R. DE GOJAME · R. DES AGAUS
R. de GOJAME
R. DAMOT

SEMEN R. DE TIGRE · DU BARNAGAS
ROY. DE TIGRE · ROY. DE BAGEMDER
ROY. de AGAUS · R. D'AMARA · R. D'OLECA · R. D'ANGOT · ROY. DE DAN
GALLA · R. de CHOA · R. D'IFAT · R. D'OGGE

ROYAUME D'ETHIOPIE ou D'ABISSINIE
Bas Choa · Haut Choa · GHEDM

ROYAUME DES GALLES
Alamale autrefois soumis au Roi d'Ethio · GALLES · GUMAR

GUINEE
les Calbongos · Haute Terre d'Amboizes
DE BENIN les Calbongos Peuples mechans et trompeurs ennemis des autres Calbongos leurs voisins

ROYAUME DE MUJAC
Biafara · ROYAUME DE MUJAC
BIAFARA
dont le Roi est fort puissant et les Sujets font des courses continuelles sur les terres du Grand Macoco qui est obligé a cause de cela d'entretenir une armée aux frontieres Septen les de ses Etats

R. de BIZAMO · R. de NAREA ou il y a des mines d'or
ETAT DU ROY DE GINGIRO
appellé GINGIR-BOMBA qui signifie EMPEREUR DE GINGIRO
Il a quinze Rois pour Vassaux
Il est allié au Grand Macoco, et leurs Sujets se ressemblent assez en humeur Coutumes et superstitions

CAMBAT · ADIAS · BORE GALLA · les Cajasos
les Peuples Dadas · les Arbores ou Asbores · les Arvisas · les Bresomas · les Maracates Peuple

ROYAUME D'ALABA
Royaume des Machidas Nation puissante dont le Roi descend des R. d'Ethiopie avec la elle est toujours en gu soit Mahometan

Pays de Bokkemeale habité par les Jagas qui tirent des dents de l'éléphant des Bakke
Forests habitées par les peuples BAKKE-BAKKE qui sont

ROYAUME DU CAP LOPO GONSALVES

# The Oases: Distant Islands

Anyone who travels away from the Nile in a westerly direction enters a living hell: all trails vanish, all water disappears, all people have fled. Nothing is left but a blinding, infinite expanse of sand. One's destination is uncertain; will the dazzling and dangerous journey end in a mere mirage? No. Color and life reappear along with abundant vegetation, a murmuring spring, the noise of human beings, and an oasis, which Herodotus called "the Island of the Blessed," anchored like an island in the middle of the ocean. Olympiodorus compared oases with islands left behind by the sea, stranded forever on the sand, where shells and marine fossils bear witness to an aquatic past.

Where does the word "oasis" come from? Professor Jean Leclant explains that the term has a long history: It has been in constant and common usage ever since the Old Kingdom. "Oasis" once designated specific places in the Libyan Desert, but now applies to all havens of greenery and peace encircled by an expanse of desert, land, or sea.

Oases benefited from favorable atmospheric conditions enhanced by the contrast with their surroundings. Their abundant water supply was even envied by inhabitants of the Nile Valley, who were at the mercy of the capricious Nile floods. Scattered from north to south like a frontier, the oases have played an essential role in forming societies. In prehistoric times, they attracted climatic refugees who had been driven from the Sahara in times of drought, enabling them to pool their knowledge of agriculture, animal husbandry, and handicrafts such as pottery, engraving, and painting. While profiting from Egyptian domination and the exchange of commercial, artistic, and cultural commodities, they also took in political exiles from the Nile Valley.

Progress in means of transportation and the construction of roads has reduced the oases' isolation, and current exploitation projects in the "New Valley" are even trying to attract new residents to live there: Once a place of exile, the oases are now being transformed into a new home for Nile Valley dwellers.

*Previous page: Map of Egypt drawn by Guillaume Delisle of the Royal Academy of Science, printed in Paris, November 1707.*

# Chapter I

# Siwa the Remote:
## *The Oasis of Myth*

### The benefits of isolation

"Upon traveling toward the interior, one finds ... the region of wild beasts; beyond this is the region of dunes that extends from Thebes in Egypt to the Pillars of Hercules. In this region one finds, about ten days' walk from one another, mounds covered with blocks of salt made up of large agglomerated crystals; from the summit of these hillocks, fresh, sweet water gushes out amid these salt blocks; the springs collect around them the last inhabitants of the country within the confines of the desert, beyond the region of the wild beasts."[1]

After several exhausting and perilous days spent crossing the desert, caravans found a magnificent sight in the midst of a striking landscape: chalk mountains of dazzling white, lapped by huge salt lakes sparkling peacefully under a thin heat haze, mountains carved with tombs or covered with houses, and still others topped by temples overhanging the rock! Mirage or reality?

Even today the encounter with Siwa remains a shock. Its geographical situation is unique, being located 360 miles from the Nile, 180 miles from the Mediterranean, and just 30 miles from Libya. To the south it is bordered by the Great Sea of Sand, and by marsh and quicksand to the east, so the route from the north provides the best access.

Because of its isolation, Siwa has had an unusual history. It has been inhabited since earliest prehistory and was a frequent point of call in antiquity. It provided an obligatory place of refuge and rest for caravans traveling from north to south—from the Mediterranean to the Sudan—and from east to west—from the Nile Valley to Libya. Later, it was also a stop on the route to Mecca.

For a long time, this area was covered by the sea, which withdrew, advanced again, then receded to its present limits. Fossils of marine animals, salt rocks, and small salt lakes still bear witness to the former presence of the ocean. In the early 19th century, von Minutoli described the oasis as follows: "the ground was wet in places, swampy and covered with small salt lakes from which little fertile islands emerged in a very odd manner. These contained freshwater springs and were covered with various sorts of luxuriant vegetation."[2] Water is trapped in the depression; rainfall, though rare, tends to be torrential and destructive. Many of the freshwater artesian springs are valued as therapeutic hot springs, but fewer than a third of them still produce drinking water, and numerous sources of water have dried up since ancient times. The lakes are too salty for fish to survive, which also prevent the Siwites from keeping dromedaries because there are no fish to feed on the marsh insects that are, tragically, fatal for dromedaries.

Only donkeys flourish in these climatic conditions. In deference to the modesty of the oasis women, an ancient local custom relegates all female donkeys to a neighboring island; a meeting of the donkeys for mating purposes is arranged once each year. Relieved of the distraction of the female of their species, male donkeys devote themselves to farming and domestic tasks, and serve as transportation for the oasis inhabitants.

Among Siwa's unique features is its situation in a 48-mile-long depression about 65 feet below sea level. It has 300 springs, 15,000 inhabitants, 200,000 date palms, and many other fruit trees. Von Minutoli tells us that crops were abundant and diverse, though their bounty has sometimes been exaggerated: One legend tells of 14,000 oranges harvested from a single tree![3] According to Guy Wagner, olives, pomegranates, figs, apricots, melons, grapes, and dates constituted the wealth of the oasis.[4]

The quality and quantity of the region's dates have been famous since ancient times, largely due to artificial pollination practices—von Minutoli writes of 5,000 to 9,000 camel loads per year.[5] Date trees bear fruit for a particularly long time; they can be harvested in their fourth year and may bear fruit for 150 or 200 years. Several varieties of date have made Siwa famous, including *elquak* (white date), *gesali* (red date), and the most tender and delicious of all, *thewa*.

1. Herodotus, translated from: *L'Enquête*, IV, 181, p. 349, La Pléiade, traduction et annotations A. Barguet, Éd. Gallimard, 1964.
2. H. von Minutoli, *Reise zum Tempel des Jupiter Ammon in der Libyschen Wüste*, p. 88f., Berlin, 1824.
3. Von Minutoli, *Reise*, p. 89.
4. G. Wagner, *Les Oasis d'Égypte*, p. 296, Cairo, 1987.
5. Von Minutoli, *Reise*, p. 90.

*A mirage at the heart of the desert? A dream of quenching one's thirst, of alleviating the heat of the scorching sand and sun? A huge expanse of water, a real oasis of sparkling white, nestled among large lakes and yet cruelly deprived of fresh water and constantly threatened by excess salinity, which drives away the fish and destroys the crops. The distant sea withdrew long ago, but has left its imprint at the foot of the immense limestone plateaus on the frontier of the sandy desert.*

A seductive lake landscape, surrounded by treacherous swamps. Palms, fruit trees, and other crops bear witness to the incessant struggle between rising salinity and sources of fresh water. Unlike the oases around it, which have been gradually destroyed by the salt, Siwa has remained prosperous, thanks to its 300 springs.

The spring water flowing in furrows at the foot of the palm trees goes on to water crops by means of an age-old, strictly regulated system of irrigation.

**Following page:** *In one of Siwa's squares, two men warm themselves in the sun early on a winter morning. Nights are cold at the gateway to the desert. The wall painted with indigo, a local pigment, reminds passersby of the unchanging presence of the sky and of water, the source of life in the oases. Indigo is also believed to keep evil spirits at bay.*

Dates, the legendary wealth of Siwa, produced by 200,000 palms of several varieties and enjoyed since ancient times, were called the "fruits of the Oracle of Ammon." Their reputed quality was amplified by Siwa's prestige as a place of pilgrimage. The various types of dates still play a role in ceremonies, not only as gifts, but also as symbols of good fortune. As dates ripen, their color changes; these colors are all represented on the embroidery of a bride's dress, to bring luck and fertility. Ethnologist Bettina Leopoldo, who has lived in Siwa, tells us that the palette consists of "five typical colors: red, green, orange, yellow, and black; each symbolizing the different stages of a date's maturity."[6]

**6.** B. Leopoldo, *Égypte, Oasis d'Amunsiwa*, p. 28, Geneva, 1986.
**7.** Wagner, *op. cit.* p. 215.
**8.** A. Fakhry, *The Oases of Egypt, vol. I: Siwa Oasis*, Cairo, 1973.

## The people and their customs

Siwa's unusual geographical position and its remoteness from the Egyptian, Libyan, and Sudanese capitals have helped the oasis maintain its independence.

Inhabitants of Siwa are proud of their uniqueness and their ability to retain economic independence despite the hardships of cultivating salt-permeated soil. Most of them are Berbers, but passing caravans have introduced former slaves of Ethiopian or Nubian origin. The people living in this magical site deep in the desert have jealously defended their identity and local language: Siwi, which is quite distinct from Arabic; according to Guy Wagner, it is a hybrid of the ancient Egyptian and Nubian tongues.[7]

Ahmed Fakhry, a native Egyptologist who lived in Siwa for many years, interviewed residents and read the famous Siwa manuscript that records the long history of the oasis. He describes the oasis in great detail, including its wealth and the Berber customs still practiced there, which differ from those of the other oases.[8]

The women are very segregated, for example; they are confined to their houses in the center of town and only leave for important occasions such as weddings, baptisms, and funerals. When they do venture out, the women are masked by a *milayah*, a large black shawl bordered with blue that covers their faces completely, with only a small opening to allow them to peep out. All outside activities are reserved for the men. They cultivate the gardens, conduct business, and add life to the town streets. Young bachelors, called *zaggalahs* or "stick carriers," live outside of town; their sole responsibility is to look after the gardens, where they also sleep, so that their whereabouts can be monitored.

### Marriage

On her wedding day, a young Siwite bride dons seven layers of garments; seven is held to be a magical number that brings good luck. The seven garments allow the bride to wear a new outfit every day for the following week, in predetermined order: The garment closest to her skin must be transparent and white, the second of a light red fabric, the third black, the fourth yellow, the fifth blue, the sixth of red silk, and the last of green silk. The bride is then ready to don the traditional black wedding gown, richly embroidered with colorful geometric designs around the neck and many mother-of-pearl buttons—tiny suns to ward off the Evil Eye. Some see the buttons as a vestige of the famous sun-

*Where is this faceless woman going, dressed in the famous black milayah, with its blue border and white stripes? Is she on her way to the wedding of a friend, who will be wearing the traditional bridal dress, richly adorned with mother-of-pearl buttons, one of the seven garments worn in layers for the big day?*

**Following page:** *The children play, the men converse, the women only leave their homes for special occasions. Surely, the sight of seven Siwites in the square is a good omen!*

rays that were a symbol of the god Aton.[9] Others describe them as a sort of magic mirror: "they not only reflect all colors, but it is believed that they attract energy from the sun and bring it to the person adorned with them. They are thus a source of personal energy, of a powerful and positive aura."[10]

Large silver necklaces decorated with suns and other traditional motifs such as dates, palms, and fish scales complete the bride's outfit. Finally, her hair, decorated with crescent-shaped silver ornaments weighing several pounds each, is covered with a large striped red silk shawl finished with multicolored woolen tassels.

### Mourning

Festive garments are black, while white is worn for mourning. Siwa is the only oasis that perpetuates a harsh tradition involving the young widow, the *guhlah*. Believed to be a victim of the Evil Eye, she is forced into seclusion, sequestered from the rest of the community so she cannot contaminate them. She must wear a white garment and is not permitted to wash, speak, look at or be seen by anyone—except close relatives and an old woman appointed to bring her food through a closed door. This ostracism

lasts four months and ten days. The night before the widow is released from her confinement, the town is warned by the sound of a drum. The woman herself is blindfolded to prevent the Evil Eye from wreaking havoc and led to a purifying bath in the Tamusi spring, which rids her of the demon forever. She is allowed to remarry a year later. A widower, on the other hand, endures no particular restrictions; he is free to remarry only weeks after his bereavement with the blessing of the community.

### The sacred number seven

The number seven, symbolic in both ancient and modern cultures and religions, is significant throughout Egyptian mythology, from birth to death. Its importance derives from the very beginning of the world, whose creation began with the "seven words pronounced by the demiurge."[11] The seven Hathor deities preside over each person's birth and over his or her destiny. The dead, moreover, have to pass through seven doors to leave the darkness and reach Osiris before they can be blessed in all eternity like him. The god Ra himself possesses seven souls and seven pairs of ka[12] to which worshippers pay homage at sunrise:

*Seven times greetings to you and your soul!*
*Fourteen greetings to you and your ka!*[13]

Time in ancient Egypt did not follow the rhythm of the seven-day week; their weeks lasted ten days. In the Muslim world, on the other hand, the seven-day week is a beneficent symbol of a regular cycle, the promise of renewal, even of eternity; its fixed cycle invokes change and progress. Seven suggests completion and perfection, like the seven heavens or spiritual spheres that one must pass through to attain them, or the seven colors of the rainbow, or the seven notes of the musical scale. Seven is also one quarter of the 28-day lunar month that is still the basis of the calendar for many civilizations. Many Islamic rites still refer to the number seven:

**9.** Aton, the solar disc, has been part of the Egyptian pantheon since the Ancient Empire; he represents the physical appearance of the sun. Amenhotep (1352–1338 BC) made him the god of the dynasty and became his worshipper by changing his name, *Amenhotep*, "Peace be to Ammon," to *Akhenaton*, "Aton's worshipper," thereby lending importance to the divine immanence and creating a direct link between the Creator and humanity. This new relationship, represented symbolically by a solar disc whose rays shoot out hands towards Humankind, and expressed in art with excessive "realism" inclining towards caricature, was a short-lived one. After Akhenaton's death and the ephemeral reign of Smenkhkare in fact, *Tutankhaton*, "the

living image of Aton," returned to the Ammonian religion and reigned under the name of *Tutankhamun*, "the living image of Ammon" (1336–1327 BC).
**10.** Leopoldo, *op. cit.* p. 49f.
**11.** D. Meeks, C. Favard-Meeks, *Les Dieux égyptiens*, p. 139, Paris, 1995.
**12.** The Ka is an abstract notion, and therefore difficult to define, because it is "a manifestation of vital energies, as much in its creative function as in its conservative function." G. Posener, S. Sauneron, J. Yoyotte, *Dictionnaire de la civilisation égyptienne*, p. 143, Paris, 1992.
**13.** P. Barguet, *Le Livre des morts des anciens Égyptiens*, p. 46, Paris, 1967.

In the old part of Siwa, ruined houses stand alongside dwellings propped up by the trunks of palm trees jutting out from the walls. Each house has a flat roof from which the women can watch all the comings and goings while they themselves remain unseen.

**Following page:** *Wearing traditional long dresses and under the watchful eye of an older sister, the little girls in Siwa love to chatter, laugh, and sing. They are veiled only at puberty.*

**14.** J. Chevalier, A. Gheerbrant, *Dictionnaire des symboles*, p. 862, Paris, 1982.
**15.** Chevalier, Gheerbrant, *op. cit.* p. 863.
**16.** Herodotus, *op. cit.* p. 350.
**17.** Leopoldo, op.cit. p. 11.

*On a pilgrimage to Mecca, one must go round the Kaaba seven times.[14]*

*When a pregnant woman is in danger, read seven verses of the sura over her.[15]*

On the walls of the temple of Idfu seven oases are mentioned, and in the desert seven mysteries await us.

### A lost name

Siwa is mentioned in the text on the "Seven Oases" engraved on the Idfu temple, but the inscription has so deteriorated that its ancient name will probably never be known. The oasis was situated in Libyan territory; the word *aman*, meaning "water," is of Libyan origin and the god of springs, Ammon, was worshipped there. When the ancient Greek culture spread and the oracle was famous, the similarity to the name of the illustrious god Ammon of Karnak determined the name, the oasis of Ammon or Zeus-Ammon: "The first people one comes across when coming from Thebes, ten days journey from this city, are Ammonians, who have adopted the cult of Zeus of Thebes (because ... the statue of Zeus in Thebes also has a ram's head)."[16]

In the 14th century, the oasis was only known as *Santarieh*, the "place of acacias," and *al-Wahat al-Asqa*, the "remote oasis." Siwa is a relatively recent name that came into use between the 15th and 17th centuries. Ahmed Fakhry attributes its origins to a Berber tribe called the Swa. Leopoldo relates that a small Berber tribe from Tripolitania with the name Ti-Swa was already mentioned by the historian Ibn Khaldun in the 14th or 15th centuries.[17]

## A turbulent history

Shaped stone tools prove that the Siwa region, like the rest of the Sahara, has been inhabited since prehistoric times; in a number of eras, the climate in the region was favorable for habitation. Still, Siwa has always differed from the other oases in that it had a so-called northern civilization based on hunting, gathering, and fishing; southern civilizations were characterized by playas, which lent themselves to agriculture.

During the 1st dynasty—between 3000 and 2780 BC—the region was occupied by small tribes from the west called Tjehenou, a Mediterranean race with brown skin like the Egyptians'. They

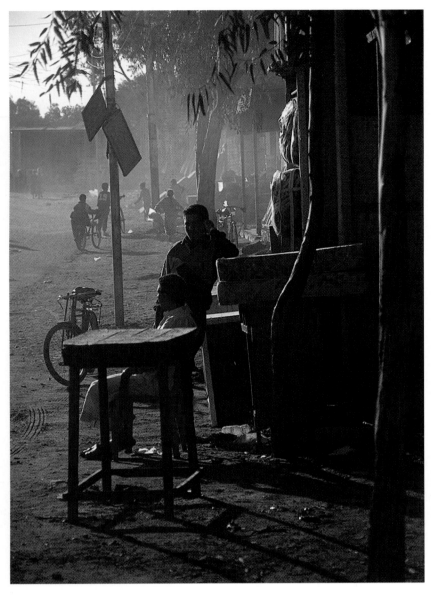

*A stall in a dusty street.*

swers to their spiritual questions directly from the god, through an intermediary, of course. The oracle of Ammon was highly respected and had an authority rivaling that of the oracle of Apollo at Delphi on the other side of the Mediterranean. Three famous examples of its prophecies have come down through history:

The first example of the oracle's power is the misfortune of the Persian king Cambyses II, son of Cyrus II, who invaded Egypt in 525 BC. Cambyses conquered the Nile Valley and then the chain of oases, though not Siwa. As king and founder of the 27th dynasty, he was disturbed by the growing influence of the oracle of Ammon, which predicted a catastrophic defeat for him. Cambyses swore to destroy the town and sent his troops to invade the remote oasis and subdue what had become an important center of commerce. An army of 50,000 men left Thebes and reached the large oasis of Kharga, from which it took the southern caravan route, which meant a difficult crossing of the Great Sea of Sand.

Herodotus relates what ensued: "This is what the Ammonians say: having left the city of Oasis [Kharga] to march against them, Cambyses' soldiers entered the desert. They had almost covered half the distance when ... the south wind suddenly began to blow violently, covering them in swirling clouds of sand. This explains their complete disappearance. Such was the fate of this expedition, according to the Ammonians."[19] The soldiers vanished without a trace, though archaeologists still search for signs of their expedition, dreaming of uncovering remnants of Persian armor. Is it not possible that the Ammonians, alerted to the threat of Siwa's prosperity and encouraged by the oracle, could have infiltrated Cambyses' army by placing their own people among the expedition's guides? This would have been simple enough, in view of the fact that Siwa's position was incorrectly marked on the maps of the time, leading travelers not to the oasis but into a 600-mile-long desert.[20] It is said that, terrified by the prospect of a certain and terrible death in the Great Sea of Sand as prophesied by the oracle, some of Cambyses' soldiers deserted and stayed in the oases, where they mixed with the local population.

The second example of the oracle's authority involves a Greek athlete from Cyrene, Eubotas, who visited Siwa. Upon consulting the oracle, Eubotas was told he would win at the Olympic Games. He immediately had a statue of himself erected, planning to have it unveiled on the day of his athletic triumph. And indeed, according to Diodorus Siculus, the statue was unveiled upon Eubotas's victory in 408 BC.

The third illustration of the oracle's power involves Alexander the Great. In 331 BC, after driving the Persians out of Egypt, Alexander was proclaimed Pharaoh. He hoped to have his divine descent confirmed by the oracle of Ammon, which was equally respected among Greeks and Egyptians. After founding the city of Alexandria, Alexander set out, hastily prepared, for Siwa. Mindful of the tragic fate of the army of Cambyses, Alexander took the less perilous northern route, which was nonetheless not without hazards. Within three days, Alexander's entourage had exhausted

were driven away by the Tjemehou, a different race that probably came from Asia Minor. The Tjemehou were light-skinned people with blue or gray eyes; they wore ostrich feathers on their heads and had a long lock of hair hanging to one side.

During the 6th dynasty, under Pepy I (ca. 2320–2285 BC), all the oases were under Egyptian control except Siwa, which maintained its independence. Much later, the founding of a Greek colony at Cyrene around 640 BC brought increased trade with Egypt. The arrival of caravans allowed Siwa to trade its already famous dates and olives for wheat and livestock from Fayum and for sylphium, a now-extinct medicinal plant, from Cyrenaica. The Siwa oasis was governed by princes of Libyan origin who, though already under Egyptian influence, were protected by their geographic remoteness. These princes maintained a high level of independence under the protection of the god Ammon.

Not until the 26th dynasty, from 664 to 525 BC, were Egyptian monuments erected in Siwa, including the temple of Aghurmi that housed the oracle of Ammon,[18] which occupied a very important position at the time. Visitors and supplicants could receive an-

**Above:** *View of the temple of the oracle and the ruined city of Aghurmi, perched on the rock that dominates the depression of the Siwa oasis. The temple of the oracle, whose entrance is still visible, was dedicated to Ammon.*

**Right:** *An old view of Siwa, "the city of mud," taken by the Kaufmann expedition before the destruction caused by the torrential rains of 1926. It shows the considerable dimensions of the city.*

18. The god Ammon is supposed to be the issue of a double union: on one side from the ram god, the ancient god of water and fertility in the whole north of Africa and in Egypt, and on the other side from Ammon, Egyptian anthropomorphic god of the same name, worshipped in Thebes with the head of a ram or wearing a headdress crowned by two large feathers. Ammon of Siwa can be distinguished by the horns curled around his ears, the last sign of his animal origin, which symbolizes strength. The link between the animal and the god is explained by Herodotus: "Herakles wanted at all costs to see Zeus, who did not want to show himself; finally because Herakles was so insistent, the god decided to put on a disguise: he skinned a ram, cut off its head which he held in front of his face, put on the animal's skin and appeared to Herakles in this disguise. That is why Egyptians put the head of a ram on the statue of Zeus, and this custom has been handed down from the Egyptians to the Ammonians."
*op. cit.* p. 159.
19. Herodotus, *op. cit.* p. 230.
20. J. Leclant, *Per Africae Sitientia, Témoignages des sources classiques sur les pistes menant à l'oasis d' Ammon*, Bull. Inst. Fr. archeol., p. 193-253, 49, Cairo, 1950.

**Following page:** *The remains of the temple of the oracle of the god Ammon in the heart of the citadel of Aghurmi.*

*View of the city of Siwa and the Mountain of the Dead in 1820 after drawings by von Minutoli, plate V.*

*The fortified city of Aghurmi, which housed the temple of the oracle, depicted by von Minutoli in 1820, plate XI.*

*View of the Aghurmi fortress through a portal of the temple of Umm el-Beyda, as drawn by von Minutoli in 1820, plate VII.*

its water supplies, though the route required enough water for a week. Alexander, along with his entire army, nearly died of dehydration, but they were saved by an unexpected downpour. Legend has it that Alexander and his soldiers, completely disoriented by a sandstorm, owed their lives to two ravens that came to their aid by showing them the way to Siwa. This place still bears the name "route of the ravens" among the Berbers.

Alexander never recounted the oracle's exact message, but Plutarch reports that the high priest, who was not fluent in Greek, made a slip of the tongue that greatly delighted the monarch, uttering a triumphal *O Païdios*, which means "Son of Zeus," instead of the traditional greeting, *O Païdon*, "my son." Alexander thus found the confirmation he sought of his divine origin, and remained faithful to the oracle until his death in 323 BC. He asked to be buried in Siwa, but this wish was never fulfilled. After receiving Ammon's blessing, Alexander the Great, venerated as both Pharaoh and god, was depicted with divine attributes in the form of two ram's horns coiled around his face, an image that appears on Greek coins.

The decline of the oracle began with the advent of the Christian era, and the politics of the Roman Empire made the oasis a place of exile for political prisoners. In the 6th century AD, the Byzantine emperor Justinian had the temples of the oasis closed at the same time he closed the temple in Philae, near Aswan.

The arrival of Islam, in the 7th century, consigned the oracle to oblivion, but as always, rebellious, independent Siwa resisted conversion longer than the other oases. Despite the Arabs' many attempts to impose it, Islam did not really gain a foothold in Siwa until the middle of the 10th century. The oasis even remained autonomous until 1798, when the political influence of Cyrene was again supplanted by that of Egypt.

It was around this time—the late 18th century—that the first European travelers appeared in Siwa, but like others before them, they had to contend with both the Siwites' legendary mistrust of strangers and a dire prophecy that if a single Christian were to

enter the town, unimaginable catastrophes would follow. W.G. Browne, an Englishman, came to Siwa disguised as a Muslim, but he was found out, beaten and expelled. The German explorer Friederich Hornemann also suffered from the consequences of this xenophobia twice during his visit to Siwa at the time of the Napoleonic campaign in 1798. Because he spoke Arabic, dressed in native costume, and was familiar with Islamic customs, he was admitted to the oasis, but his conspicuous interest in the temple of the oracle betrayed him. He was suspected of being an infidel and found it prudent to call a halt to his investigations. As he was leaving the area, he fell into a trap set by the Siwites some distance from the oasis. To clear himself of suspicion, he presented the Koran to their leader who, to Hornemann's surprise, asked whether anyone of the company understood it. Realizing that he and his companion were the only ones in the assembly with any education, Hornemann courageously put the Siwites at a loss with his knowledge of the Koran: "We were ordered to read so they could see if we belonged to the religion. Our knowledge in this regard went far beyond just being able to read. My companion knew all the Koran by heart, and as for me, I could write Arabic, even well—which for these people was proof that one had made

the most extraordinary progress in the sciences. We had barely given a sample of our respective talents when the leaders of our caravan, who until then had kept their silence, spoke up openly in our defense, and several of the Siwahans also exerted their authority in our favor. Thus, the character of a Muslim that I had assumed was firmly established and I will no longer be subjected to such interrogations in the future."[21]

Hornemann was followed by French mineralogist F. Cailliaud, who was sent by the pasha Mehemet Ali in 1818; after Cailliaud came the Prussian von Minutoli. They were better received, even in the heart of the city, and have left a priceless trove of descriptions and sketches—the only witnesses to monuments that today are in ruins or have vanished completely.

Just as the legend predicted, these visits by Christians were followed by disastrous events: Rebellious Siwa was vanquished and subjugated by Mehemet Ali in the early 19th century. Ali finally compelled the Siwites to respect the law of the oases and to pay him taxes, including 2,000 camels loaded with provisions.

Alternating periods of submission and revolt ensued until an Egyptian governorate was established in 1829. Outsiders remained unwelcome, and this changed only when the founder of the Sanusi

**Above:** *An ancient Greek tetra-drachma from the time of Ptolomy I showing Alexander the Great, wearing the horns of the god Ammon and an elephant's skin; on the reverse, an Athenian warrior, an eagle at his feet (Paris, BNF, Cabinet des monnaies, médailles et antiques).*

**Left:** *View of the depression of Siwa taken from the temple of the Oracle of Ammon.*

**Following page:** *Bust of Zeus-Ammon, possibly with the features of Alexander the Great. The horns of Ammon—a ram's horns curling around its ears—symbolize Alexander's divine origin, confirmed by the Oracle when he visited the temple of Siwa (Avignon, Calvet Museum).*

**21.** F. Horneman, *Voyages dans l'intérieur de l'Afrique, pendant les années 1797, 1798*, p. 118, Paris, 1802.
**22.** Leclant, *Per Africae Sitientia*, p. 218.
**23.** Leclant, *Per Africae Sitientia*, p. 218.
**24.** Herodotus, *op. cit.* p. 350.
**25.** S. Aufrère, J.-C. Golvin, J.-C. Goyon, *L'Égypte restituée, vol II, Sites et temples du désert*, p. 146f., Paris, 1994.

religious movement—a Sufi brotherhood created in Algeria in 1837 by al-Sayyid Muhammad al-Sanusi—settled in Siwa. The Grand Sanusi, who had fallen ill while emigrating to Libya, convalesced in Siwa and established a center of learning there, the second most important in Egypt after the university of al-Azhar in Cairo. At first the Sanusi movement advocated nonviolence, unification of the various tribes, and a return to strict religious practices, even a certain asceticism including a ban on tobacco and alcohol. The Grand Sanusi brought peace to Siwa, reconciling the inhabitants of the east and west of the oasis, whose legendary conflicts only ceased when they were compelled to unite against a common enemy: foreigners. The movement's influence is still palpable today, and the offer of a cigarette might well be declined with a stoical: "No, I am Sanusi."

This apolitical and nonviolent movement spread over a vast territory from the Sahara to the Sudan. Sayyid Alhmed al-Sharif, grandson of the founder, became involved in World War I. Defeated by the English and Egyptian armies, he took refuge in Siwa. The oasis finally surrendered to the English without a fight toward the end of the war, and the Sanusi leader was sent into exile.

Siwa remains a city of mysteries and legends. Here is one told by Pomponius Mela and confirmed by Pliny the Elder (1st century AD): "[There is] a particular rock dedicated to the south wind. If you place your hand on it, a violent wind blows up, raging like a wind at sea, driving the sand before it like waves."[22]

## Ruined splendor

### The temple of the oracle

Several myths recount the origins of the temple of the oracle, including Publius Nigidius Figulus (1st century BC): "While Liber led an army into Africa, his troops began to die for lack of water. At last, after several days, [a ram] suddenly appeared and miraculously led Liber and his army to water. Liber called the ram Zeus-Ammon and built a magnificent temple to him on the spot where water was found, honoring the site with an immortal monument. This temple is nine days' journey from Alexandria in the midst of sands where serpents abound. And it is from the word 'sand' that the name Ammon derives. The ram ... was also deemed worth immortalizing and was placed among the heavenly constellations."[23]

The temple of the oracle has a commanding position on the peak of Aghurmi mountain and is hidden within the town as if its divine nature needed to be concealed, its secrets protected. Unlike the town itself, which is built of dry mud bricks, the temple was built of stone in the Egyptian style by the Pharaoh Apries and his successor Ahmose II during the 27th dynasty (624–525 BC). Greek influence can be seen in the Ptolemaic columns added later.

Alexander the Great loved this sacred place that dominates the oasis and provides a stunning view of crystalline lakes surrounded by palm and date trees. Even in Greco-Roman times, Siwa was sought out for its oracle, hot baths, and sand baths. Cleopatra is said to have been there, and one spring still bears her name: The famous "Spring of the Sun," also known as "Cleopatra's Pool," is known for its temperature changes in the course of a day. Pilgrims purified themselves here before ascending to the temple: "lukewarm at dawn, and coolest at that time of day when most people visit; as noon approaches, the water turns icy ... As the day draws to a close, the pool gradually warms up, and at sunset it is lukewarm again. The water temperature climbs continuously until the middle of the night, when the water boils furiously; after midnight it cools down again until dawn."[24] Legend also tells of a secret underground passage leading from the temple to the Mount of the Dead. Sydney Aufrère, Jean-Claude Golvin, and Jean-Claude Goyon give us a glimpse of the splendor of the city and its monuments, especially the temple of the oracle of Ammon.[25]

Despite the poor condition of the buildings and cracks in the rock itself, the ruins and the twisted path to the temple entrance are still very moving. The complicated interior architecture, suggesting an intimate, close character, takes the visitor to the famous stairway that, according to legend, once led to the secret chamber that concealed the priest responsible for proclaiming the oracle.

### The temple of Umm el-Beyda

At the foot of the rock mountain Aghurmi is the temple of Umm el-Beyda, built by King Nectanebo II (360–341 BC), the great

builder of the 30th dynasty. According to the Siwa manuscript, the name of the temple comes from *umm ma'bad*, and means "the mother temple." Like the temple of the oracle, Umm el-Beyda is built of limestone that bears traces left by the sea, and fossilized shells are buried within its walls.

The path toward the temple's demise began with an earthquake in 1811 and was completed by dynamite blasting ordered by a police official who wanted stones to build an office—as well as a house for himself.

Sadly, just a single remaining wall bears witness to the temple's past splendor. On it are three groups of representations of divinities on a restored stele. Beneath the columns of text along the top of the wall is an image of the temple's architect, Ouenamon, kneeling before the god Ammon, to whom the temple is dedicated. Ouenamon wears an ostrich feather, signifying his Libyan origin, on top of his head; he might well have been called the "great desert chieftain."

Along the lower length of the wall march the gods—Atum, Shu, Tefnut, Geb, Nut, and Nekhbet. Von Minutoli's precise reconstructions bring these marvelous bas-reliefs to life against a blue background. A particularly striking drawing depicts the now-defunct ritual of the opening of the mouth, meant to breath life into a dead person or a divine statue and to give the person or the statue the use of the senses and of speech. The ritual consisted of more than a hundred specific steps and required various hand tools such as an *adz*.

Unfortunately, von Minutoli's reproduction of the hieroglyphics is less than accurate; hieroglyphics had not yet been deci-

phered at the time he was in Siwa. Still, he did leave us drawings of panels that no longer exist, evidence of what once was.

### The tombs of the Mount of the Dead, Jebel el-Mawta

The many tombs carved into the Mount of the Dead date from the 26th dynasty and the Ptolemaic era. Despite reuse of the land and systematic pillaging, there are still mummies to be found there, showing that Egyptian funerary rituals were in general use in these regions. Some decorated tombs have been rediscovered, but they were badly damaged during the two world wars, which contributed noticeably to Siwa's destruction. Each time people took refuge in the tombs of the Mount of the Dead, they undertook further excavation without taking care to preserve the paintings, ornaments, or ancient artifacts. It is only through the reconstructions and descriptions left us by Ahmed Fakhry that we can know them.

### Shali, the abandoned fortress

About 600 AD, a group of survivors of a violent Bedouin attack decided to build a fortress on one of the hills in the oasis. The fortress was called *Shali*, a Berber word meaning "the city." It was intended to fortify the Siwa oasis against invasion by Egyptians or by Libyans. As part of the fortification plan, Shali originally had only one gate. Two additional gates were built later, one on which was exclusively reserved for women to allow them discreet access to the gardens.

The houses of Shali were built of a dried-mud mixture that could not withstand rain well. In 1926, Shali was destroyed by torrential rains that beat down on the city for three consecutive days. A few abandoned and unsafe ruins remain, but the only living creatures still enjoying the shade of the ruins are rams, goats, and sheep.

### The surrounding oases

Traces of other oases, now abandoned because of the extreme salinity of the waters, can be found near Siwa and the depression of Qatara, including Nuwamisa, Sitra, and Bahrein, as well as the two saltwater lakes, *el-Areg* and *el-Zeitun*. These oases once played a critical role in the protection of Siwa and in its economy and daily life. They served as outposts to guard Siwa from attack from

**Previous page and right:**
*Jebel-el-Mawta, the Mount of the
Dead, contained many painted
tombs, including that of Si-Ammon.
They were discovered at the
beginning of the 18th century
and suffered heavy damage in
the following years.*

**Below and following pages:**
*The impressive dimensions of
the age-old walls of Shali, the
old citadel that was destroyed by
torrential rains in 1926, still recall
its past splendor and power.*

the east and supplied the capital Siwa with produce. They were also valuable bases where caravans traveling either to or from the south could stock up on supplies. Most of these surrounding oases are in depressions below sea level, surrounded by quicksand, and thus dangerous to approach. Now there is little more left than some palm trees encircling a few small saltwater ponds. However, it is still possible to find fossils, so-called "nummulites," occasionally glistening in the sunlight like coins or mother-of-pearl (see page 45).

Of these lesser surrounding oases, two are especially noteworthy. *El-Areg*, or "the cripple," is an important necropolis in an area of eroded limestone. There one may still find traces of a temple, though the inscriptions and ornamentation have faded.

*Qaret Umm el-Sughayar*, or "the little mother," dominates the Qatara depression. A strange and somewhat foreboding "tradition" helps maintain a constant population here, sustaining the economic equilibrium of the community. Frédéric Cailliaud relates the same phenomenon, but in his time, at the beginning of the 19th century, the population numbered 40: "Sheik Kouroum told me that ... the number of inhabitants can never be more than 40.... If a woman bears a child, one can be sure that someone else will die soon afterwards; in this way, the number 40 neither increases

nor decreases."[26] The present population seems to have stabilized at 120 people: that is, three times 40! Each birth compensates for a death or demands someone's departure.

Alexander the Great is said to have set up camp here en route back to Memphis. In the end, as in Siwa, the ancient city was destroyed by torrential rains.

In all important cities, whether ancient or modern, the title of capital city appears to be greatly coveted. Some cities manage to reach this goal, others fail ever to gain such a universally recognized distinction. Siwa, situated at the crossroad of well-travelled trade routes, and with a long history of both internal and external conflicts, has managed to retain its power, its influence, and its grandeur without ever becoming a capital. If anything, one might consider that its greatness surpassed that of a capital as the home of the great oracle of Ammon—a distinction shared by no city other than Delphi.

Siwa, the most remote, the most Saharan, and the most mysterious of the oases, without ever having possessed a large kingdom, still symbolizes independence, resistance, and hegemony. Far more than a capital, it has held peripheral influences in check and maintained constant command over civilizations and the memory of humankind.

**Above:** *Twilight falls on Qaret Umm el-Sugayar, or Qara, the abandoned city that still dominates the Qatara depression. Legend tells us that Alexander camped there after leaving Siwa on his way back to Memphis.*

**Right:** *El-Areg seen from the Qatara depression.*

**Previous page:** *El-Areg, an ancient oasis near Siwa, protected by limestone hillocks resembling forts erected for its defense, possessed a temple of which only ruins remain. The many chalk-encrusted shells create a magical contrast with these dark mounds shaped by erosion.*

**26.** F. Cailliaud, *Voyage à Meroé,…à Syouah et dans les autres oasis, fait dans les années 1819, 20, 21, 22,* p. 53, Paris, 1826.

**Above:** *Qaret Umm el-Sugayar, which, like Siwa, was destroyed by torrential rains in 1926, watches like a phantom ship over the new city built nearby by the inhabitants, who still observe their ancient custom, maintaining a constant population.*

**Previous page:** *On the road to Qara, the wind and the sand have shaped the landscape. Eroded mushrooms are scattered over the plain: The softer chalk layers are gone, while the hard cap remains— but could collapse at any moment.*

*Nummulites cover the ground with a glittering silvery carpet.*

## The Nummulites of the Libyan Oases
by Didier Basset

*Nummulites are fossils dating from the start of the Tertiary Period—that is, the Paleocene Epoch. They lived from 65 million years before our era until the Oligocene Epoch 23 million years ago.* Shaped like extremely flat discs, they are so-named because of their resemblance to coins. In fact, popular stories speak of them as the petrified treasure of a giant.

Although they are relatively large—they range from the diameter of a lentil or a small bean to the size of a coin—they belong to the group foraminifer, which are protozoans, or single-celled organisms, covered with a calcium shell. Their surface is marked by several lines following a spiral pattern, not unlike the tracks on a vinyl record album. The shell is pierced by holes through which the filaments they use to collect their food used to pass, just like the foraminifers that still populate the oceans on chalky or sandy beds in warm, shallow seas.

Nummulites are particularly abundant in the area surrounding the Siwa oasis. One can also find them in the white limestone mounds of the oasis of el-Areg, associated with so-called sea lilies and giant sea-urchins. The ground near Siwa is virtually littered with nummulites, numbering in the billions, reflecting the intense light and sparkling like a salt lake. For good reason, the people of the region call this "the desert of lentils."

# Chapter II

# Bahariya, Oasis of the Black Desert:

## *Hidden Splendor*

### A crossroad for caravans

On the western plateau on the left bank of the Nile are a row of depressions, the northernmost of which is Bahariya. This depression plunges down into the heart of the stunning shiny black rock escarpments that constitute the Black Desert, a stark contrast with the Yellow Desert. The valley is roughly 400 feet below sea level, runs 54 miles from north to south, and is about 24 miles across at its widest point. Within this vast region are numerous springs around which many small oases have arisen. They have also enabled inhabitants to cultivate fertile green gardens producing a variety of crops.

The vastness of the Bahariya Valley promises wealth, while its location makes it a special site in an otherwise hostile environment. Caravans passing through could be sure of finding refuge and refreshment there, so it became an obligatory point of call. The oasis itself stands at the intersection of several popular routes: It is a stopping place along the pilgrimage to Mecca from Siwa and Cyrenaica, 240 miles from Siwa and 110 miles from the Nile; it is a center of trade and commerce en route from the Sudan to the Mediterranean, 115 miles from the nearest oasis, Farafra, and 230 miles from the coast; and it is 251 miles from Cairo, making it a convenient stop for travelers from the city. Bahariya is not a discreet entity, but consists of many small oases. Four villages dominate the area culture, including El-Qasr, formerly the capital, and Bawiti, the administrative and commercial center.

In geological terms, the Bahariya depression was formed in several complex stages. The sedimentary deposits that form the base of all the depressions in the Western Desert are here mostly covered with black rocks of various origins. They are primarily a sign of volcanic activity and of the fact that the area is rich in iron. Whereas in the other oases, quartz glitters in the sun as transparent and reflective crystals, in Bahariyah it is in the form of plentiful black quartzite, making the landscape dark. Bahariyah is the only oasis that wears this somber attire. We should remember that recent volcanic episodes have penetrated the Cretaceous strata (Mesozoic Era) and formed the basalt columns that dominate Bawiti. The iron mine situated about six miles north of Bawiti, accessible by railway, is one of several local assets.

The dark color of the area owes a great deal to volcanic activity; in some spots, the basalt outflows have risen to the surface. The presence of both iron and recent volcanic rock accounts for the heat of the ferruginous springs. The hot water in these springs is full of iron and sulfur, offering travelers passing through these torrid, parched regions a welcome salutary bath.

The climate here is healthy: Rainfall is rare and moderate, and the atmospheric conditions allow various fruits and vegetables to thrive, which has been greatly appreciated since ancient times. Vines grew in abundance, and the fine reputation of wine from Bahariya spread as far as the Nile Valley—or even beyond, though transporting it required long caravan journeys.

### A mixed population

A minority of Bahariya's population are immigrants from Siwa sent into exile for committing crimes or moral offenses. There is also a small, extremely old Christian community known for having resisted conversion to Islam. But most of the inhabitants are no different from those of the other oases: a mixture of settled Bedouins, original oasis dwellers, and migrants from Cairo who came to work, in this case in the iron mines. An extensive development project in the oasis also accounts for immigrants from various places, but these are all farm laborers.

Some ancient customs have survived in Bahariya, especially those surrounding major social events such as the birth of a child.

*Panoramic view of the Bahariya oasis and its gardens, overshadowed by black mountains: There is a vivid contrast between the green of the palm trees and the rocks made dark by their iron and basalt content. Silica is also present in the form of black quartzite.*

*Prehistoric people lived in the mountains and left some traces of their presence. When the dry period began, the inhabitants descended to the plain so they could use the springs.*

**Above:** *Bahariya's famous wine was much appreciated in ancient times on the banks of the Nile. Theban tombs give proof of its fame, as here in the tomb of Sennefer in the Gurnah necropolis, the Valley of the Nobility.*

**Below:** *The tomb of Bannentiu, a rich landowner of Libyan origin, contains paintings dating from the 26th dynasty depicting different gods. Here, Horus, in human form, takes part in the funeral procession.*

When a boy is born, the child's male relatives give him one or more palm trees. On the evening of the sixth day, a ewer filled with water is placed at the head of the newborn infant. The next day, "early in the morning, the father takes the ewer in his hand, goes to the gardens, and pours a small quantity of the water on the trunk of each palm tree given to the child; later the same day, the same male relatives draw up a document which is signed by each of the donors."[27]

After a burial, custom demands that specially made pots be placed near the place where the head of the deceased lies and be filled with water every week. The soul of the dead person can then come in the form of a bird to quench its thirst: an old Egyptian belief says that the soul of the deceased is represented by an anthropomorphic bird, the Ba bird.

## A name and history marked by trade

Bahariya was called the "northern oasis" or "the small oasis" to distinguish it from the others, and the wine produced there was said to come from *Djesdjes*, a name found on the Idfu temple. Bahariya was called *Psôbthis* in Greek times, meaning the "capital of the small oasis."[28]

Owing to trade and its location as an obligatory stopping place for caravans, Bahariya flourished in independence for a long time. It only became Egyptian during the 18th dynasty, when the Pharaoh Thutmose III took power and named Amenhotep governor of Bahariya. During the following dynasties, the Libyans and Egyptians wrangled over control of the oasis, and lasting peace was reached through a compromise, namely, the accession to the throne of a Libyan Pharaoh, Sheshonk I, founder of the 22nd dynasty. In the 26th dynasty, the oasis was greatly developed during the reigns of the Pharaohs Apries and Amasis, who already ruled Siwa. It was during this period that the most important monuments were built, some traces of which remain today.

## Tombs of extraordinary riches

Other than tombs, there are few traces of prehistoric and later inhabitants in the oases. Some romantic illustrations by Frédéric Cailliaud have fortunately preserved the memory and beauty of these.[29] One can still see some of the walls from monuments dating from the 18th dynasty (1584–1314 BC). The tomb of Amenhotep, governor of Bahariya, is currently being excavated and dominates a palm plantation on top of *Qaret Helwa*, the "Beautiful Hill."

Four tombs dating from the 26th dynasty were rediscovered and described by Fakhri in 1938. They are found in the middle of the village of Bawiti. Two—the tombs of Djed-Ammon-ef-ankh and his son Bannentiu, who were probably rich landowners or prosperous merchants of Libyan origin—are adorned with pic-

Above: *Several tombs still contain mummies in a relatively good state of preservation, thanks to the dry climate. The large number of tombs and mummies found at Bahariya, dating from different epochs, is an indication of the importance of this oasis.*

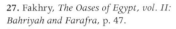

27. Fakhry, *The Oases of Egypt, vol. II: Bahriyah and Farafra*, p. 47.
28. Wagner, *op. cit.* p. 197.
29. Cailliaud, *Voyage à Meroé*, vol. I, ch. VII and IX.
30. F. Dunand, R. Lichtenberg, *Les Momies et la mort en Égypte*, p. 97-124, Paris, 1998.
31. Dunand, Lichtenberg, *op. cit.* p. 19.

Right: *A scene of the judgment of the dead in the tomb of Bannentiu. The Great Devourer awaits the verdict of the god Anubis after the dead person's heart has been weighed.*

tures. Although it is not finished and was reused during the Roman period, the tomb of Bannentui is the best preserved and most spectacular: The gods Thoth and Horus, represented in almost human dimensions, frame the entrance, pouring streams of purificatory water. They invite the visitor to join the funeral procession that progresses along the walls and columns, sometimes against a bright yellow background that throws the colors of each divinity into relief.

Recent excavations have uncovered an important necropolis dating from 332 BC in Bawiti, capital of the oasis. It contains 200 mummies wrapped according to the rites customary in Greco-Roman times, and enclosed in sarcophagi painted with scenes representing the gods.[30] Adorned with expressive gilded masks bearing the features of the deceased, and wearing crowns or decorative headdresses, they wait to be gathered by Osiris, their wide-open eyes turned toward heaven. Their rich ornaments and the cult objects surrounding them reveal the level of civilization that had been attained by the inhabitants of the oasis shortly after the visit of Alexander the Great, during Alexandria's golden age. This

discovery raises hopes that research will reveal more about the identities and lives of these princes and princesses, and that excavations will uncover the full extent of the necropolis, which is built in the same style as those found in the southern oases by the French Institute of Oriental Archaeology.

## Mummification in the oasis

The practices of burial of the dead provide valuable information about the evolution of religious and social customs. We know little about the origins of these rites. According to Françoise Dunand and Roger Lichtenberg, the determining motives were probably a mixture of altruism and self-defense: "the desire to preserve the bodies of the deceased from damage, and perhaps also to prevent their reappearance, led to a progressive elaboration of inhumation methods as well as methods of preservation."[31]

In neolithic times, graves were simply pits in the ground containing one or more bodies wrapped in skins and adorned with

*Several gilded mummies have been found in the Greco-Roman tombs near Bahariya, including this child's head.*

In the Old Kingdom, it was customary to place a bust or statue of the deceased next to the sarcophagus so the Ba bird, which flew about freely, could find the deceased and instill them with life. The paintings, at first done directly on the wrappings, were gradually replaced by funerary masks made of precious metal for high-ranking people like the Pharaohs, or of stucco, "often gilded or painted yellow to imitate the golden 'skin of the gods'."[34]

The painted *wadjyt* eye reminds of the eye of the god Ra that was lost but grew again. It is set off by black spots, like those on falcons, painted on the cheeks and in a line from the outer corner of the eye toward the back of the head. These eyes are often found in temples and in the form of amulets, and are painted on the richly decorated sarcophagi as symbols of physical rebirth.

In the New Kingdom, people began using tombs called *hypogea*. These underground burial chambers were dug into natural cliffs or the ground, both in the oases and in the Nile Valley. In the Late New Kingdom, bitumen was used to preserve bodies. The Arab word for bitumen, *mumia*, came to denote mummies themselves.

The practice of mummification continued and became widespread during the Greco-Roman period, but declined in quality due to the increased demand. There were not enough tombs, so they had to be reused many times. In this period, a new technique of decoration as a sign of privilege was used on several mummies of important persons in Dush and Kharga; gilding the body itself was meant to confer divinity on the deceased: "You will appear as a golden being, you will shine like electrum."[35]

The stucco masks adorning most bodies reflected the personality and expression of the deceased, and were made more vivid by the use of enamel eyes and realistic colors in the style of the Fayum portraits. Bandaging was a time-consuming, meticulous process, dictated by strict custom, that often required more than a month's work. The sarcophagi were made from boards of compressed papyrus in order to conserve precious wood, so rare in the oases. The tombs then took on the appearance of catacombs. They contained both individual and collective burial places and housed funerary urns of those cremated according to Greek ritual as well as sarcophagi. The advent of Christianity did not change the practice of mummification, which was consistent with their expectation of physical resurrection, but the Christian method of burial was simplified. The mummies were wrapped in a shroud, or in Bagawat, in a monk's habit. Later, mummies were dressed in their finest clothes and jewels, and only around 600 AD did the spread of Islam bring mummification to a halt by demanding that the dead be buried in the earth, quickly, wrapped only in a shroud.

Mummies of several kinds of animals have been found, likely of sacred animals—in the 1st dynasty, rams with horizontal spiral horns, then others with coiled horns, the animal emblems of Ammon and Khnum, could be mummified. A necropolis from that period containing a number of ibis and raptor mummies has been discovered in Qaret el-Farargi, not far from Bawiti—evidence of a former cult site. The mummies of falcons are even accompanied by

shells. Over time, the pits grew larger and more elaborate and the quantity and quality of the objects accompanying the dead increased, marking social differences: Jewelry of gold or silver, precious stones, sometimes even imported stones like lapis lazuli have been found in graves. The first, rather makeshift tombs found in the oasis date from 4000–3200 BC, and are attributed to farmers and herdsmen who came from the desert to settle. Wooden or terra cotta sarcophagi only appeared in the late predynastic period, and the construction of brick mastabas,[32] which started at the same time as mummification, only began in the oases in the 6th dynasty.

The first attempts at mummification using a resin coating were ineffective at preserving the body, but techniques developed over 2,000 years and were finally perfected in the New Kingdom. The five steps of mummification were already described in detail by Herodotus: (1) evisceration, (2) a natron bath (natron is a naturally occurring mixture of sodium chloride, sodium carbonate, and sodium sulfate), (3) removal of the brain, (4) application of ointments and resin, and (5) careful bandaging.

These advances made it possible to preserve bodies, which were deemed necessary for a person to take part in the next, eternal life. At first reserved for people of high social standing, mummification spread to the other classes as well. Herodotus tells us of three types of mummification: "When a dead person is brought to [the mummifiers], they show their clients wooden dummies of cadavers painted with meticulous precision. The most finished model represents, they say, the one whose name it would be sacrilege for me to mention in a matter such as this; they then show the second model, less expensive and less finished, then the third, which is the least finished of all. After this they ask their clients to choose the method they would like to see used in the case of their deceased. The family agrees on a price and leaves."[33]

**From top to bottom and left to right:**

*A group of mummies inside the tomb.*

*A small divinity.*

*Detail from the plastron of the mummy shown below showing the god Thoth, the "master of liberty," in the middle in the shape of an ibis, worshipped by two figures: on the left, Osiris, and on the right, Anubis or a priest of Anubis.*

*Bust of a woman.*

*Bust of a man.*

*Bust of an important person, probably a rich oasis land-owner. The decoration on the plastron depicts traditional funeral rites. Under the face, covered with gold leaf, Osiris is depicted surrounded by the four sons of Horus.*

**32.** Mastaba is a word of Arab origin which means "bench" and refers to a tomb of the Ancient Empire distinguished by sloping walls made of brick or stone which generally are of a rectangular shape; the tomb consists of an underground vault and an outer chapel: "The vault was made out of the bottom of a mostly vertical well and contained a sarcophagus made out of stone commissioned by the sovereign, and also the necessary equipment for the dead person's life beyond the grave. The vault was walled up after the burial and the well used for access to the tomb was buried under loose stones and earth ... The chapel was richly decorated with bas-relief or paintings featuring scenes of life on earth ..." Posener, Sauneron, Yoyotte, *op. cit.* p. 163.
**33.** Herodotus, *op. cit.* p. 174.
**34.** Dunand, Lichtenberg, *op. cit.* p. 102.
**35.** J.-C. Goyon, *Rituels de L'Ancien Empire*, p. 102, Paris, 1972.

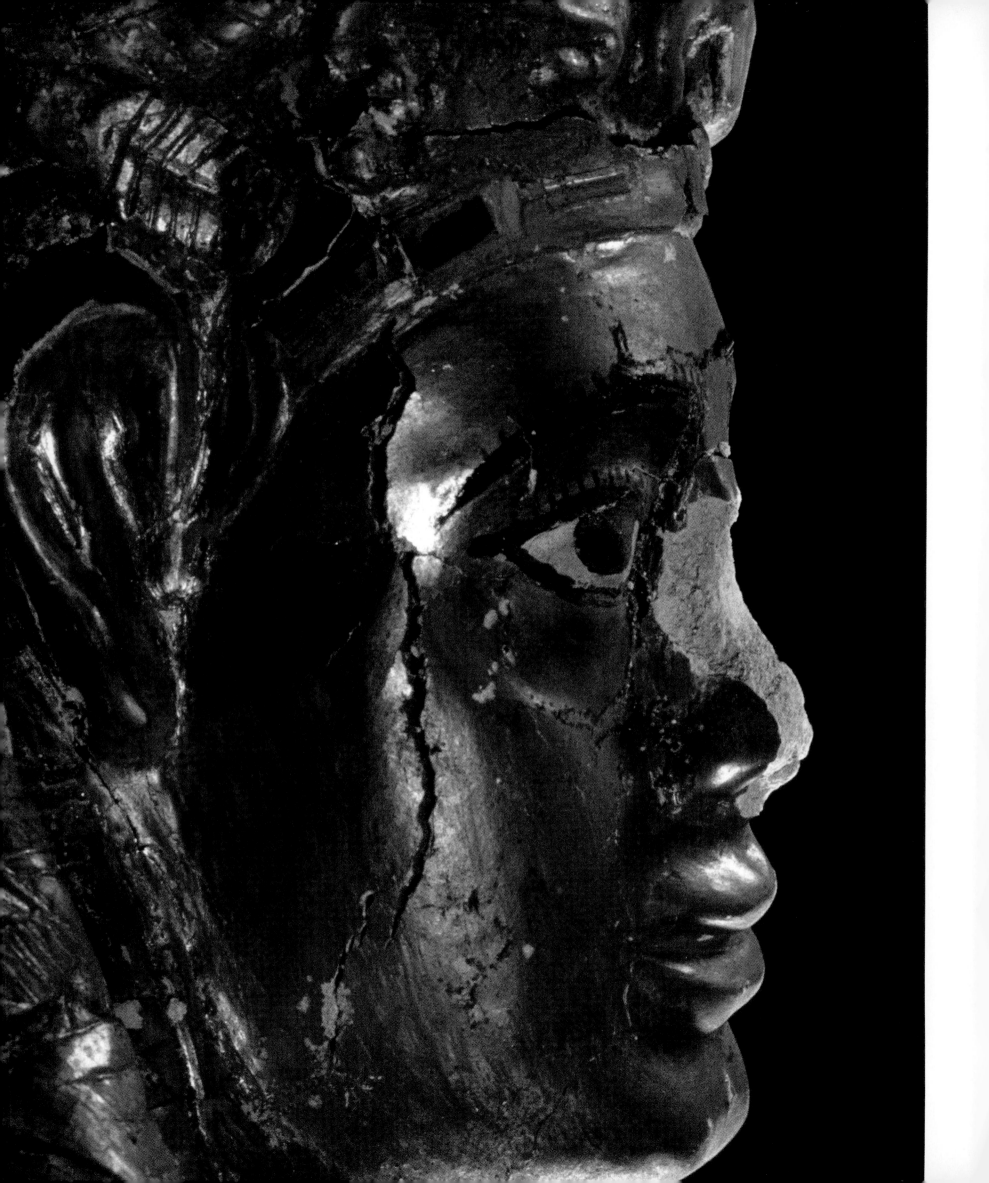

mummies of shrews for the falcons to eat in the afterlife. Fake mummies, probably used as votive offerings in temples, show that production was sometimes insufficient for the needs of the time.

## Temples: Great sites in ruins

Two ruined temples dating from the 26th dynasty still exist in Bahariya, although they are barely visible. One was built by King Apries in el-Qasr, the other by King Amasis in Bawiti. When returning from Siwa, Alexander the Great chose to take the eastern route back to the Nile Valley. He stopped in Bahariya and marked his visit with the construction of a huge temple in Bawiti: the temple of Qasr el-Mesguebe.

The many gardens in the oasis soothe the gaze with their myriad shades and hues of green. The thermal properties of the water gushing from underground enhance the fertility of the land, and crops thrive. These qualities were noted by a khedive who was in poor health and in need of recuperation. He built a palace of black quartzite on top of a promontory overlooking the oasis depression. Unfortunately, this particular governor succumbed to his

illness before it could be completed. The ruins remind us of his story and message: Contemplate the splendor of proud Bahariya.

Thirty miles southwest of Bawiti, on the road leading to the neighboring oasis of Farafra, is a small oasis surrounded by abundant springs: el-Heiz. El-Heiz played a central role in Bahariya's history, for it was the site of a large Roman fort built to defend the southern approach against invasion. The fort's high, imposing walls still recall this role, as they tower over the governor's palace and its outbuildings, and stand watch near an important town, a wine-making center, a chapel, and a huge necropolis that is currently under excavation. Not far from this fort stands a large church, probably dedicated to St. George, near a huge well. For several centuries it was certainly one of the most important churches in Egypt, and a center for Christianity. It was built in early Christian style in the late 4th or early 5th century. Cailliaud's pictures capture the grandeur of this edifice, which is currently being reconstructed in sunbaked brick according to the original plan and using the same materials.[36]

The presence of all these various buildings demonstrates the essential role the el-Heiz oasis played in the region. This oasis is

*The curator of the khedive's palace keeps constant watch over the ruins.*

*Portrait of a young oasis dweller.*

**Right:** *Palm plantation and gardens irrigated by springs and wells, in this case, of Roman origin. Maintained with great care using traditional techniques, they are the pride of the inhabitants—a haven of peace and place of refreshment for travelers.*

**Previous page:** *Nestling among black rocks shaped by the natural forces of erosion, the palace of the khedive towers over the Bahariya depression.*

36. Cailliaud, *Voyage à Meroé.*

**Top and previous pages:**
*Remains of the ramparts of a large Roman fortress that surrounded the township in the oasis of el-Heiz. This settlement probably consisted* *of a small chapel and numerous houses, including that of the governor, a place for making wine, and cellars, where pots stained with tannin can still be found.*

the fourth of the seven oases mentioned in the famous list of the Idfu temple, bearing the name "the oasis established in the place of the *noun* (13,000 trees)." *Noun* was the name given to the primordial ocean from which the creation and the Creator emerged, and thus suggests the promise of life nourished by an original liquid element.[37]

Despite its apparent modesty, Bahariya has had its hour of glory, and the two extremes of the depression, el-Heiz and Bawiti, 30 miles apart, are still active centers of excavation that will no doubt yield further evidence of past grandeur. The "small oasis" has a modest, self-effacing name that does not do justice to its historical importance. Indeed, its history is distinguished by magnificence and a certain sacral quality, as shown by the recently unearthed Roman necropolis.

The special past of the Bahariya oasis is also revealed in the evidence of Christianity provided by monuments found in its far southern end, in el-Heiz. This town served as guardian of the civilization of the Bahariya oasis, but also as a beacon of Christianity directed toward the southern oases.

The church at el-Heiz, in Early Christian style. It is one of the oldest churches in Egypt, dating from the end of the 4th century, and contained paintings and capitals that are no longer extant. Cailliaud made a touching engraving of it (plate XXXVI), showing the ruins as they appeared before the reconstruction that is now in progress.

**37.** Fakhry, *The Oases of Egypt*, vol. II, p. 110.

# Chapter III

# Farafra, Oasis of the White Desert:

## *A Center of Irrigation and Intensive Agriculture*

### A pleasant stop

After receiving a blessing at the basilica, pilgrims leaving el-Heiz followed the southern route and crossed a rock barrier composed of thousands of sparkling crystals reflecting the sun: the Crystal Mountain. Remarkable multicolored rocks, blue and red, frame the quartz and calcite rising from their geodes like flowers of stone. Carried by the wind, grains of sand patter on ridges formed of "desert diamonds," small citrines that catch the sun's rays and send out brief flashes of gold, competing with the pearls of carnelian said to have been left behind by Isis, and thus known as the "blood of Isis."

Finally, the path plunges into a new depression of blinding white: the White Desert surrounding Farafra. This oasis is situated halfway between Bahariya, 115 miles to the north, and Dakhla, 120 miles away via the caravan route over the eastern plateau, or 180 miles if one takes the route across the plain. Although it is longer and quite monotonous, the latter route is much easier to travel. In the west, a trail leads to the small oasis of Aïn-Della, a strategic point stranded on the edge of the Great Sea of Sand. It is the starting point of the route to the Libyan oases in the Qatara depression and, despite its extreme isolation, has always been a well-defended military outpost.

At the foot of an imposing massif, Qus Abu-Saïd, the small village of Farafra is dominated by a medieval fortress and surrounded by gardens that are irrigated with water from a well built in Roman times. Farafra was thought to be a small oasis, nestled in a moderate-size depression, and therefore of limited use for agriculture. But the relatively recent discovery of the actual dimensions of the depression and its huge underground reserves of water has changed this view of Farafra, opening up new prospects for the oasis as an intense system of cultivation is being developed. The landscape is constantly changing, and the irrigation canals and green fields expand every year, so much so that the development is seriously interfering with access routes. Now, far from being insignificant, Farafra appears to be turning into the most important agricultural center in the chain of oases.

Because of its ancient trading connections with Libya and the Nile Valley, Farafra's destiny has tended to run parallel to that of its nearest neighbor, Bahariya. Both oases were governed by the same "Egyptianized" Libyan princes, but Farafra, unlike Bahariya, retains no trace of this epoch.

The oasis also has an old name, *To-ihe*, which means "the country of the cow." This is a tribute to Hathor, the goddess of love and fertility, an anthropomorphic deity with a cow's head. It is also a reference to the Bedouin nomads who came to pasture their herds on the Farafra plain.

Here, the Bedouins live according to the rhythm of the stars, attentive to their slightest movements as they guide their daily tasks. The people of all the oases, but especially those in Farafra, have always been enamoured of astronomy. Their knowledge of the stars allows them to precisely measure the passing of time, and thus maintain a water distribution program, day and night.

Most people are familiar with Venus, the Evening Star, which is visible at twilight. But in the oases, the pure, clear skies allow learned Bedouins to observe this planet in broad daylight, even from the bottom of a well. Venus is the "Bedouin's star," the clock of the desert.

**Above:** *In contrast to the black universe of Bahariya, the White Desert is made up of mountains and massifs that reflect a dazzling light.*

**Right:** *The Mountain of Crystal conceals ochre and blue pigments in its hollows, as well as flowers of stone: Calcite and crystalline gypsum sing the beauty of the desert.*

*The fortified city of Farafra with its thick medieval walls,*
*only rarely pierced by apertures.*

*There are many springs in the gardens. Some are hot mineral springs,*
*while others are used to irrigate the crops that constitute Farafra's wealth.*

## Ghostly places

### An ancient fortress

A single fortress dating from the Middle Ages can still be seen today in Farafra. Built on a rocky outcropping, it has a commanding view of the region. Its imposing walls surrounded approximately 100 rooms used to store the provisions—olives, dates, and grain—of all the families in the oasis, guarded by one woman. The interior is protected by beautiful doors made of acacia wood, but there is just one door to defend the fortress from external attacks.

Sadly, the central structure of this citadel was weakened by exceptional rains. It collapsed in 1958, but is still surrounded by noble residences decorated with scenes of daily life or images from pilgrimages to Mecca. The acacia doors to the fortress, carved with magnificent lintels, have been recovered and tell us of the oasis' history. The doors' ancient wooden locks, still in working condition, demonstrate the skill and ingenuity of local craftspeople able to make wooden keys that could withstand the ravages of time.

### The legend of King Hennis

The ancient route leading to Farafra passes by the foot of two immense rocks made of sedimentary deposits. Through erosion, they have taken the form of gigantic towers, and they mark the entrance to the realm of an ancient ruler, King Hennis. Paths wind along the rocks across reddish, treacherous quicksand to bring us to the remains of his dwelling. The route is difficult, strewn with boulders that have tumbled down from the surrounding mountains. The remains of the king's castle are hidden on top of one of these. Small rocky escarpments mark its limits, and a strange yellow cement joins the blocks. The view from this site is oriented toward the east, and the solitary acacia standing out against the horizon reminds us that one of the rich resources of this region, the water of the Aïn el-Wadi, is not far away. Legend tells us that King Hennis owned huge herds of livestock and was extremely wealthy, in part because this magical place was also supposedly rich in gold mines; his story is told in the Siwa Manuscript.

*The White Desert even contains "chapels" and "candles" that are lit in the twilight, though others may see camels or the entrance to a secret kingdom in these formations.*

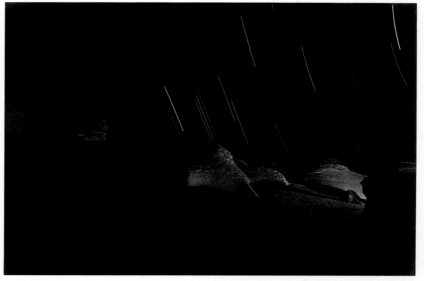

*Like little metallic flowers, these hematite pseudomorphs throw their dark shadows onto the sand, heralding the night, which will reveal Orion rising to lead the dance of the stars.*

**Following pages:** *Someone has been walking over the White Desert: These giant footprints lead to the domain of King Hennis, whose turret is already visible, an outpost of his chalky kingdom.*

### The White Desert

The trail that leads to King Hennis' mountaintop continues past the castle and its towers and crosses a vast expanse of chalk desert, the White Desert. Farafra is the only one of the oases situated on the crumbling remains of a limestone massif from the Cretaceous era. The purity of the limestone can be inferred from the dazzling whiteness it produces. The retreating sea left behind ripples that were formed from chalk and sand, now frozen in time. In these are imprisoned numerous marine fossils including sea urchins and shells.

The region looks as though it has been frequented by a giant sculptor who has created people, animals, and monuments on his own, enormous scale. This oversized statuary invites visitors to take a phantasmal stroll. The path passes "Our Lady of the White Forest" and its adjoining chapel, leads to an encounter with "Nefertiti," and then with a reclining princess, who is watched over by a "man with a pipe" and the grimacing figure of the devil. Further on, a gendarme searches for his horse, while a camel chases a mouse. Suddenly surrounded by gigantic meringues, the visitor, disconcerted by so many fantastic forms, looks to the horizon for refuge. But where have all these white tents on the sand come from? Is it a huge prehistoric campsite, or are they shelters for people fleeing from Cambyses—or the dwellings of *jinni*?

Across the white chalk carpet, strange small black stones sparkle and crunch with a metallic noise underfoot. Their shapes vary—they may be round like a cherry or a pomegranate, elongated and rough like the branches of a shrub, or surprisingly geometric. They look like flowers of crystallized iron but are actually composed of ferric sulfides and oxides: They are pseudomorphs of hematite or limonite that have assumed the shape of the calcite crystals or marcasite "flowers" they have replaced.

Is the wind the creator of these sculptures, which never cease to evolve according to the caprice of a seemingly wild imagination? Never satisfied with its work, it occasionally destroys them, leaving us to blame the "Abominable Chalkman," who takes refuge in his palace, which is hidden by thick white walls, assailed by the howling winds, and sometimes disappears under thick whirling clouds as in a sandstorm. But time passes, and the setting sun throws pearly shadows onto this magical whiteness, washing the sky with preternatural rosy hues.

Farafra the White defies the White Desert that had almost obliterated it. To travelers who discover it, the land of the cow offers greater sustenance than the arid whiteness of the surrounding desert. But, hidden under a cloud of dust raised by the intensive clearing of land and the laborious excavation of many canals, Farafra expands, surrounding itself with fields and greenery.

# Chapter IV

# Dakhla, Gateway to the Desert:

## *The Inner Oasis*

## An ancient capital

On the southwesterly route out of Farafra lies the small oasis of Bir Abu Minqar, whose strategic importance stems from the fact that it is the last town where travelers can obtain provisions of water. The vast and nearly impassable ranges of dunes of the Great Sea of Sand rise up on one side; on the other, to the southeast, begins the route to the Dakhla oasis, dominated along its entire length by a steep cliff, the edge of the chalk plateau. This is the route taken by caravans from Farafra.

Unlike the oases to the north, Dakhla is clearly laid out along an east-west axis, 40 miles long and 15 miles wide, and it encompasses three very distinct regions. The first of these is rocky terrain and the site of ancient fortifications and more recent temples. The second region is green and fertile, and the third is a sandy area where one finds the pharaonic city and its necropolis.

## A history wrestled from the sands

In prehistoric times the Dakhla region was inhabited by nomadic peoples who settled in lake villages. These villages flourished because it was possible to cultivate the indigenous grains—barley and wheat—and because the settlers could keep domestic animals, particularly dogs, cattle, and sheep. The carved wooden and stone tools from the era testify to the highly advanced techniques used by craftspeople. Groups led by the Egyptian Supreme Council of Antiquities and the Royal Museum of Ontario (Canada) have excavated 13 sites near Dakhla, one of which appears to have been something like a slaughterhouse. They have unearthed bone fragments and the teeth of a variety of animals—elephants, aurochs, gazelles, deer, an ostrich, and a horse—all likely to have lived in savannah regions, with plentiful grasslands and water.[38]

Changes in climate, the gradual cessation of seasonal rains, and a dwindling water supply drove the inhabitants of the subdesert zones toward the oases. In the 6th dynasty, during the reign of Pepy I (ca. 2320–2285 BC)—long before the northern oases fell under the rule of the Libyan princes brought up in the Nile Valley—Dahkla became an important Egyptian colony administrated by local governors according to pharaonic law. The governor's residence stood near the modern village of Balat in what is known as Ayn Asil, then the principal town in the eastern part of the oasis.

The history of Dahkla seems unremarkable until the 18th dynasty (ca. 1553–1295 BC), when all the oases came under the direct administration of the Nile Valley nomarchs[39] during the reign of the Pharaoh Thutmose III.

## A population of artisans

### *Pottery*

Egypt has an ancient pottery tradition. Pottery was highly valued because of its association with the divine creator, Khnum, who was himself a potter. Khnum was a ram-headed deity whose role was central to the ancient belief system: "One may imagine everything modeled by him on his wheel with a mere breath from his lips, with an unknown form of clay."[40]

Khnum had horns like the god Ammon, and his creative powers enabled him to bring animals, humankind, and the gods themselves into the world. He even set creation itself in motion, recounted metaphorically, by giving birth to the sun: "He ... modeled the primordial egg from which the sun sprang at the beginning of the world."[41]

There is a certain moving quality to finding large pottery artifacts, whether jars or bowls, not only in the obscurity of a potter's studio, but also smashed and abandoned in the desert sun in Abu-

*Bir Jebel, the mountain well, a small oasis nestling at the foot of the steep escarpment of the Mountain of the West.*

**38.** A. Mills, *Research in Dakhla Oasis, Origin and Early Development of Food-producing in North Eastern Africa*, p. 205-210, Polish Academy of Sciences, Poznan, 1984.

**39.** A nomarch is the governor of an administrative, economic and fiscal province that corresponds to the division of the territory and its system of irrigation. *Nome* is the name given by the Greeks to these districts, called *sepat* by the ancient Egyptians. Posener, Sauneron, Yoyotte, *op. cit.* p. 190.

**40.** Meeks, Favard-Meeks, *op. cit.* p. 76.

**41.** Meeks, Favard-Meeks, *op. cit.* p. 308.

**Above:** *An ancient tower, taken over by pigeons, rises like a lighthouse over Qasr, a city famous for its pottery.*

**Left:** *Khnum, the potter god with a ram's head, depicted on the left pillar in the vestibule of the Deir el-Haggar temple.*

*Thou who holds the secret of the trade*
*O Sheik Abd al-Rahim, be with us.*[43]

At the decisive moment when a clay object is removed from the potter's wheel and sent into the world, the artisan expresses his pride in creation. Henein recounts, "One day I silently observed one of the master potters. He was completely absorbed in his work. While removing his pot [from the wheel], he said to me: 'If I were able to give it a soul, my pot would speak.'"[44] The influence of human representation on the art of the potter is evident even in traditional terminology: a piece of pottery has feet, a belly, hips, shoulders, a neck, and even lips.

In the Badoura quarter, the ancient knowledge is passed down within seven families, all of whom live in what is known as "Potters' Lane." Henein describes their way of life and methods of production in detail. The studios are in the hands of 175 people from these families, 36 of whom are potters. Each family studio has an intensive work load that at times calls for the talents and skill of the group's expert, the master potter, to build a kiln dome or to fire the pottery. The work is long and arduous, not merely creative, including gathering fuel, collecting and preparing the clay and other materials, actually making the forms, drying the pots, heating the kiln, and firing and cooling pottery.

Two kinds of clay, red and white, are commonly used. The exact choice of materials depends on the demands of a particular pottery design and an economical use of energy.

Red clay has a number of advantages: it is found nearby in large quantities on the top layer of the soil, so it costs nothing and

Ballas. The remarkable power to embue inert matter with life is still passed down among master potters. Nessim Henry Henein lived with some of these masters in Dahkla for several months to learn their views and try to grasp the essence of their art. "The potter of Al-Qasr," he tells us, "describes his wheel as a soul that engenders life, and the act of potting as gestation and birth."[42]

Potters, it is said, have inherited their knowledge from a distant ancestor, Sheik Abd al-Rahim al-Qenawi, who came to the Nile Valley from Qena. Near their studios, a small, white, commemorative cupola has been erected to offer the potters support, and they never fail to invoke its protective charm before engaging in a delicate task:

is easy to obtain. After it is mixed with a kind of vegetable ash, it can be used to make almost anything. This mixture makes the pottery more watertight and more resistant to stress and jarring, thus making it easier to transport. Objects made with this kind of clay tend to include those used for storing foodstuffs, such as oils, vegetables, or date paste. Common shapes are flat bowls and basins for various purposes, such as the kneading trough used to make bread dough, which can also be turned into a cradle if necessary! Large jars known as *sega* (meaning "to give a drink" or "to irrigate," see page 74) are used for carrying water. Their ovoid shape, common in Egypt and the oases, dates back to well before the Roman epoch. Their size—about 16 inches long and eight inches tall—is perfectly suited to the width of the irrigation canals next to the wells, which makes it easy to fill them quickly; the water simply flows into the opening at the top. They are marked with hastily drawn zigzag motifs to distinguish them from butter churns, whose shape is identical.

White clay, on the other hand, is only found some miles from the village in the potters' hill, Qaret Chanda, where it is increasingly dangerous to mine. The white clay, naturally enriched with limestone and iron, and mixed with silica, may be more fragile, but its extreme porosity is ideal to cool hot water drawn from the springs, filter it if necessary, and store it at a low temperature. While on a scientific expedition in the Napoleonic campaigns, Vivant Denon sang its praises: "We spent the night in Balasse, which has given its name to the earthen jars it supplies not only to all of Egypt, but also Syria and all the islands of the archipelago. These jars have the property of allowing water to seep through them, thus purifying and cooling it ... Nature provides the material in the neighboring desert ready for use: a fat marl, fine, soapy and compact, which does not need to be moistened and kneaded to be easy to form and resilient; and the vessels that are made from it, first fashioned on the wheel, then dried and half baked in the sun, are finished in a few hours using a single fire of straw."[45]

This type of clay is used for fewer objects than the red clay, primarily those reserved for water and beverages. Henein writes about kettles and traditional water jars, which, due to considerations of time and profit, are the only item decorated these days: "Perhaps the purity and sacred character of water, which is difficult to obtain in the oasis, has led to a respect for the receptacle that holds it."[46]

The skill of the potter gives him license to produce all the various items needed for domestic and commercial usage. An ancient code dictates a unique purpose for each shape, so that anyone can recognize its purpose immediately upon seeing it, with no need for painting or decoration. The absence of ornamentation enhances the purity of form and the nuances of ochre coloring produced by the firing process.

In conformance with the religious traditions and hospitality of the oases, large jars called *sabil* or *garra* are filled with water and set out in the shade of a roof for the use of passersby. These jars

*The cupola of Sheik Abd al-Rahim protects the potters.*

*Pots drying in the sun.*

**Following pages:**
*Watercolor paintings of different types of pottery (from left to right, and top to bottom):*
*– rabbit hutch (adus al-araneb)*
*– basin (test) and colander (masfa)*
*– pot (dest)*
*– drinking bowls (adus sagir)*
*– water jug (olla)*
*– ewer (abri)*
*– water jug of the seventh day (ollet el-subu')*
*– jars for transporting water (sega)*
*– basins*
*– water jars (zir)*

42. N. H. Henein, *Poterie et potiers d'Al-Qasr*, p. 40, Cairo, 1997.
43. Henein, *op. cit.* p. 217.
44. Henein, *op. cit.* p. 40.
45. D. Vivant Denon, *Voyages dans la Haute et la Basse Égypte pendant les campagnes de Bonaparte, en 1798 et 1799*, volume I, p. 320f., London, 1807.
46. Henein, *op. cit.* p. 111.

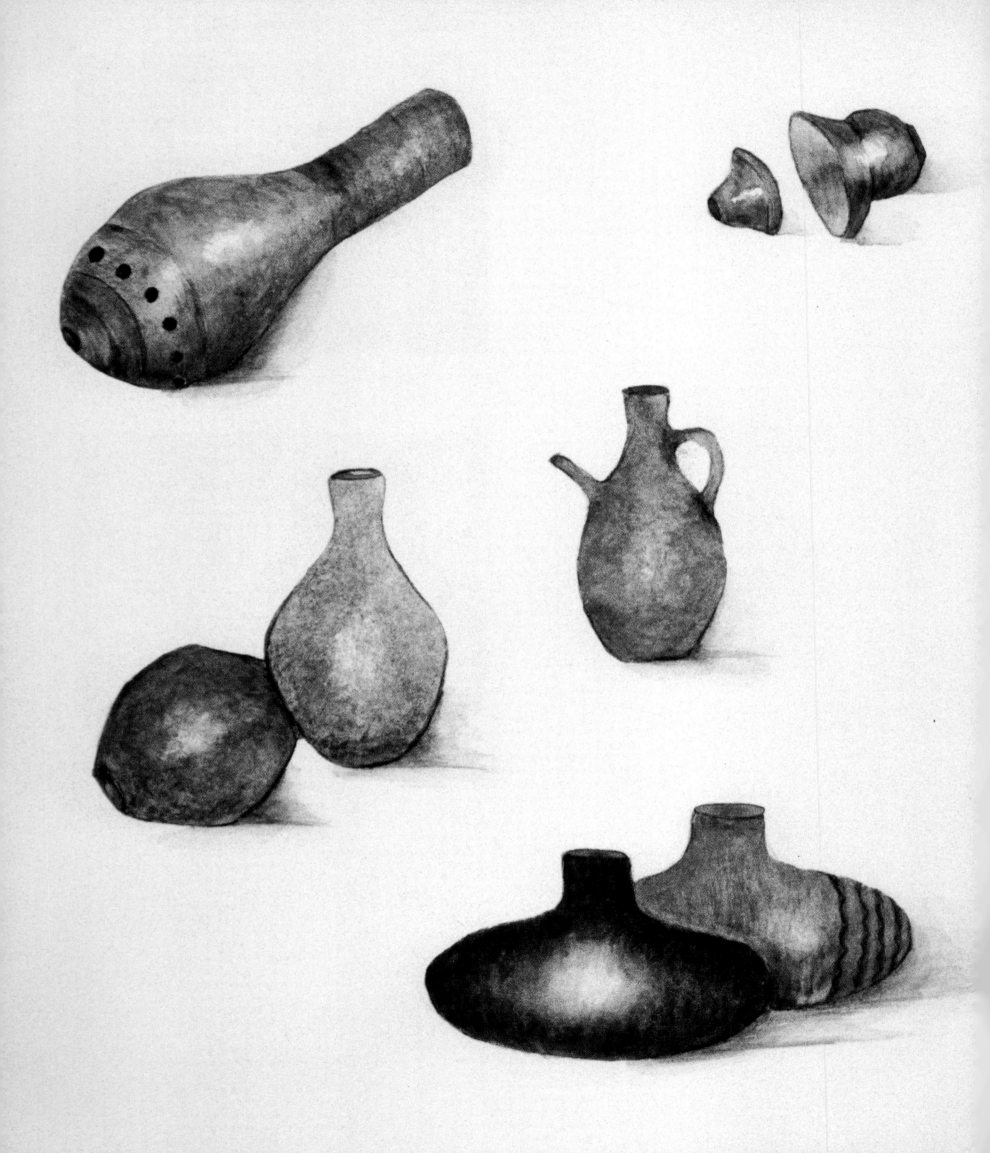

*Baskets, platters, chests: Basketry is a tradition passed down from ancient times, as can be seen in the above engraving by von Minutoli showing mat-weaving, plate XXIV.*

**Following page:** *The temple of Deir el-Haggar, the Monastery of the Rock, 1st century AD, before its reconstruction.*

are taller than they are wide and are sometimes fitted with "ears" for transport. During the harvest, it is customary for *sabil* to be hung in the trees edging the fields and to give one to farm workers as a gift in addition to their seasonal wage. In return, the laborers offer a sheaf of wheat, called "the dinner of the jar." Members of the community help one another and still live largely by bartering, getting grain or services in exchange for pots.

Certain pottery items are used for ritual ceremonies, such as the birth of a child. "The water jug of the seventh day," or *ollet el-subu'*, is a peculiarly shaped pot that resembles a fountain with several tiers, becoming smaller toward the top. It has seven openings meant to hold a candle, each of which celebrates one of the past days and guarantees a secure future for the new child. Parents of a newborn wait a week to buy the jug, then light the seven candles—seven being a magical and lucky number—and joyfully celebrate the happy event.

The child's sex determines the choice of vessel: rounded water jars are used for girls' ceremonies, while spouted ewers or pitchers are associated with the male sex. The appropriate vessel, decorat-

ed with blue beads as protection from the evil eye, is placed in the center of a large tray, surrounded by seven grains and several coins. The family encircles its oldest female member in a candle-light procession, while she exorcizes the evil eye by singing and throwing salt. Fast sprouting of the grains is a good omen for the child.[47] This custom recalls the ancient ritual of Osiris as the god of vegetation, when rapid germination of grain placed in small statues of Osiris was a good sign for the next harvest and all sorts of other events as well. This ancient potters' tradition is threatened by the advent of metal kettles and washbasins made of durable plastic in gaudy colors—but these lack the *jinni*!

### Basketry

The art of basketry is still practiced in all the oases: Palm leaves are cut into thin strips and then woven into mats, baskets, large platters, various sorts of covers, and even chests. The tradition dates back to the time of the Pharaohs. The most common technique is the sewed coil, which is similar to that used in pottery—plant fibers are rolled into a spiral to form a base and are then sewn together to create the desired size and shape.

Both the men and the women of the oasis wear pretty straw hats with a blue band to match their *galabiyah*, a special woven cloth. A Dakhla marriage custom calls for the manufacture of two special cloths to be used only once by the young married couple, "oval-shaped, with bright colors for the bride and more somber tones for the groom."[48] What better symbol for the union of two people than a cloth shaped like the original egg, hatched from an "Ammonian" spiral, with weaving that in itself illustrates the art of harmoniously and patiently "marrying" two strands!

## Sites of distinction

As you enter the Dakhla oasis after crossing the escarpment, you may sense that the access road is being guarded by a sentry post. This is a temple dedicated to the god Ammon, built in the

Roman era in the 1st century. It was begun under Nero, continued under Vespasian, and finished by Titus and Domitian: Deir el-Haggar, or "the Monastery of the Rock," whose Egyptian name is *Set-Ouha* or "Oasis of Seth," was later occupied by Christian monks. The name fits the temple well: It is made from impressive blocks of stone that have been cleverly cemented together. The temple and its outbuildings were surrounded by a brick wall which was, until a few years ago, barely accessible. Ruined in a landslide, anyone who wanted to see the cartouches and the wall inscriptions required mountaineering skills to scale it. Though this adventure did have its appeal, the entire compound has now been restored and visitors can easily reach the temple's interior and admire the bas-reliefs in their original setting.

The antechamber entrance is crowned by a lintel with a figure of Horus as protector, leaning on two decorated pillars. The emperor Vespasian pays homage to various gods including Ammon-Min[49] and Khnum. The walls bear scenes of temple patrons alternating with the cartouches of the four Roman emperors who set their signature to this edifice.

Not far from the temple of Deir el-Haggar, two hills form the actual entrance to the oasis. Bones have been found on one of them, leading archeologists to believe it was used as a cemetery in ancient times. The other hill is a veritable necropolis, *Garet el-Mussawaga* ("the Hill of Paintings"), containing two tombs decorated with zodiacal signs, which were built during the Roman era between the 1st and 2nd centuries AD. Both the walls and the ceilings of these tombs, which were built for two of the city's notable citizens, Petubastis and Petosiris, are richly ornate. The walls

**47.** D. Ammoun, *Égypte, des mains magiques*, p. 92f., Cairo, 1993.
**48.** Ammoun, *op. cit.* p. 78.
**49.** Min is a very ancient god of fertility whose religion is linked to the harvest. He is pictured holding his erect penis in one hand and brandishing a flail in the other over his shoulder. He wears a crown with the two large feathers of Ammon in it. Linked with the latter, he was frequently likened to Ammon from the time of the New Empire onwards; he was depicted with the appearance of Ammon and was also called Ammon-Min.

*Temple of Deir el-Haggar: portico with a lintel decorated with the disk of the sun flanked by a protecting uraeus and a spread wing on each side.*

**Following page:**
*Necropolis of Mussawaqa*

**Top left:** *Tomb of Petosiris, scene of the judgment of the dead (psychostasis). On the right, Osiris is seated on a throne in front of the Great Devourer; Thoth can be seen behind the latter. On the left is a scene of the weighing of the soul. On the left in the middle, the deceased, with his arms raised, is introduced by the goddess Maat.*

**Bottom left:** *The Ba of Petosiris, a representation of his soul in the form of a bird with a human head, receives a libation from Isis, who is followed by the solar scarab.*

**Right:** *Tomb of Petosiris, spirits armed with knives ensuring the protection of the dead person. At the top is a spirit with the head of a jackal on the left, and one with the head of the god Bes. Below, Khonsu is shown spearing an animal, and the child Horus is depicted with two faces. The two scenes are decorated with the "wadjyt eye."*

**50.** Anubis, "the god of the necropolis," is shown with the head of a dog or a jackal. He presides over the embalming ceremony, of which he is the initiator and specialist. He guards the kingdom of the dead.

in the tomb of Petubastis depict the dead man being judged and his soul being weighed—the classical scene of psychostasis as described in the *Book of the Dead*. The god Osiris presides at the judgment of the dead, while the jackal-headed god Anubis[50] brings him the deceased person who "confesses" his innocence. Anubis uses scales to verify that the heart of the dead person weighs no more than the effigy of Maat, the goddess of justice, or the feather that represents her. "The Great Devourer," a monstrous hybrid, bides its time, hoping to make a good meal of the damned. The Ibis-headed Thoth, patron god of scribes, records the result on a tablet and, if the good and bad acts balance one another, the deceased is taken into the kingdom of the blessed.

The paintings in this tomb are enhanced by an exquisite ceiling decorated with the signs of the zodiac, and the whole construction displays fine workmanship.

The tomb of Petosiris also shows a scene of psychostasis, but its context is more provincial and its execution displays less artistic skill. Depictions of battles and agricultural scenes transport us

back to the world of that era; the wealth of the palm plantations and the cultivation of wine are emphasized over the curve of the vault and joining the starry sky.

These two tombs clearly express the importance of funerary gifts to secure eternal salvation for the soul of the dead person.

Finally, there is the city of el-Qasr, which was once a fortress built in the Middle Ages on the foundations of an older Roman village. Originally built to defend the oasis, el-Qasr became the medieval capital of Dakhla. Narrow lanes wind between four- and five-story houses whose high walls are dotted with impressive windows and doors. The doors are flanked by temple pillars decorated with hieroglyphics and crowned by wooden lintels bearing inscriptions, generally the homeowners' genealogy accompanied by verses from the Koran. An ancient mosque stands atop the city; climbing its 65-foot high minaret is a perilous undertaking. Some steps have vanished, and those that remain are defended aggressively by pigeons. Attaining the top is well worth the trouble, however, where you are rewarded by a magnificent panorama of

**Left and below:**
*Narrow streets with ancient doorways surmounted by lintels with carved symbols, inscriptions, and verses from the Koran.*

**Previous pages:** *The old city of el-Qasr, former capital of Dakhla during the Ayubidd period, 11th–12th centuries.*

**51.** C. Drovetti, *Journal d'un voyage à la vallée de Dakel, vers la fin de 1818,* in F. Cailliaud, *Voyages à l'oasis de Thebes et dans les déserts situés à l'orient et à l'occident de la Thébaïde, fait pendant les années 1815, 16, 17, 18,* p. 103, Paris, 1821.

**Left:** *El-Qasr's minaret, the domain of pigeons. Pigeon breeding is still a local tradition, and a pair of pigeons given as a wedding present is said to betoken a happy future.*

**Above:** *Market gardens near Mout, the administrative capital of the oasis.*

**Following pages:** *View of the city and the flat roofs of the houses from the top of the minaret.*

the green oasis at the foot of the dazzling white cliff that dominates it. Pigeon breeding is another local custom developed from ancient roots: at celebrations, particularly weddings, it is traditional to give a pair of pigeons or turtle-doves as gifts.

El-Qasr has one famous spring, described in 1818 by Chevalier Drovetti: "El-Qasr ... is situated at the foot of the mountain. An abundant spring, which rises in the middle of the village, waters the surrounding gardens. This water source is thermal and impregnated with sulfur. In the pool that it forms, women gather in groups to bathe at night: next to it, a closed chamber has been built for men ... It is the same at Genah, whose spring provides water like that in el-Qasr. These two springs display the same qualities as the famous Fountain of the Sun [in Siwa] mentioned by Herodotus."[51]

In the town itself, goods produced by local artisans are displayed in the squares, including a variety of baskets, silver jewelry, and small painted clay figures depicting traditional trades and everyday scenes, ranging from farmers and craftsmen to musicians, dancers, or even chess-players.

Not far away is the site of the city of Amheida, originally called Trimithis, which had been inhabited since prehistoric times and enjoyed great prestige in the Greco-Roman era. Amheida had its heyday in the Byzantine era but was abandoned quite early on in favor of the neighboring city of Mout. The area around Amheida is still littered with remnants of pottery, but few other traces of it remain. The site is marked by one simple monument, like a boundary mark of this forgotten Greco-Roman town.

Situated at the center of the Dakhla oasis, Mout, or Mothis, is still the administrative capital, with a large, active population, mostly farmers. This city has drawn together the inhabitants who from ancient times had settled around the small lakes as the environs grew too arid to sustain them. The cultivation of vines and palms was developed here, as attested by the paintings in the tomb of Petosiris. There are many, many fields whose strong and vibrant green contrasts almost violently with the pastel hues of the northern cliff at dawn; the latter change to mauve, then to a dazzling white at noon, and finally into the color of flame at sunset. The green carpet around Mout is enlivened by tiny white dots—the oxpeckers, graceful long-necked white birds that quench their thirst and serenely contemplate their reflections in the irrigation canals. They wait, immobile, for the caravans coming from the south, for Mout marks the end of the long journey from the Cufra oasis in Libya.

In ancient times, a vast city stood at a place today called Mut el-Kharab. It was built during the 22nd dynasty (945–715 BC), contemporary with the stele in Dakhla that regulated the use of the springs, and thus irrigation as well.

The ancient city of
Balat with its shady
lanes conducive to the
occasional chat.

**Following page:**
*Returning from the
gardens in the golden
light of sunset fringed
by growing shadows.*

52. Wagner, *op. cit.* p. 195.

The ancient Byzantine city of Kellis, which became Smint el-Kharab, then Smint, boasts several ruined chapels whose stone arches follow one another like waves stranded on the sand. One leading to the next, they offer a hint of the importance of this city near Mout.

According to Wagner, the name of the town of Balat comes from the Roman term *Palatium*, and is used for other Middle Eastern cities as well, particularly in Turkey.[52] Balat's ancient center is in many ways similar to that of el-Qasr; it also has narrow, winding lanes shaded by large palms that offer protection from sand and sun. At its feet is a bustling modern city, a center of commerce in many areas.

Until the middle of the 20th century, no one suspected that the sands at the eastern end of the oasis covered a town and a necro-polis of monumental proportions at the foot of the city of Balat. But in the wake of an unusually violent storm in 1947, the top of some massive walls began to emerge from the sand, attracting the keen eye of the archaeologist Fakhri. This was the greatest discovery ever made in the oasis: Protected for such a long time by its blanket of sand, the town of Aïn Asil and the mastabas of Qilat el-Dabba today bear witness to the form and dimensions of a city dating from the Old Kingdom. The excavations, conducted under the egess of the IFAO in Cairo, continue to reveal more and more of the city, which was a residence of the governors of the Dakhla oasis in the 6th dynasty, the era of the Pharaohs Pepy I and Pepy II. Surrounded by several wells, the town included a governor's palace, funeral chapels, an administrative district, and large pottery studios.

There are about a dozen mastabas for the governors in Qilat el-Dabba, which vary in importance. Five of them have been explored by archaelogists, most notably those of Khentika, governor of the oasis during the reign of Pepy II, around 2250 BC, and of Ima-Pepy, dating from the end of Pepy II's reign, around 2160. They differ mainly in the style of their funeral chapels, one of which is vaulted and one not.

At the far eastern end of the Dakhla oasis is the small town of Ezbet Bashendi, which contains funerary monuments from several different epochs. One of these is the tomb of Kitinos, a rich Greek landowner in the region in the 1st century AD. A pillar at the entrance to his tomb still bears a bas-relief, sole witness to the wealth and refinement of the former inhabitants of this area. Another ancient tomb near that of Kitinos was reused for the burial of Sheik Bashendi. Crowned by a cupola, it resembles a small mosque and invites contemplation. The name *Kitinos* is not Egyptian, of course, but of Greek origin, and means "the pomegranate flower." Still, the name can be found on the temple of Hibis in Kharga, and according to Wagner, it may very well refer to the same person.[53]

Near the village of Tenida, the last in the oasis, stand imposing rocks of variegated sandstone with striations of different colors. Since ancient times, the splendor of this moiré stone has compelled people passing by to pause and admire it, and to carve

**Top:** *Colorful houses girdled by the ramparts of the old city of Balat.*

**Above:** *Ancient doorways, some open, others walled up and outlined by bricks or plaster, show the passage of time. The apertures in the walls allow light to enter while keeping out excessive heat.*

53. Wagner, *op. cit.* p. 195.

*A trio of riders, knights of the oasis.*

messages and signatures into it. The muddle of engravings, both ancient and modern, makes them extremely difficult to decipher and date, but the sight is fascinating.

From Tenida, there are two possible routes to Kharga. The path through the valley, the Darb el-Ghubari, is easier and faster, but there is no water along the way. The route across the plains is longer and more difficult, but the Aïn Amur oasis halfway through the journey provides a pleasant break and along this route one may see the fortresses guarding the Kharga oasis.

The oases of Dakhla and Kharga have often been considered a single entity, and even administered as such at times. In the 5th century BC, they were even given the collective name of "Great Oasis." They both define themselves according to their relationship to the desert and to the Nile: *Dakhla*, which means "inside" in Arabic, is further from the Nile Valley and closer to the Great Sea of Sand, and thus to the desert; the more southerly oasis near the great river, and thus on the fringe of the desert, is *Kharga*, which in Arabic means "outside."

The remoteness of Dakhla from the civilization in the Nile Valley has probably played a large part in the direction in which the oasis developed—such a level of isolation would necessitate a strong, autonomous local government. This is precisely what the recent discoveries in Balat indicate, further justifying Dakhla's title of the oasis "inside" the desert.

The Abu Muharek, an immense, solitary dune moving over the limestone plateau like a mastodon with a wrinkled skin, encroaches slowly upon the Kharga oasis on its way south.

**Previous page:**
*A pass for madmen: the extremely steep limestone escarpment that towers over the Kharga depression at a height of around 1,300 feet offers few alternatives for reaching the valley. A slight case of madness complemented by a thorough knowledge of the terrain is necessary if you want to venture onto these dizzying slopes.*

*All tracks have disappeared. Only the telegraph poles, which the sand is inexorably burying, mark where they used to be.*

found here; its quality is renowned throughout the Mediterranean. There is ochre as well, of mineral origin, used to decorate houses and drive away evil spirits.

The name Kharga is not mentioned in the list on the temple at Edfu, but the oasis was known formerly as *Ouhat Resyt,* or "Oasis of the South." It was also called Kenmet, a designation that may link it to Dakhla. It has been inhabited since prehistoric times, and the population is demographically similar to that of the other oases. To an original mixture of Berbers, Bedouins, and Arabs, other influences were added—from the Nile Valley through frequent trade, and from intermarriage with Nubians taken in from the caravans using the Darb el-Arbaïn. During the New Kingdom, Kharga was also a place of exile due to the inaccessibility afforded by the vast and inhospitable desert.

## A long history of domination

Archaeological evidence proves that Kharga was already inhabited in the Paleolithic and Neolithic eras. It then came under Egyptian domination during the New Kingdom, from 1553 to 1069 BC, as shown by paintings in Theban tombs. No buildings from this era have survived—the local stone was so rare and highly prized that the oasis dwellers constantly reused it. One possible exception is the city of Hibis, which may date from this period. The stele of banishment, which originated in the 21st dynasty (ca. 1069–950 BC), explicates the laws of exile in effect in this oasis. Exile may have been imposed for religious or political reasons. The stele, "dating from the pontificate of Menkheperre, [tells us]

that in the Third Intermediate Period, Kharga had become a place of exile for people judged undesirable on Egyptian territory, a situation that continued in ensuing periods."[56]

A period of Libyan control and oversight was followed by Persian domination in the 27th dynasty (525–404 BC). After the misfortune of Cambyses's army (see page 30), Darius I (522–485 BC) launched a new program of development. During his reign, agricultural methods diversified and new techniques made it possible to greatly expand irrigation, both in area and in depth, thanks in particular to the introduction of the *sakia* and of *qanats*.

The *sakia,* consisting of a vertical shaft attached to a horizontal cog, is used to raise the level of the water, which makes it possible to irrigate new areas via a network of canals. The cog is turned by an animal, which then drives another vertical cog attached to buckets for drawing water.

*Qanats* are underground water conduits that are dug, reinforced, then buried under a layer of soil of varying thickness to prevent evaporation and covered by a wellhead, where they are sheltered from encroaching sand. Large enough for a person to walk in, these tunnels are used to fill the reservoirs or water distribution basins that feed the irrigation canals. Brick manholes are placed at regular intervals; these have to be high enough to remain free of sand and are used to supervise the running of the qanats. These structures are part of a network that makes it possible to irrigate large and distant cultivated tracts of land.

Transportation was radically transformed around 500 BC by the introduction of the dromedary, which replaced the donkey on long journeys, and by the creation of new terra-cotta vessels that were more suitable for camel caravans. The dromedary could travel farther and faster than its predecessors, and could carry heavier loads. This helped diversify the range of traded goods, thereby expanding commerce with the oasis.

The 28th, 29th, and 30th dynasties (404–332 BC) were the time of an Egyptian revival, after the first Persian period. The construction of temples continued, most notably the famous temple of Hibis, before the short-lived second Persian period (343–332 BC). A period of Greek domination followed (332–30 BC). It was during this time that the Ptolemaic builders added new splendor to many places in the oasis, including the city of Hibis, which developed rapidly in these years. Improved means of transport allowed increased trade with the Nile Valley, whose influence is manifest in the architecture of oasis monuments dating from this time.

Roman domination and the beginning of Christianization (30 BC–395 AD) were marked by an intensification of commerce. This necessitated fortifications to protect and to supply the trade caravans, as well as to maintain security for the surrounding villages. A large network of tracks was also built, maintained, and guarded by Roman legions. Kharga, still a place of exile, took in important communities, and at least two famous bishops, Athanasius and Nestorius, found refuge there.

Kharga converted to Christianity without resistance under the reign of the Roman emperor Constantine the Great (306–337 AD). Constantine ended the years of intense persecution of Christians led by the emperor Diocletian by officially establishing freedom of religion with the Edict of Milan in 313, and actually encouraged Christianity. He thus launched a policy of unity within the empire, and chose a Greek city as his capital: Byzantium was proclaimed the "New Rome" in 330. The emperor himself never officially converted to the new religion, and was only baptized on his deathbed. Since at that time people believed they could only call upon divine forgiveness once in a lifetime, it was thought best to wait until the final hour.

Constantine I defended the Christian religion, but occasionally supported heretics. For example, he opposed one of the Fathers of the Church, St. Athanasius (295–373) of Alexandria. He studied at the School of Alexandria, a renowned theological center that opposed the idea of divine duality—the paradoxical and theologically fruitful idea that Christ is both fully human and fully divine. A celebrated preacher, he was elected Patriarch of Alexandria in 328 and became one of the first Christian writers. He was a friend of St. Anthony, the renowned Egyptian and Christian hermit, who had taken refuge in the desert near Thebes. Anthony, blessed with exceptional longevity (250–356), is best known through the many paintings by famous artists depicting the temptations he faced in the desert: His struggles have been interpreted by Hieronymous Bosch, Brueghel the Elder, Veronese, and in the famous Issenheim altarpiece by Matthias Grünewald. Called the "Father of the Desert," St. Anthony initiated monasticism; the monks of Mount Athos and others still live according to his order. Athanasius supported Anthony's establishment of monasticism and, shortly after

*A stele of banishment (in the Musée du Louvre, Paris), commemorating an amnesty granted in the 11th century BC during the reign of Smendes, 21st dynasty: "Through the judgment of an oracle, the god Ammon of Karnak orders the repatriation and amnesty of people banished to the Great Oasis [Kharga]."*

The Temptation of St. Anthony: *painting by Hieronymus Bosch, 15th century, known for his fantastic visions of terrifying hybrid monsters (in the Museo da Prado, Madrid).*

**56.** C. M. Zivie, "En Égypte les temples de l'Oasis méridionale témoins d'une intense vie religieuse," in *Archéologia* 110, p. 34, Sept. 1977.

*Hibis, the largest temple in the oases, is situated in the center of Kharga and dedicated to Ammon and Osiris.*

**Following page:**
*An engraving of the temple of Hibis by Cailliaud (ca. 1817), plate XIX: "View of the facade of the great temple of el-Khargeh, as seen from the east .... Oasis inhabitants busy clearing away the sand using a wooden tool made of vertical and horizontal struts (on the left)."*

**57.** Aufrère, Golvin, Goyon, *op. cit.* p. 76f.
**58.** The triad regroups a family, consisting of a father, who is a god, his wife, and their son, who is considered a child god. Amongst the most famous are the Theban triad and the Osirian triad.

*General view of the great temple and surroundings, seen from
the northeast of the temple, Cailliaud, plate XVIII.*

the latter's death, wrote *The Life of Saint Anthony*, which was translated from Greek into Latin and was widely read. Thus, the Egyptian desert became a symbolic place of trial and encounter with God when the Christian persecutions came to an end, three centuries after Christ himself withstood his trials in the desert.

St. Athanasius, who fought against heresy, was exiled no fewer than five times for his intransigence and for refusing to compromise on the question of Christ's full divinity. Condemned and exiled by Emperor Constantine I, he found refuge in Kharga, where he may well have been inspired to preach the benefits of the desert and isolation.

The emperor Theodosius I (379–395) proclaimed Christianity the official religion of the Roman Empire, outlawed pagan cults, and ordered that the oasis temples be destroyed in 391. The only oasis spared was Siwa. Theodosius thus robbed us of the shrines of the desert gods; only those temples that were transformed into churches survived his reign—the last witnesses of this era, more ravaged by man than by sand or wind.

During the Christian and Byzantine eras (395–640 AD), disputes between Rome and Constantinople gave Kharga the opportunity to shelter Nestorius, former Bishop of Constantinople, for 20 years. After long, intense debate and some political intrigue, Nestorius was condemned and exiled by Cyril, Patriarch of Alexandria, at the Council of Ephesus in 431 AD for challenging the principle of divine duality. Nestorius emphasized Christ's human nature over his divine one, and maintained that only his human nature had suffered on the cross. Logically, he also honored Mary as bearer of the earthly Christ, but not as the mother of God, since this

implied that there was a time when God (as Christ) had not existed. Nestorius continued to preach and disseminate this heretical view, known as Nestorianism, in Persia and the East. There are still pockets in India and the Middle East today where the Christian community remains faithful to his ideas.

The extensive necropolis of Bagawat is a clear indicator of the early fame and standing of the great oasis as a refuge for committed Christians who taught a growing number of disciples, which ensured the influence of Christianity until the arrival of Islam.

The city of Hibis—in Egyptian, *Hebet*—was built on the edge of a lake overlooked by a temple reconstructed in an imaginative yet alluring way by Jean-Claude Golvin.[57] The city was known in ancient times and fortified against attack by nomadic tribes.

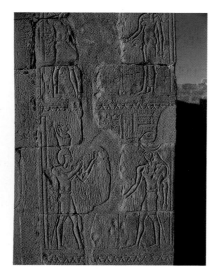

*Gift for Khonsu, temple of Qasr el-Zaiyan.*

*The king making an offering of the head of a ram to Maat and Ammon, temple of Qasr el-Zaiyan.*

*Elements of the Osirian triad: Osiris followed by Isis (temple of Deir el-Haggar).*

58. See p. 98.
59. The atef-crown is composed of a white mitre with a solar disc on top and framed with two high white ostrich feathers, placed horizontally on the ram's horns.

## The Theban Triad: Ammon, Mut, and Khonsu[58]

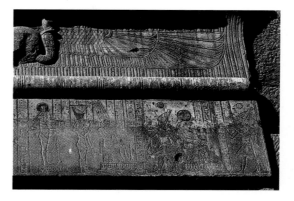

Ammon, "The Hidden," was at first a wind god to whom people who were suffocating called for aid. Linked to the Theban dynasty, his popularity grew with the rise in fortune of the princes that repelled the Hyksos and recomposed Egypt in the middle of the second millenium BC. Associated with Ra in the form of Ammon-Ra, he became the key to the pantheon, entering a union with Mut, goddess of the sky and divine mother. Mut, depicted with her head adorned with the feathers of a vulture, or even with a vulture's head herself, bore Ammon a son, Khonsu. Khonsu changed form many times, but essentially remained a moon god, divine son, and healer, all in one.

The Theban triad was first venerated in Thebes in the temples at Karnak and Luxor, where almost all successive sovereigns made a point of building, decorating, and restoring. Cults associated with these deities were also created in most provincial capitals, where the cultural institutions sometimes followed a Theban model.

## The Osirian Triad—Osiris, Isis, and Horus—and Seth[58]

Osiris, god of the soil and vegetation, taught humans the art of agriculture. Killed by his brother, Seth, the ministrations of his wife, Isis, and his sister, Nephthys—who together carried out the first mummification—brought him back to life. Wrapped in a shroud, wearing the atef-crown,[59] and holding a crook and flail with his arms crossed, he presided at the judgment of the dead and guaranteed kings a destiny like his own—that is, resurrection. In the 5th dynasty, only kings became Osiris after death; later, in the Middle Kingdom, resurrection was available to all the dead. Osiris still travels the desert sky as the constellation Orion.

Isis was goddess of the delta and in reference to her name, which means "seat," wore a royal throne as headdress. She was the most worshipped goddess, as archetypal woman and mother: distressed widow of Osiris, weeping with Nephthys, and mother of Horus. Her humanity, maternal nature, her sufferings, and her abilities as healer and even magician made her very popular, and her cult spread through the entire Mediterranean basin. Wearing a feather from her emblematic bird, the kite, she sometimes appeared with a cow's head as a reminder of an episode from the combat between Seth and Horus: She wounded Horus while trying to help him, so he cut off her head in a fury; Thot saved her by lending her a cow's head. This demonstrates her proximity to and quasi-assimilation with the goddess Hathor. Associated with Sirius, Isis is now also represented in the night sky.

Horus took on many identities: a celestial god with a falcon's head and sometimes body as well, or a child-god, the posthumous offspring of Osiris and Isis, depicted with a finger in his mouth. Every Pharaoh became a Horus, a model of the divine king, son of the god Ra, upon ascending the throne, and then an Osiris at his death.

Seth, the red-haired god of the desert with a voice like thunder, presented two facets of an aggression more or less under control: Wearing the white crown, which designated him as king of Upper Egypt, he was a valiant warrior at the prow of the solar bark and daily conqueror of the serpent, Apopis, who threatened the rising sun. But his temperament also led him to excesses: He was a drinker and jealous, and of such a violent nature that he killed his brother Osiris. He then became the incarnation of evil, battling constantly to gain power over Egypt against his nephew, Horus, king of Lower Egypt, who wore the red crown and was the incarnation of good. Seth was responsible for cosmic disorder and exiled by the gods, where he haunted the darkness and the deserts in a bizarre form: He had the body of a greyhound, built for running, and ending in a long forked tail. His head was a huge, narrow, aquiline snout with piercing black eyes and long, pointed, erect ears.

*Temple of Hibis: the god Thoth, patron of scribes and magicians, wearing the atef crown.*

*Temple of Hibis: Darius I brings offerings to Maat, the goddess of justice.*

**Right:** *The temple of Nadura, dedicated to the goddess Mut, wife of Ammon: view toward the temple of Hibis in the distance.*

## The temples

### The temple of Hibis

Kharga is home to the largest temple in the oases, which is dedicated to Ammon of Hibis, or Amenebis, and to Osiris. Various bas-reliefs in this temple reveal how two important constellations of gods—the Theban triad of Ammon, Mut, and Khonsu and the Osirian triad of Osiris, Isis, and Horus—were brought together.

Many Pharaohs played a role in the temple's history. Psamtek II (595–589 BC) had it built during the 26th dynasty, probably on top of a more ancient structure. The Persian king Darius I (522–486 BC) began the decorations. Additions were made by Hakor (393–380 BC), Nectanebo I (380–362 BC), and Nectanebo II (360–343 BC) in the 29th and 30th dynasties. Finally, in the Greek era, Ptolemy II Philadelphus (285–246 BC) ordered further ornamentation and permanent carved inscriptions. Though the temple was built over the course of various epochs, the Egyptian style is quite uniform. The proximity of the lake enabled the sacred bark to moor at a dock; from here processions moved up the Avenue of the Sphinx and passed through successive doorways that regulated access to the hypostyle hall and finally the *naos*, or innermost shrine, where all the Egyptian gods are found. Some are grouped, like the triads or the god Seth, who was combined with Horus, depicted with the head of a falcon, demonstrating the complementary nature of the two guardian deities of the pharoanic royalty.

The era in which Psamtek II began construction of the temple was a prosperous one in Egypt, seen as a rebirth after a series of civil wars that occured during the Third Intermediary Period. Restoration work done by the Metropolitan Museum of Art in the early 20th century made it possible to save the temple, at least for a time, from the threats posed by underground water, the clay subsoil, sand from the dunes, and the fragility of the pink sandstone of which it is built. This delicate, sometimes variegated stone that sparkles in the sunlight adds its charm to the images that adorn it, but is very sensitive to the ravaging effects of violent winds blowing in from the desert. Whistling between the temple's columns, it continues to threaten the survival of the gods.

### The temple of Khonsu and the temple of Nadura

Not far from the temple of Hibis, two temples were built in the Roman era by Antoninus Pius (138–161 BC). The first, at the foot of a hill, was dedicated to Khonsu and received many pilgrims, while Nadura, perched on top of a hill and encircled by a now-collapsed brick wall, served as protector of the area and of the city of Hibis. If, as has been speculated, it was dedicated to the goddess Mut, the three sites would have honored the Theban triad.

### The temple of Qasr el-Ghueida

The Qasr el-Ghueida temple is situated just a few miles south of Nadura and Khonsu, high atop a hill that dominates the region.

**Left**: *The temple of Qasr el-Ghueida, "The Deep Spring," dedicated to the Theban triad.*

**Above**: *The temple of Qasr el-Zaiyan, showing the contrast between the stone of the entrance portico and the walls of sunbaked bricks surrounding it, which protect the temple and its many storerooms.*

The site includes a temple and several outbuildings, which are all built of sandstone and surrounded by a thick brick wall. Its name derives from the spring on which it was built: *ghueida* means "the deep spring." Construction of the fortress began during the reign of Darius I and continued in the Greek period under Ptolemy III Euergetes (246–221 BC) and Ptolemy X Philopator (107–88 BC). This temple, like the one in Hibis, was originally dedicated to the Theban triad.

### The temple of Qasr el-Zaiyan

Called *tchonemyris*, which means "the great well," this temple was built in the Greek era, dedicated to the town god Amenebis, and later restored by Antoninus Pius. An inscription confirming this was found and recorded by Drovetti and Jomard in 1825: "to Amenebis, great god of Tchonemyris, and the gods honored in the same temple..."[60]

The many storehouses and ovens found near Qasr el-Ghueida and Qasr el-Zaiyan indicate that they served not only religious functions, but also defended the cities and their crops. The local wine was also famous.

## Dush

Dush is an exceptional site at the southern tip of the oasis, about 60 miles from Kharga and 320 feet above sea level. Tools found in the area show that it was inhabited in prehistoric times. Dush consisted of a garrison and a town built around two temples, and stone and Greco-Roman necropolises. There were also villages and cultivated land irrigated by a network of *qanats*. The pass at Dush is a critical spot where the plain narrows, bordered by the sheer cliff of the depression to the east and threatened by encroachment of the dunes in the west. The fortifications were surveillance posts for trade routes between the Nile Valley and the Sudan. Several small forts built in the Ottoman era maintained this defensive role, notably the one called *Meks el-Quibli*, a Turkish word meaning "toll-house of the south." This elevated site, which the Egyptians called Cush—probably due to commercial links with the country of Cush in the Sudan—was called Kysis by the Greeks before it became known by its present name of Dush.

The slave caravans that took the Darb el-Arbaïn passed by the foot of the Dush fortress without ever knowing there was a temple

**Right**: *The southern outer wall of the temple: detail showing the cartouches of Domitian.*

**Following pages:** *View from the temple of Dush looking down onto the 40-Day Road at sunset.*

*Citadel of Dush el-Qal'ah: engraving by Cailliaud, plate XIII, showing the imposing walls of the temple enclosure. The temple is almost completely covered with sand; only the top of the left-hand part of the portico is visible.*

*Series of archways leading to the sanctuary of the temple.*

**60.** Cailliaud, *Voyage à l'Oasis*, Paris, 1821.

hidden behind unscalable walls. Traders from the north had to climb the steep hill before they entered the temple dedicated to Isis and Osiris. Two doorways and two inner courtyards led to the sanctuary. The temple was built by Domitian (81–96 AD) and completed during the reigns of Trajan and Hadrian (98–138 AD), according to the cartouches engraved on the pillars. The walls surrounding the temple seem to be of Roman origin and are designed to protect the compound from sand.

Isis and Osiris are depicted in scenes on the outer wall, which legend claims was once covered with gold. Discovered in 1988 during IFA excavations, the "Dush treasure"—2.5 pounds of solid gold jewelry in a vase, either forgotten or hidden in a niche behind the intrados of a vault—lends support to this legend. The treasure includes a magnificent diadem worn by the high priest while performing cult duties, as well as a heavy necklace and two bracelets. These are today on exhibit in the Cairo Museum.

The necropolis in Dush displays the simple architecture and systematic reuse of tombs characteristic of the Ptolemaic and Roman eras. This early recycling was necessitated by "the general spread of mummification, and the lack of available land to extend

the huge necropolises [that were] wedged between arable land that had to be preserved, and the desert, into which no one wanted to penetrate very far."[61] The study of mummies *in situ* is particularly interesting, as their provenance is certain. The work of Dunand and Lichtenberg has taught us a great deal about the life and health of the inhabitants of these cities over a long period—from the 1st century BC to the 5th century AD. They systematically took radiographs of 120 mummies between 1978 and 1992. Comparison of these mummies with 60 others discovered in the necropolis of Aïn Labakha corroborates current theories: The standards of living and of health were clearly better in Aïn Labakha than in Dush, where life was harder in part because of a dearth of pack animals, and people died younger, at an average age of 38.

## Fortresses

A network of fortresses, most of them built by the Romans, defended the northern part of the Kharga oasis, which had more access routes than the south. Unlike the fortress in Dush, which was

**Left:** *The Aïn Umm Dabadib fortress, one of very few fortresses with a rectangular tower.*

**Previous page:** *Procession of divinities on the outer southern wall of the Dush temple. The cornice at the top is decorated with the cartouches of deities with a text by Trajan. In the center on the left, Domitian makes an offering of incense to Harsiesis, in front of Isis holding a sistrum. On the right, Domitian is facing Ammon-Ra (or perhaps Osiris), followed by Isis.*

*Interior view of Aïn Labakha.*

designed to protect the temple at its heart, these were built for military purposes. All were built around springs and the water supply was augmented with *qanats*, a system of irrigation canals of Persian origin (see page 96).

Though these fortresses are now mostly ruins, they are still mighty and impressive, and convey a sense of the considerable scale of works from their period. Three forts seem to have been especially critical: *Aïn Umm Dabadib*, "The Spring of Scorpions," on the road from Farafra, *Aïn Labakha*, and *el-Deir*, "The Monastery," along the route from Abydos in the Nile Valley.

### Aïn Umm Dabadib, Aïn Labakha, and El-Deir

After passing a rocky spur on the plain at the foot of the cliff, you reach a 50-foot-high wall forming a tremendous square over 300 feet across. The corner towers of Aïn Umm Dabadib, breaking with local tradition, are rectangular rather than cylindrical and the result is spectacular: The towers' colors and scope harmonize so well with the mountain that they seem to have been taken from it in order to defend the plain. The largest fortification in the oasis, it allowed surveillance of the roads and was a refreshment stop for the many caravans that rested here.

Between Aïn Umm Dabadib and Aïn Labakha stretches a 19-mile caravan route. Aïn Labakha is a desolate spot, graced by the ruins of an abandoned village built around a well, now dry, and surrounded by stunted palm trees. But the fortress that overlooks this village, though more modest in scale than Aïn Umm Dabadib, still reminds us of the importance of the garrisons. Brightly

*Fortress of El-Deir, "The Monastery," with its twelve cylindrical towers.*

colored paintings on the walls and the circular vaulted entrance of a small, well-preserved temple made of sun-baked brick dating from the 3rd century AD have survived and stand out against the backdrop of sand which, in this unusual case, has protected rather than destroyed the site. A dilapidated brick wall juts out from the cliff like the silhouette of a petrified dromedary with an ochre-colored coat, guarding the entrance to the temple for all eternity.

The Darb el-Arbaïn runs halfway between the fortress of Aïn Labakha and the imposing el-Dar fort, built on a small hill in the

---

61. Dunand, Lichtenberg, *op. cit.* p. 119.

age of Diocletian (284–305 AD) and more impressive even than Aïn Umm Dabadib. It is enclosed by high, 10-foot-thick brick walls, including 12 cylindrical towers and topped by a sentry walk overlooking the plain. Nearby lie the remains of a building that was probably a small fort with a tower protecting a well.

## Christian monuments

### The necropolis of Bagawat

To the north of the temple of Hibis at the foot of *Gebel el-Teir*, the "Mountain of Birds," lies the Bagawat necropolis—one of the most famous, best preserved and perhaps most moving Christian sites in all of Egypt—a collection of funerary chapels scattered throughout the desert hills. They were built between the 4th and 8th centuries AD, some in Romano-Byzantine style and others in proto-Coptic manner: "The funerary chapels are built of sunbaked

*The necropolis of Bagawat. It is one of the oldest known Christian cemeteries and contains 263 chapels; some of these have Coptic inscriptions and paintings inside the cupolas.*

**Left:** *Shrine of St. Thecla in the church Notre Dame de Chamalières, Puy de Dôme. The shrine is said to have housed relics of this early martyr until the French Revolution.*

**Right:** *Bagawat, cupola of the Chapel of Peace: The circular frieze contains the names of figures from the New and Old Testaments, including St. Paul preaching to St. Thecla, depicted with long blond hair.*

**Right, below:** *Detail of the ceiling of the Chapel of the Exodus showing the Pharaoh in pursuit of the Hebrews. Vine branches extend down from the ceiling, connecting and ordering the figures.*

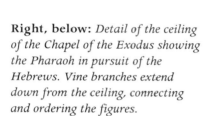

62. M. Capuani, *L'Égypte copte*, p. 229, Paris, 1999.
63. A. Fakhry, *The Necropolis of El-Bagawat in Kharga Oasis*, p. 67-78, Cairo, 1951.
64. R. P. du Bourguet, s.j., *Art paléochrétien*, p. 176f., Lausanne, 1970.
65. Wagner, *op. cit.* p. 65.
66. Wagner, *op. cit.* p. 67.

brick and represent an extraordinary example of proto-Coptic art. Their architecture, which features a cupola as roof, takes various forms in terms of shape (square, rectangular, circular, composite), height, and architectural decoration. The facades and outer walls are ornamented with engaged columns, capitals, niches, arcades, and pilasters, all made of sunbaked brick."[62]

The majority of the chapels in the necropolis consist of a single room topped by a cupola; only three have ceilings painted with biblical scenes or representing significant early or local Christian figures. Fakhri has made a detailed study of these paintings, particularly of those in the Chapel of Peace, which dates from the 5th century.[63] He admires the fine, intricate workmanship of the figures against a colored background. Portraits and depictions of historical personages alternate with allegories that are suffused with elements of Egyptian culture. For example, Peace is personified as a woman with long, blond hair, shown in a frontal view, dressed only in a pharaonic loincloth decorated with geometrical motifs; in her right hand she holds the traditional *ankh*, the Egyptian symbol of life, and in the other hand a scepter. Not far from her is a painting of a horned serpent whispering in Eve's ear; Eve is shown to be embarrassed by her nakedness as she dries

her tears. Meanwhile, St. Paul is shown preaching to an Egyptian virgin, St. Thecla, the first Christian martyr.

The Chapel of the Exodus houses the most ancient paintings, probably dating from the 4th century, but the variety of subjects, depicted in light colors on a white background, make it difficult to distinguish the many overlapping scenes and identify individual figures. Nonetheless, the decor "follows a plan that is not without method ... in fact, the themes spread out in concentric waves starting at the top—the flight of the Hebrews pursued by the Pharaoh ... next to which stand St. Thecla and the seven virgins—then scenes illustrating salvation: the sacrifice of Isaac, Noah and the ark, Daniel in the lions' den, the three Hebrews in the furnace..."[64]

The importance of the Christian presence in this region, and particulary in this location, is attested to by Greek, Coptic, and Arabic graffiti. Some of the inscriptions are quite remarkable, such as this text quoted from St. Paul's letter to the Romans: "If God be for us, who can be against us,"[65] or this passage from the tomb of Petechon: "I have left my betrothed in this world to participate in the Spirit."[66] The rays of the setting sun let the ochre stone of a multitude of chapels glow warmly, and cast

**Following page:** *Chams el-Din, dating from the 4th century: Remains of the church and monastery that are said to have been called Munesis in memory of Isis.*

## Saint Thecla,
### the First Woman Martyr

*"Hail to Thecla the Apostolic, whom God has strengthened; the lions did not harm her and the furnace did not burn her. Because she believed in the doctrine of justice, she left her parents, as Paul told her to do, and rejected her wealth."*[67]

The life of the first woman martyr seems like a mythological tale, and Thecla herself seems to be the incarnation of Daphne. Her story is so full of incredible events that many people find it hard to believe she existed. A disciple of St. Paul, she was known as St. Thecla of Iconium, and was martyred during the persecutions of the emperor Septimus Severus.[68]

When Paul preached in the city of Iconium, Thecla, a young woman of 18, heard him and was so fascinated that she did not leave the window of his house for three days and nights. Denounced by her neglected fiancé, Paul was thrown into prison, but Thecla joined him so that she might hear him again. She was condemned to be burnt alive, but was saved by a miracle: *"God sent a great rain, hail, and lightning, and the furnace became like a cold dew."*[69]

Delivered from this punishment, Thecla followed Paul to Antioch, where a great man, overwhelmed by her beauty, wanted to marry her. Annoyed by her refusal, he denounced her. Thecla was condemned to be delivered to the wild beasts; they, however, merely licked her feet. After other attempts to kill her also failed, Thecla was pardoned. She joined Paul again and continued to preach the gospel, at first in Iconium, then in Seleucia in Syria, where she lived as a hermit in a mountain grotto until her death, performing many miracles and conversions. The story of her death adds to her mystery: Surrounded by blasphemers with evil intentions, she escaped them by calling on God, and disappeared miraculously:

*"She saw the rock stand open, ran to it and entered in, and the rock closed in such a way that there* was no trace of a crack ... a piece of cloth which she used to cover her head ... remained outside the rock as a sign for those who were present."*[70]

Other versions of her story speak of an arm remaining in front of the rock, a relic of which is said to be in Catalonia in the Church of St. Thecla.[71] A richly decorated sanctuary built above the grotto where she is said to have lived and disappeared attracted many pilgrims in the 5th century, because the miracles apparently continued, sealing her fame.

According to the Ethiopian synaxarion, Thecla was buried in Sengar (Babylon), near modern-day Cairo. Her feast is held on September 23 according to the Coptic calender, and September 24 by the Armenian synaxarion.

Her sanctuary was later associated with St. Menas, because of their geographical proximity and many miracles relating to water. St. Menas, martyred in the 3rd or 4th century under Diocletian, had a sanctuary in Abu Mina, and was represented there with St. Thecla above some phials of miraculous water that were removed by pilgrims. Three of these phials (ca. 6 in. high) can still be seen in the Louvre in Paris; others were lost in the French Revolution.[72]

Additional relics, whose legends are explained on a metal plaque, are located in Chamalières, France, where the saint is also honored on September 23rd.[73]

St. Thecla was venerated in the Libyan Desert and appears in two chapels in Bagawat: being converted by St. Paul in the Chapel of Peace, and being delivered to the flames and leading her followers in the Chapel of the Exodus.

In England, a carved stone represents her with bare bosom, under attack from two ill-defined or composite animals, her arms raised in the stance of a supplicant; this pose may be related to the hieroglyph "Ka," adopted by Christian art to symbolize prayer.[74]

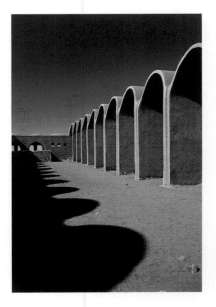

*New Baris: Light and shade play on this architect-designed city, built by Hassan Fathy as part of the New Valley project.*

**67.** I. Guidi, *Le Synaxaire éthiopien,* Patrologia Orientalis, volume VIII, p. 407f., Paris, 1911.
**68.** *Vie des Saints et des Bienheureux, selon l'ordre du calendrier, avec l'historique des fêtes,* by the RR.PP. Benedictine monks of Paris, volume XVIII, September, p. 477–482, Paris, 1950.
**69.** Guidi, *op. cit.* p. 407.
**70.** T. Israël, *Le Synaxaire arménien,* Patrologia Orientalis, volume VI, p. 285, Paris, 1911.
**71.** *Vie des Saints et des Bienheureux...,* p. 480.
**72.** *Christian Subjects in Coptic Art,* p. 540.
**73.** *Vie des Saints et des Bienheureux...,* p. 482.
**74.** A. S. Atiya, *The Coptic Encyclopedia,* vol. 2, p. 536, New York, 1991.
**75.** Wagner, *op. cit.* p. 29.

shadows of their arches and gentle curves on the ground, progressively effaced by the encroaching night. At the top of the hill, a majestic basilica recalls the past and stands watch over the city of the dead.

### The church of Chams el-Din

On the Darb el-Arbaïn, not far from the road to Dush, are the remains of a Romano-Byzantine village, Chams el-Din. At the heart of these ruins stand some columns from a 4th-century AD church. A number of Greek inscriptions have allowed archaeologists to discover the name of the village, *Munesis*, which may mean "the water of Isis."[75] This suggests that here again, in the south of the oasis, a Christian monument was built on a site previously devoted to the cult of Isis.

Over time, the Kharga oasis has been exposed to many influences, most of which came from the Nile Valley. Independently of the origin and purpose of the monuments built before our era, these have been strongly marked by Christianity. Ancient temples were used as cult sites and new churches were built, some in villages, others inside fortresses. Kharga was a center from which Christianity spread and over time also became accepted in the other oases, with the exception of Berber Siwa.

### An interrupted project: New Baris

New Baris is the brainchild of architect Hassan Fathi, conceived as part of the New Valley development. A modern city was built in the 1960s near the ancient city of Baris, of which few traces remain. The new city was intended to be the home of artisans and their families, but it was never finished or inhabited. It was designed to resemble ancient architecture, with vaulted ceilings and cupolas offering views where, in the course of the day, shadows and light play and cool air is held captive. The intersecting arches, the lines of pillars, and the dark lanes all wait patiently for the magician who will bring this small, forgotten city to life.

Kharga opens two doors: Through one, it is possible to reach the well-known civilization of the Nile Valley; through the other, you may venture into the mysterious, sandy expanse of the desert that skirts along the line of oases.

The Darb el-Arbaïn, the infamous 40-Day Road, hardly tempts you to follow it further. Toward the west, toward the setting sun, lie the riches, but also the mysteries, of the Libyan desert waiting to be discovered. In this setting, tentative steps through the sand may take you to places inhabited since prehistoric times, and perhaps even to the mythical lost oasis.

# Colors as Symbols:

## *Green, king of the oases; Red, ruler of the desert*

*As things show a likeness to each other in many ways, we should not suppose there is any rule saying that what a thing signifies by similitude in one place it signifies everywhere else.*

**St. Augustine, *The Christian Doctrine***

Unlike Western convention, in ancient Egypt, the color black indicated neither death nor mourning; rather, it announced fertility: The darkness allowed the goddess Nut to regenerate the sun before giving birth to it at dawn each day. In the same way, the black soil, engorged by the nourishment of the Nile, prepared to receive the seed and start germination to produce a new harvest. The black robes of bridal couples in the oases are reminders of this phase prior to creation, and are thus a sign of fertility.

White evokes the light of the splendid sun, conqueror of dark forces, who helps nature regenerate and presides over the celebration of rebirth.

In a dissertation on colors in ancient Egypt, Gautier explains the value of the two most popular colors: "red and green are not only dominant, but also ... constitute the organizing principle of Egyptian use of color."[76]

Green—the color of life, the color of the oases—is fundamentally positive, revitalizing, and fresh like vegetation. These qualities stand in contrast to the ambivalence of red, which is hot, dynamic, and vital like blood; but also dangerous like fire or the scorching sun of the desert.

Green essentially refers to nature, growth, and renewal. The papyrus chosen by the scribes "as a sign crystalizing all the symbolic nature of green,"[77] provides a fitting image of vitality through its many applications. The green of the oasis betokens life: springs and flourishing crops, symbolic of a happy life. Vegetation is fundamentally beneficial, for, as a metaphor it promises vigor and vitality; and as a metonym, prosperity, happiness, and

regeneration. The majestic forests of papyrus-shaped columns supporting temples are possibly intended as reminders of the Egyptians' hope for an after-life.

Osiris, the god of vegetation, is often represented with green face and hands that symbolize resurrection and regeneration after death. It was considered an omen of a good harvest when small effigies of the god filled with grain and watered daily by the priest germinated vigorously and rapidly: "I am the one who makes the plants grow, who makes the banks of Upper Egypt become verdant again, master of the desert regions, who makes the oases green once more" (*Texts of the Sarcophagi*).

Min, the god of fertility, was offered gifts of green romaine lettuce with white sap because of its putative aphrodisiac qualities. The bright green of malachite provides an image of the celestial fields, evocative of fertility, as opposed to turquoise, whose pale green suggests stagnant water.

Red, the color of life and death, the color of the desert, bears more ambiguous and complex connotations. Red immediately suggests blood, symbolic of life and vitality, but it has to remain hidden, or death may threaten. When fire is mastered, it is a symbol of life, warmth, and purification; but its force becomes destructive when it escapes our control. Red may be malevolent, associated with hostile expanses of desert scorched by the sun and haunted by the red-haired god Seth, whose hot breath is the wind of the desert, and by the goddess Tefnut of the flaming eye.[78] Breaking red pottery is supposed to reestablish order and secure effective protection by destroying the evil forces contained in it.

*Green, the color of the oases, a symbol of life and regeneration taken from the plant world.*

The red crown of Lower Egypt draws on the positive side of aggression and of royal power, which may be usefully directed against the enemy. It is complemented by the white crown of Upper Egypt, which brings in the sun's brightness and helps to govern both regions.

Egyptian scribes used red ink—facilitated by the abundance of ochre—to underline certain elements in texts written in black. Thus, it could strengthen the effectiveness of magic formulas, whether positive or negative, to cure people or to cast spells. The aggression of red was then neutralized and returned to the enemy.

The scribes chose to symbolize red by the long, curved beak of the pink flamingo. This bird lives peacefully in the middle of lakes and green papyrus, and reminds us of the complementary nature symbols must have, and of the play of contrasts, from birth to death, and rebirth again.

*Red, the color of the desert, symbol of life and death, blood or fire, destruction or purification …*

**76.** P. A. Gautier, *Le Rouge et le Vert: sémiologie de la couleur en Égypte ancienne*, Egyptology thesis presented at the University of Paris IV-Sorbonne, UFR: Archeology, History of Art, Oct. 1995, volume I, II.

**77.** Gautier, *op. cit.* p. 93.

**78.** Gautier, *op. cit.* p. 383.

Part Two

# The Desert

*It is nothing but sand,
terrible aridity, pure desert*

**Herodotus**

# Mysteries of the Great Egyptian Desert

Originally called the *Profundum Aequor* by Curtius Rufus Quintus, meaning deep water or sea, the word "desert" comes from the Latin *desertum* and only appeared in Europe in the 11th and 12th centuries, with no synonym. It was first used as a military term, with the negative connotation of desertion, suggesting abandonment of the established order for a place set apart from the world. The idea of deprivation eventually pervaded the very concept of deserts, and it became associated with the ideas of extremes—extreme temperatures, winds, erosion, distances—and severe shortage of water and of life forms. Over time it came to connote abstract ideas, like solitude, emptiness, and nothingness.

For ancient Egyptians, the desert, or *desheret*, was a place verging on chaos beyond the protective barrier of mountains that separated it from the valley. Jean Yoyotte called the mountains, or *djebel*, whose colors and silhouettes marked the entrance to and boundaries of the desert, "a running hieroglyph on the monuments represent[ing] three round summits, separated by passes. The symbol was painted pink and dappled fawn, looking exactly like a mountain as it appears from afar in the high noon sun."[79] The desert mountains also belonged to the world of the dead, since graves were dug at their base and deep inside them were rich veins of ore to be mined.

Today, Arabic has a wealth of terms concerning the desert. There are words to distinguish between a rocky desert dune (*reg*), sand deserts (*erg*), and high pebble-strewn plateau deserts (*hamada*). The preferred term, however, remains *sahra*, from which the name Sahara derives. Oddly, this word expresses a sensorial feeling of color and touch, without corresponding to an actual geographical meaning. The Sahara Desert represents a vast, borderless region that is fundamentally defined by its characteristic golden-fawn color, and by its wildness, burning heat, and fierce, mysterious, often hostile wildlife. Still, today it has been circumscribed with carefully defined limits and borders so that it has assumed the clearly defined status of a geographical entity.

The word desert thus designates a bare, untouched, and authentic landscape against which other landmarks stand out in relief, color, and light, allowing us a glimpse of infinite diversity. The seemingly endless space provides a deep silence where we can listen to ourselves, and a naked essence that let us know that wholeness and happiness exist.

The desert is, of course, dangerous to cross. It is a harsh place that tries its inhabitants and visitors in many ways, and yet it had to be conquered. It is a place where unimaginable treasures have been conveyed, all worthy of the tales of the Arabian Nights.

*Satellite view of the northern art of the Great Sea of Sand, near the oasis of Siwa. Great rocky massifs bordering on the Mediterranean erode and are transported by the wind to form this immense sea.*

**79.** J. Yoyotte, "Désert" in *Dictionnaire de la civilisation égyptienne*, p. 84, Paris, 1992.

On the Ammonite Hill, in the middle of Thetys, marine fossils bear witness to the former presence of the sea, which left behind seashells and ammonites (cornua Ammonis or "horns of Ammon") as well as beds of ochre, a pigment that has been used by artists since ancient times.

## History of a name: the Libyan Desert

The Egyptian Nile has its source in two countries far removed from the Mediterranean Sea. It actually consists of two rivers: the White Nile, born in the heart of the "Lunar Mountains" of the Ruwenzori mountain range in Uganda, and the Blue Nile, which flows from Ethiopia, considered by many to be the birthplace of humanity. The two branches come together in Khartoum, Sudan. After twisting through the Nubian Desert, this king of rivers enters Egypt, carving out a valley between two deserts: the Arabian Desert to the east, and the Libyan Desert to the west.

The Libyan Desert is less well known than its Arabian counterpart, its identity confused by its many different names. It is spread across three countries. The largest portion is indeed in Egypt, but it also covers eastern Libya and northern Sudan. It is called the Egyptian Desert in order to distinguish it from the Libyan Desert, which is located entirely within Libya's borders as they are known today. The Egyptians themselves prefer to call it the Western Desert, or the Occidental Desert. However, Sahara experts call it the Eastern Desert, since it is the easternmost part of the largest desert in the world.

The Libyan Desert begins just beyond the limestone plateau of the mountains that form the western border of the chain of oases parallel to the Nile Valley. It consists of a vast area of sand, called the Great Sea of Sand, crowned to the north by the Berber oasis of Siwa. The desert extends as far south as the rocky plateaus of *Gilf Kebir*, "the Great Escarpment," and the granite range of *Uweinat*, "the Land of Springs." The Libyan Desert remains relatively unknown, and is considered to be impenetrable and full of mystery.

## The geological history of the Great Traveler: the Sahara

The Sahara Desert, an integral part of the African tectonic plate, migrated northward from the South Pole 420 million years ago, during the Paleozoic era—toward the end of the Ordovician and the beginning of the Silurian period. It crossed the equator roughly 140–130 million years ago during the Mesozoic era—at the end of the Jurassic and beginning of the Cretaceous period—but did not reach its current location until the beginning of the Cenozoic era, 65 million years ago, when the dinosaurs disappeared.

According to Saïd, the geological history of the Sahara begins on very ancient land: the crystalline shelf that just touches the southern extremity of the Libyan Desert.[80] Granite-type formations from this period dating back 600 million years ago thus correspond to the end of the Precambrian period or the beginning of the Paleozoic. The geological adventure continues with a continental episode that settled in around 600–530 million years ago, and lasted until roughly 430 million years ago—from the Cambrian to the Ordovician periods. Erosion scraped away the mountains framing Egypt, and great masses of sand began to cover the peneplain and fill in the holes and valleys. Outcroppings from the Silurian period, about 410 million years old, may be found at the foot of the southern flanks of the Abu Ras plateau, in the Wadi Abd el-Malik, and at the Aqaba Pass.

Approximately 400 million years ago, a warm, shallow, tropical sea called Thetys deposited a series of thick marine layers that can be seen in the Gilf Kebir in the central Sahara. These graptolite clay deposits are the mother rock of Saharan oil deposits and of marine fossils. Eventually this sea disappeared over the course of 70 million years, leaving a layer of "Nubian sandstone." This famous Nubian sandstone actually consists of alternating marine sediments and continental deposits—either airborne or carried by rivers. This process, so evident at the Gilf Kebir site, continued until the middle of the Cretaceous era.

**80.** R. Saïd, *The Geology of Egypt*, p. 253, Rotterdam, 1990.

Toward the end of the Cretaceous period, 100 million years ago, the sea coming from the West covered the Sahara for the last time. By this time the Sahara had reached the equator and extended into the northern hemisphere, to the 15th parallel, resulting in a hot and humid climate.

During the Cenozoic era—at the end of the Eocene period—40 million years ago, the sea withdrew one last time, leaving behind a vast limestone plateau. The Western Desert underwent great changes and was impacted by rivers, ice, and wind, giving it its current form. The Great Sea of Sand constitutes the most typical example of this desert, bordered to the east by a string of oases nestled into valleys like the beads on a rosary.

## Marine fossils from the dawn of time

"How can it be that two or three thousand leagues inland, there are endless places where seashells, bivalves, cheramydes, and even brackish lakes can be found ... like an enormous bed of seashells?"[81] The advancing and retreating of the sea over millions of years left its marks, depositing sediments on the seafloor and burying marine fossils that testify to its former presence. In the Great Sea of Sand, one can encounter many ancient fossilized creatures. You can admire a sea urchin shining in its limestone matrix, come across an oyster stranded in the hollow of a hill, or find a miniature scallop on the crest of a dune. Before leaving the region, the Thetys sea left its signature: Many types of seashells and magnificent ammonites proliferated in its warm muddy waters during the Mesozoic era, the Jurassic era, and part of the Cretaceous period.

Why were these fossils dubbed ammonites? Pliny the Elder was the first to take an interest in these petrified shellfish. In his book *Natural History*, he named them *Ammonis cornu* because their spiral shape resembled the horns of Ammon, the ram-headed god worshipped in Siwa. According to the 1752 edition of the dictionary of the *Academie Française*, the Ethiopians believed Ammon's horns could attract dreams that allowed people to predict the future. Perhaps the priests of the oracle of Siwa sold magic amulets found nearby? The seashells kept the name "Ammon's horns" for many centuries and only appear under the name "ammonite" in 19th-century editions of the *Academie Française* dictionary. Gerhard Rohlfs was the first European explorer to come to the Great Sea of Sand, and in 1873–1874, he and his German team found an unusually large deposit and declared: "This region that we came across for the first time was rich with oysters and ammonites: because of these fossils, Zittel named the place 'Ammonite Hill'."[82]

The geologist Karl von Zittel published a book about ammonoids after another expedition in 1884. Ammonites were cephalopods with spiral-shaped shells that could be either plain or patterned or even ribbed. The geometric shape of the spiral varied from one species to another, though a progressively uncoiling spiral indicated either an aging specimen or an aging species showing signs of disruption and degeneration. Their great numbers in the secondary layers between 200 million and 65 million years ago were followed by a sudden disappearance that remains a mystery. Several, as yet unproven, hypotheses have been proposed to explain their disappearance, including a species of marine predator, destruction due to underground geological phenomena, climatic swings that affected their habitat, a cataclysm similar to the one that caused the extinction of the dinosaurs, or that they vanished with the receding of the sea.

Ammonites are still found in this remote place. Their remarkable condition suggests that the Thetys receded gradually, leaving them covered and protected in muddy silt. Just a few are visible to remind us of their existence, and their mystery.

*Various coiled ammonites, protected by their bed of sand since the Mesozoic era.*

81. Strabon, *Géogr.*, quoted by Leclant, *Per Africæ Sitientia*, p. 226.
82. G. Rohlfs, *Drei Monate in der libyschen Wüste*, p. 169, Kassel, 1875.

*Right: Aerial view showing the courses of ancient Saharan rivers, the wadi of the wet era; they used to water these expanses, which are now desert. Traces of the dried-up valleys still furrow the base of the mountains.*

*Fossilized seashells of the brachiopod family—turritella and helix—and various mollusks.*

# Ancient Rivers in the Sahara
## by Rushdi Saïd

*The Western Desert of Egypt (also called the Eastern Sahara) was elevated from under the sea some 40 million years ago, forming a great tableland of limestone beds. During the long period of time that has elapsed since then, it has undergone enormous changes that have brought it to its present shape. Many of these changes are related to the great geological and climatic events that the desert has witnessed during that time. Shortly after the emergence of the land and the retreat of the sea, there occurred the great tectonic event of continental dimensions that elevated the Red Sea mountain range and began the process of the rifting and spreading of the Red Sea. This event apparently affected the climate, as well, bringing great rains over the land of Egypt. These rains seem to have formed an extensive drainage system. The only remains of this now totally defunct system are the great Oligocene delta of the Fayum region, as well as some isolated gravel beds on top of the plateau of the middle latitudes of the Western Desert that are assumed to be of fluvial origin.*

*The most dramatic event that helped shape the modern landscape of Egypt occurred some 6 million years ago when the Mediterranean Sea was isolated from the world's oceanic system, then dessicated, and became a desert of salt. The new lowered base level of the vanishing Mediterranean subjected Egypt to intense erosion; the modern Nile Valley was excavated and developed into an enormous gorge toward which many rivers emanating from the Red Sea were graded. Active sheet wash erosion caused the leveling of the sandstone plains of the Nubian Desert and the excavation of the Kharga and Dakhla depressions. Apart from the river Nile, the only marks of this system are the exposed rock-cut surfaces in the south and the incised and deeply buried channels in the north.*

*The last of the major drainage systems that the Western Desert has witnessed occurred some 3 million years ago. The channels of this drainage system are covered by a veneer of wind-blown sands and are difficult to trace in the field, although they were known to exist and were recognized as representing the remnants of the third major drainage system that affected the desert. Their presence and extent have been confirmed by the images of the Shuttle Imaging Radar obtained by the Space Shuttle in 1981 and in 1994. The image strips that cover Egypt show the existence of a network of vast buried channels under a veneer of sand that the radar imagery technique was able to penetrate. There is no consensus as to the direction of the flow of these channels. Some claim that they form part of a trans-Atlantic drainage system that flowed across Africa toward the Atlantic Ocean; others claim that they were part of an interior drainage system that ultimately led to the great depressions of Selima and Chad. This would not preclude a possible drainage line that could have flowed into the Nubian Paleonile.*

*Following that last rainy period, the desert became extremely arid during most of the Pleistocene era, which witnessed the great climatic fluctuations of the northern hemisphere. There were short intervening pluvial episodes in Egypt during that epoch, which for the most part coincided with the interglacial episodes of the northern hemisphere. The deserts of Egypt were extremely arid and void of habitation during the last glacial period, which ended about 10,000 years ago. Intensive wind action produced the great sand dunes that accumulated along large stretches of the desert and are still seen to this day. It also excavated the many playas of the Western Desert. The last ice age was followed by a nearly 5,000-year interval of meager summer rains that filled the excavated playa ephemerally, and made possible the appearance of Neolithic pastoral communities that flourished in the climate of the desert at that time.*

# Chapter I

# The Desert,
# Keeper of Tracks

## Persistent tracks, witnesses to the passage of the first explorers

The joint impact of wind and sand makes spectacular disappearances seem plausible, such as that of the army of Cambyses 2,500 years ago. For example, von Minutoli describes the probable demise of a large group in 1805 on the road to Darfur. "The troops of Cambyses and the caravan of 2,000 people that was supposedly buried in 1805 may have succumbed to *khamsin* (sandstorm) or to thirst, and the corpses would then have been covered with sand, as can happen in the sandy North in very little time."[83]

The Great Sea of Sand has doubtless witnessed many other tragic adventures of which, seemingly capriciously, certain traces remain. Today remnants of the camps of the desert pioneers—Almasy, Bagnold, Clayton, or Kemal el Dine—lie washed up in the sand: empty food cans, oil drums polished by the wind and shining in the sun, broken wooden crates, even military survival rations with their instructions still legible: "Emergency Ration. Contents to be consumed only when no other rations of any kind are procurable. To open strip off band. NOTICE: not to be opened except by order of an officer."

Even more fascinating are the inexplicably still-visible tracks of automobiles that crossed the desert between 1920 and 1940. One can still encounter the twin wheel ruts of the Rolls Royces or Renaults used by Kemal el Dine or Beadnell, probably the only people who ever attempted to traverse the desert by car. The sand and wind have left these tracks only on a particular type of ground, where the surface consists of tiny, dark pebbles covering a layer of sand and soil. The weight of the vehicle compacted the soil and left a shallow but highly visible rut. Blown by the wind, sand fills in the smaller indentations, leaving two light-colored tracks that contrast sharply with the surrounding dark pebble surface. This phenomenon often occurs between two rows of dunes, where these seemingly permanent tracks are protected, "forming marks that might easily last for a century."[84]

## Impassioned explorers

According to Major Peter H. Clayton, the desert expeditions led by the British, by the Hungarian Count Almasy, and by the Egyptian prince Kemal el Dine all shared the same objectives: to explore a hostile landscape, to reconnoiter in order to draw maps, and to contain the Sanusi people. In the same period, the French were also trying to establish routes to penetrate and pacify African countries from the Sahara to Madagascar, from Morocco to Sudan. These were the 1923–1924 Renault and the 1924–1925 Citroën reconnaissance expeditions across Africa, the latter using what were known as "halftracks" or *autochenilles*, to test the capability of autos to travel over challenging and diverse terrain.

### Major Patrick A. Clayton and Major R.A. Bagnold: Two experts on sand

The cartography that was accomplished under the direction of Major Patrick A. Clayton is the result of a number of forays into this decidedly hostile and inaccessible land. This was a formidable task at a time when instruments were rudimentary and fragile, demanding considerable skill and care to use them. Reconnaissance using a sextant generally involved constant stopping and the performance of tedious calculations, but such was the technology of the time, and Clayton was able to generate many maps with these techniques. By 1938, his biographer (his son, Major Peter Clayton) tells us, over 74 original maps carried his name.[85]

Today, modern instruments like the Global Positioning System (GPS) can instantly record one's position and the planned or actual trajectory, and can be superimposed on existing maps. Nonetheless, the cartography created by Clayton and his team, using the means available at the time, is still essential for anyone venturing into this landmark-free desert. Indeed, these early maps tally impressively with more recent satellite maps, which confirms the exceptional quality of Clayton's work.

*Explorers of the year 2000, their presence betrayed by a cloud of dust, also leave traces that will be found again ... many years from now.*

**Right:**
*English army survival rations, "only to be opened upon the order of an officer."*

*Remains of the Hungarian explorer Count Almasy's camp.*

**83.** Saïd, *op. cit.* p. 201f.
**84.** Harding King, *Mysteries of the Libyan Desert*, p. 83, London, 1925.
**85.** P. H. Clayton, *Desert Explorer, A Biography of Colonel P. A. Clayton*, Cornwall, 1998.

## GPS (Global Positioning System)

*The Global Positioning System is a modern navigation tool that uses at least three satellites to guarantee reliable data—since a point is defined by three coordinates in space (latitude, longitude, and altitude); using more satellites yields a more precise position. The pinpoint data it provides are recorded and allow you to backtrack the traveled path exactly. The GPS can do much more: If, before departure, you enter data for your destination and consult the system constantly, GPS will tell you the difference between your ideal and actual trajectories, as well as calculate how far you have yet to travel. It can record past and present geographic positions, identify unusual terrain, and tell you the direction to follow. It cannot, however, anticipate future geographic positions. This remarkable device is barely larger than a compass: It fits in your palm, can be worn like a wristwatch, or fit into a car. Though the GPS cannot prevent you from getting lost, it will always tell you your exact "theoretical" position!!*

**Previous page:** *Tire tracks, probably left by a Rolls Royce.*

**Right:** *(from top to bottom and left to right)*

*Rolls Royce command car with its tracks, 1916.*

*P. A. Clayton's Model TT Ford, 1926.*

*Rolls Royce in the Libyan Desert, 1916.*

*Model A Ford with "balloon tires" owned by Sir Robert Clayton, 1936.*

*Vehicles of British forerunners: Model T Ford, 1916–1918.*

**86.** P. Dumont, *Les Ford d'Henry Ford,* "La vie de l'Auto," p. 35, Fontainebleau, 1984.
**87.** Dumont, *op. cit.* p. 107.

## Automobiles in the Desert

The first motor vehicles used in the Egyptian desert were English Rolls Royces and American Fords. In particular, "the [Ford] Model T, with its high suspension and tight, all-terrain steering, could overcome obstacles that other more powerful cars could not."[86]

In 1926, Major P.A. Clayton chose a Model TT Ford, which is in fact a Model T stretch that was modified in England and then manufactured in the United States. This model was also used for trucking, since it could carry much larger loads.

Prince Kemal el Dine preferred the French-made Citroens with caterpillar tracks; these vehicles had already proved themselves suited to crossing the difficult, sandy terrain of the Sahara. The British later used the more modern Model A Ford, fitted with a more powerful engine: These modified engines "have torque and give the model A Ford spectacular acceleration and great ability to climb steep slopes."[87] Over the years, technical progress in automobile design and manufacture allowed desert lovers to drive cars that were equipped with improved gears and wider tires, so-called "balloon tires," first used by Count Almasy. These and other improvements enabled those impassioned with the Great Sea of Sand to venture ever further.

The mission of Major (later General) R.A. Bagnold went hand in hand with that of Major Clayton. Bagnold was in charge of preparing the expeditions, including the equipment, and was thus responsible for the well-being of his men. He was supposed to monitor the Sanusi, who considered the desert their territory and were quite capable of annexing oases from their base in Cyrenaica. Apart from his military activities, Major Bagnold's passion for the desert and the dunes led him to study how the desert was shaped, expanded, and moved. He well understood the particular difficulties of the desert and the best means to overcome them. His theories, published in many articles, described sand as a liquid; he pointed out how grains of sand move depending on their density and changing wind speed. These studies were translated into mathematical calculations of the relation between wind velocity and sand particle density. Bagnold carried out much of this aspect of his work in England, where he constructed a sand laboratory in his garden. His results were published in 1939 in his book *The Physics of Blown Sands and Desert Dunes*. His research was so seminal that it was later used by scientists at NASA to explain dune formations on Mars. About this surprising application of his early work, Bagnold wrote: "To my astonishment, it soon became the standard textbook on the subject, and still remains so. Indeed, when NASA's spacecraft were able to examine the Martian landscape at close range, the book was found to allow the sand-driving mechanism to be adapted to the very different and far more tenuous atmosphere of Mars."[88]

### Prince Kemal el Dine Hussein: An extraordinary character

Prince Kemal el Dine, son of the khedive Ismail, was attracted to the desert at an early age and crossed the north many times by camel over the years, giving him unparalleled knowledge of the desert. Passionately interested in science and discovery, he undertook to penetrate completely unknown regions of the desert, not unlike the Frenchman Bruneau de Laborie who crossed the Sahara Desert from south to north all the way to Alexandria. Kemal el Dine explored the desert systematically. An expedition he led in 1923 with Dr. J. Ball (Director of the Desert Survey Department, or DSD) was the first expedition to use a fleet of Citroën caterpillar vehicles manned by French mechanics. He recounted his adventures in his journal, where he noted the sites he discovered and the names he gave them, names that are still used today. Here is a sample journal entry: "10th of January, we are within sight of Djebel Ouenat, heading toward it, leaving to the north the edge of the plateau we've been following for two days, which here rises into impressive cliffs (altitude higher than 3,000 feet). I had already spotted these cliffs from the south in 1925, on my way from Ouenat to Tarfaoui. Dr. J. Ball had determined the approximate location of the highest point of these cliffs. I named them *Gilf Kebir*, the 'Great Escarpment'."[89]

Illness and a premature death unfortunately put an end to his extraordinary explorations. At the southernmost part of the Gilf Kebir, a rocky spur topped by a cairn (a man-made rock pile marking the site) dominates a small pyramid of stones. At the foot of this pyramid is a commemorative plaque set in 1933, written in Arabic and translated into English by Major Peter H. Clayton praising Kemal's exceptional qualities:

"To perpetuate the Memory of
His Excellency His Royal Highness Prince Kemal el Dine
the Great Explorer of the Libyan Desert,
Remember without fail his enormous ability and public esteem."

### Count Ladislas E. von Almasy: A prodigious man of the desert

While Majors Bagnold and Clayton continued to criss-cross the desert, and Kemal el Dine led motorized expeditions, an enigmatic, rather unsettling character arrived in Cairo who would later play a major role in exploring these unknown regions and make an important contribution to the discovery of sites, caves, cave paintings, and rock drawings: the famous Hungarian Count Ladislas E. von Almasy. When he first arrived in 1932, he joined up with Kemal el Dine and organized an expedition with the collaboration of Major Clayton, the cartographer, a Royal Air Force pilot named Penderel, and Sir Robert Clayton, who owned an airplane. Thus, the count inaugurated a totally new way of prospecting. He traveled all over the Great Sea of Sand and Gilf Kebir, enduring great hardships along the way despite the modern technology he had at his disposal: "The region covering the last 100 kilometers [ca. 60 miles] south of Siwa is the worst desert country I have ever come across, and I would readily label this northern part of the Great Sea of Sand a region 'unfit for cars, camels, or humans.' If the Persian army got as far as this desert region, I wouldn't be surprised by their failure to get past this obstacle."[90]

Almasy also noted the intensity of the extreme atmospheric conditions: "I had to face the ordeal of another experience that reminded me of the 'deadly South Wind' mentioned by Herodotus."[91]

Later, when the world was on the verge of World War II, the Hungarian Almasy joined ranks with the Nazis, with whom he shared his extensive knowledge of the desert. This was the dawn of a new era in the desert. Among the missions assigned to Bagnold, who was director of the Long Range Desert Group, was to capture his former desert colleague. The dramatic chase that ensued is recounted in the book *The Cat and the Mice*, which is now out of print; it also served as the historical inspiration for the novel *The English Patient*, by Michael Ondatje.

Because both Almasy and Bagnold were intimately familiar with the desert and could anticipate one another's moves, the infernal pursuit in the sand led to neither capture nor triumph. Almasy joined a German counterintelligence unit and thus came to be of service to Rommel. His mission was to prepare the 1942 counteroffensive and to establish spies in Cairo. A statement by German Admiral Canaris in 1941 underscores how vital Almasy's missions were: "Every piece of information garnered from the enemy is worth more than 20 tanks."[92]

Both of the count's missions were failures, as he chronicles in detail in his own work, *The Libyan Desert*. Count Almasy was buried in Austria, and his epitaph includes the title of *Abu Ramla*, meaning "Father of the Sand."

*Monument to the memory of Prince Kemal el Dine Hussein, built in 1933 to the south of the Gilf Kebir massif to honor this exceptional Egyptian explorer, who died at an early age.*

**88.** R. A. Bagnold, *Libyan Sands, Travel in a Dead World*, p. 285, London, 1993.
**89.** Prince Kemal el Dine Hussein, "L' Exploration du désert de Libye III, expédition de 1925-1926", p. 234-325, *Revue de Géographie*, vol. 50, 1928.
**90.** L. E. von Almasy, *Récentes Explorations dans le désert Libyque*, 1932-1936, p. 96, Cairo, 1936.
**91.** Almasy, *op. cit.* p. 96.
**92.** J.-F. Sers, T. Monod, *Désert Libyque*, p. 177, Paris, 1994.

*Regenfeld, or "field of rain,"
an alam, or cairn, built by
Rohlfs and his companions at
the site of a torrential—but
providential—downpour
lasting more than 48 hours.*

**Below:** *The signatures of the
explorers Rohlfs, Zittel, and
Jordan from 1874, Kemal el
Dine from 1924, and Almasy
from 1933.*

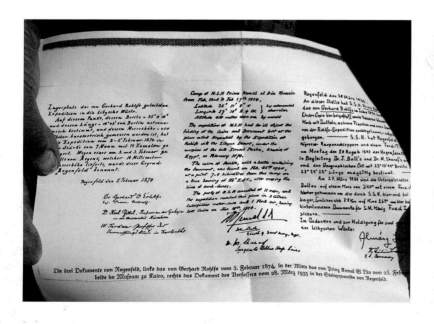

Die drei Dokumente von Regenfeld, links das von Gerhard Rohlfs vom 5. Februar 1874, in der Mitte das von Prinz Kemal El Din vom 25. Feb.,
beide im Museum zu Kairo, rechts das Dokument des Verfassers vom 28. März 1933 in der Steinpyramide von Regenfeld.

# Chapter II

# The Enigmatic Desert

## The paths of the caravans: The camel routes

*…for many thousands of years the routes of the desert have remained unchanged. Since they were first used in ancient times, millions of men and animals have trodden there, and so in the course of time they were marked on the face of the desert*.[97]

In the heart of the desert, amid a vast, desolate area, travelers may find traces of something quite different from the more recent geometric patterns left in the sand. There is a certain poignancy to these endlessly meandering, seemingly random tracks. Where might they lead? All along the route are *alams*, or cairns, that in ancient times guided the caravan travellers and marked their painful journey. Many camels walked ahead, each choosing its own path, following the footsteps of previous caravans and their fellow camels in a loping gait. These routes were maintained by the repeated passages of heavily loaded animals, the so-called ships of the desert.

A scholar who accompanied Napoleon Bonaparte's campaigns in the late 18th century, Vivant Denon, described one of these great caravans making its way from Darfur in Sudan to Assiut, in the Nile Valley in Egypt. The number of camels and their burdens seemed disporportionate compared to the distance to be traveled: "Each year, these caravans in Egypt carried three or four hundred camel-loads of elephant tusks, 2,000 rhinoceros horns, 20 or 30 kantars of ostrich feathers, 2,000 kantars of arabic gum, 1,000 of tamarind and as much natron as was gathered along the way, as well as food supplies that are eaten along the way…. Every year, two caravans travel to Darfur, each comprised of four to five thousand camels; the trip to Siut takes 40 days and the camels are driven by two to three hundred people."[98]

If the sand itself has preserved these emotionally moving tracks, it seems imperative that we should also respect them, in memory of the people whose travels they mark. Now and then one finds bones, bleached white by the relentless sun—a grisly reminder of the very real dangers of following this endless route, transient cemeteries that bear witness to the past.

## The pottery heap at Abu Ballas: The mysterious vanishing jars

Two large rocks tower protectively over the road between Dakhla and Kufra to the south of Gilf Kebir. One of them actually resembles a warrior; its sharp outline attracts the eye, dulled as it is by the monotonous landscape, dotted with little more than a few distant clay cones. Thirst for shade and a sudden irrepressible curiosity compels the traveler to stop for a closer look at these odd hills. But upon approaching, you are faced with a clear sign that visitors are not welcome: Any attempt to scale the hills launches a disastrous rockslide. This is surprising enough, but if you explore the base of the escarpment, you will find the ground here suddenly littered with fragments and shards of broken clay jars, abandoned in this pitiful state. How they came to be here is a mystery begging for an explanation, which is unfortunately lacking.

Rohlfs' team had heard of the existence of two minarets in the desert guarding a watering hole but had never tried to find it. Prince Kemal el Dine passed through this place, dubbed "Pottery Hill" by J. Ball in 1919, and decided to call it *Abu Ballas*, which means "Father of Jars": "There is no water at Abu Ballas. The name 'place of the jars' that I gave to it in 1923 comes from the fact that several hundred large terra cotta jars were found at the foot of this 40-meter high [ca. 130 feet] sandstone rock. The jars were no doubt left there by nomads at some undetermined time."[99]

A few years later, Count Almasy noted the number and nature of these pots in precise detail; they are quite similar to the pottery still made in the region today: "The *zeir* is a porous pottery, a clay jar that keeps water cool thanks to continuous evaporation; these have been used in Egypt and Sudan since time immemorial. Similar sites have been found in various places in the Libyan Desert. The largest of these pottery sites, with over 300 jars, is marked on maps by the name of Pottery Hill or Abu Ballas."[100]

Although the pots at Abu Ballas vary in shape, size, and thickness, they fall into two different basic types. One is round, cylindri-

*Traces left by ancient caravans:
The camel tracks meander and
wind to the rhythm of the "ships
of the desert."*

**97.** A. Fakhry, *The Egyptian Deserts,
Bahriya Oasis,* vol. I, p. 8, Cairo, 1942.
**98.** *De la caravane de Darfour,* by P. J. G.,
member of the Egyptian Institute, *Appendix
CCL,* in Vivant Denon, *Voyages,* vol. II.
**99.** Kemal el Dine, *op. cit.* p. 323f.
**100.** Almasy, *op. cit.* p. 3.

*Abandoned to the raptorial birds, the bones of animals that died exhausted by the rigors of the 40-Day Road lie in the sand.*

**101.** Vivant Denon, *op. cit.*, vol. I, p. 275.
**102.** Sers, Monod, *op. cit.* p. 1227.

## The route to Darb el-Arbain
### by Vivant Denon

*Here at last is the route to Darfur, where the people of Tombut arrive; a trader whom I met in Kene who had often made this journey gave me the exact itinerary that I note here.*

*The route from Siut to Darfur and Sennar via Dongola:*

*From Siut, you enter the desert heading southwest for four days before you arrive at Korg-Elouah, the most populated and cultivated oasis; there you will find sweet, fresh running water that gushes from the earth and returns to it; there is a fortress and a large village. From Korg-Elouah to Boulagh, another oasis, is half a day's journey; there is a little village with good-tasting water that may, however, give you a fever if you're not accustomed to it. From Boulagh to el-Bsactah is one day's journey, there is brackish water there. From el-Bsactah to Beris is again half a day; you will find a large village and the water is fairly good. It takes two hours from Beris to el-*

*Mekh; again there is water, and you should stock up because there are no more oases after el-Mekh and you will only find salt water for the rest of the trip. If you keep walking in the same direction, after ten days you will come to Desir. From Desir to Selima is three days; there is only salt water but it is not quite as bad. From Selima to Dongola, where you come to the Nile, is four days; you should stock up on supplies here. From Dongola, head more toward the west, and el-Goyah is four days away. From el-Goyah to Zagone is six days; you'll find salty but cool water. From Zagone to Darfur is ten days with neither water nor villages. When you come to Dongola, it takes 17 days of walking to reach Sennar, heading south; and from Sennar to Darfur is a twelve-day trek from east to west. You have to remember that on such a route the person who can't keep up will be left behind, because waiting for a straggler means jeopardizing the entire caravan."[101]*

cal, gray on the inside and covered with red clay, and has a thick, rough hand-built lip, with a pointed bottom that allowed the jars to stand upright like amphoras. These are likely the older of the two types. The other type is more of an elongated oval; it is narrower and beige or light brown in color. The first kind resemble the jars used in the Pharaonic period, and the kiln firing date has confirmed their age. The oval jars have been proven to be newer. Studies into the dates and origins of these pots prove that this ground was used as a depository from ancient times until a recent era.

The purpose of the pottery heap is less clear. Was there once a deep well that only produced a trickle of water, so that reserves of water were set aside for the passing caravans? Filled jars would probably not have survived the trip intact, so jars would be more likely to be filled on site. If there was once a well here, what happened to it? Has it simply disappeared, or was it filled in or hidden by nomadic tribes trying to stave off invaders of their territory? Or was there never actually a well? If there was no well or watering hole, the jars could have been left to replenish others' supplies. Perhaps one caravan might bring fresh water in goatskin bottles called *guerbas* and leave it in the jars for the next caravan, before continuing across the desert to Dakhla? If that were the case, why were the jars not made on site using the local colored clays? Is it possible that there was once firewood in the area to fire the kilns, though obviously there is none today? We have no solution to this mystery, and meanwhile the jars continue to disintigrate.

Why are the jars broken? One explanation is that the oasis inhabitants were tired of being raided by invading tribes, and they may have destroyed the jar depository. This draws some credibility from

the strategic location of Abu Ballas, which could easily have served as a hideout or rest stop for attackers: "At the beginning of the 19th century, the Tibu, who belonged to the Bideyat tribe from Ennedi, habitually raided the oasis at Dakhla. The khedive [or viceroy of Egypt] therefore decided to send his Mamluks to chase them away, and [the Mamluks] destroyed the well where they refilled their water supplies, seven to eight days' walk from Dakhla ."[102]

Count Almasy, moreover, noted that the water jar depository is situated on the caravan route about one-third of the way from the Dakhla oasis to the Kufra oasis. He presumed that there must have been another depository halfway between Abu Ballas and the final stop at Kufra. He searched for it in vain, but that is another story …

### Zerzura, the lost oasis

Zerzura is a familiar word to oasis dwellers and to everyone who has explored the sands of the Great Sea of Sand, the sandstone of Gilf Kebir, and the granite range of Uweinat. The very mention of the name Zerzura elicits a flood of stories, legends, explanations, and theories, all essentially serving to perpetuate rather than to remove the shroud of mystery in which it is wrapped. The word zerzura comes from the Arabic *zerzur*, which means starling, a small bird, or from the ancient Berber word *izerzer,* meaning a gazelle. In both languages, it suggests the hidden domain of wild, free birds and other animals.

What is it about this Zerzura that arouses such passion? The first European guidebook to mention Zerzura is the *Handbook for Travelers in Lower and Upper Egypt,* from 1896: "Zerzura, or the Oasis

Pottery fragments found at the foot of the rocky hill of Abu Ballas, a stop on the route from Kufra oasis to Dakhla. Both the origin of the jars and the source of the water they once contained remain mysterious.

of the Blacks," the handbook informs us, "is only known from the vague descriptions of Arabs."[103]

Arab legends describe it as an oasis of astonishing beauty, abundant riches, and hidden treasures, with luxurious gardens that are watered with crystal-clear life-enhancing spring water. Some people claim to have been there, while others say they have only glimpsed it from afar. So far, though, although no one has actually found a trace of it, many Arabs will indicate where this dream oasis may be found: over there, follow the sunset, it's a long way …

Some describe it as nestled in the mountains, so far away and so well hidden that only its inhabitants can ever find it. They jealously guard the secret of its whereabouts and never reveal themselves to strangers from the city. According to Harding King, some people even believe Zerzura to be an enchanted town whose inhabitants and herds were turned to stone by a spell, and who still await a miracle to release them from their bondage.[104]

Zerzura may also have been a water source. Perhaps it was the same site as Abu Ballas, or another jar depository in the desert. The Arabic word *zeir* means "porous pottery" or "clay jar," so it is conceivable, by extrapolation, that Zerzura means "the place of the jars," but even Almasy was not truly convinced by this theory.[105]

Wouldn't this oasis have been an essential layover for caravans, a resting place halfway between two watering holes that are quite far

apart—for example, between Abu Ballas and Kufra on a level with Gilf Kebir? Almasy was taken with this legend and, while flying over this part of the desert, discovered a green valley filled with trees (the first of the three wadis found later), but he did not solve the mystery of Zerzura. Kemal el Dine had also heard of Zerzura and vowed that it was identical with the Wadi Abd el-Malik, named after an old man of the Zwaya tribe who left Kufra to take refuge in the Fayum. Almasy had also met this man, who swore that the valley now named after him had been called Wadi Zerzura before he rediscovered it.

No one seriously believes it could have been a rain oasis, known only by a distant nomadic tribe such as the Tibu, who regularly fled the drought of the plains, bringing their herds to the greener pastures in mountainous areas in the wet season when rain and vegetation were abundant. The Tibu kept the location of such watering holes secret, and traveled from one spring to the next with the changing seasons. Such sites, whose exact locations remain unclear, receive only random rainfall and are therefore called ephemeral or short-lived oases.

Most likely, Zerzura is only an oasis of legend, a lost paradise, protected by the secrets of the sands, the tale of a shining white town encircled by high walls, guarded by a dove who carries the key to the city gates in its beak—a kind of tale of the Arabian Nights.

**Previous page:**
*Gigantic walls and pertrified monsters guard the well-hidden and forgotten citadel.*

**Right:**
*The secret path of Zerzura, paved with silver; this phenomenon, which occurs at sunset, is so short-lived that even the initiated do not have the time to find the path again.*

**Following pages:**
*This could be Zerzura, the legendary oasis—a dazzling whiteness that emerges from the heart of the desert just beyond the path.*

**103.** *Handbook for Travelers in Upper and Lower Egypt*, p. 607, John Murray's, London, 1896.
**104.** Harding King, *Mysteries*, p. 63.
**105.** Almasy, *op. cit.*

*Whalebacks.*

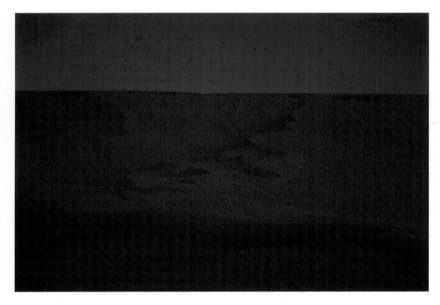

*Seif dunes.*

*Barchan dunes on the planet Mars.*

the cone will change according to, first, the intensity, regularity, and direction of the wind; and second, the size and density of the grains of sand. All dunes become significantly asymmetrical in the presence of wind: The dominant wind will push the sand toward the crest, creating a shallow incline, while the other side will naturally collapse in a much steeper slope, equaling the "angle of the natural slope" of sand, which is roughly 33°. It is this angle that makes dunes impossible to surmount from this side.

### Whalebacks

The Great Sea of Sand lies on a bed of compact, flat, and stable sandstone. In the northern region, the sand can be up to 1,000 feet deep; of this mass, only the crest of the dunes will move when blown by the wind, while the underlying mass remains stationary. As a result, the region lacks a clearly defined shape, and, depending on the seasons, the dunes are swept and pushed in unpredictable ways. The dominant winds, however, are north by northwest and south by southeast. If there are no corridors between dunes, this characteristic wind pattern gives rise to enormous contiguous dunes in the northern area called whalebacks. Whalebacks can spread out to a few miles in width and reach lengths of a few hundred miles. One ought not to imagine thousands of great beached whales here, but rather seemingly endless rounded dunes that really do resemble whales. Like the massive northern ranges that spawned them, these dunes are immobile, rooted in their place by the elements.

### Seif dunes

Only the crests of so-called *seif* dunes (*seif* is Arabic for "saber") are "alive." The wind pushes these dunes into long festoons of sword- or saber-like crests. They move like a snake, slithering along with a length of up to 60 miles, their pointed tips heading south, their stationary tails extending north to the high plateaus. "This dune head is always low and often tapers out into a pointed tip, while the tail of the dune fans out across the base of the sandstone hills, whose erosion by the wind supplies the dune with its accumulation of sand."[111]

The serpentine, undulating shape of the seif dunes is the product of periodic lateral crosswinds that blow at an angle to the dominant wind; the collapsing side of the dune is where the crosswinds hit, while the median line of the dunes' progression aligns with the direction of the dominant winds. This snakelike formation only occurs if the crosswinds are strong enough to forge the saber curve and to hone the crest into a sharp blade. Although it looks solid, this sharp crest is highly unstable, and many spontaneous small landslides streak the flanks of these dunes.

### Barchan dunes

According to Monod, the *barkhanes*, or barchan dunes, take their name from Asia, specifically from Turkistan. This category of dunes can be found in two distinct shapes: single barchans and wedded barchans. Single barchan dunes are isolated and symmetrical; they

*Crescent- or horseshoe-shaped barchan dunes. With their convex side to the wind and pointed ends directed forward, they move inexorably through the desert, swallowing up every obstacle in their path.*

111. Kemal el Dine, *op. cit.* p. 335.
112. Bagnold, *A Further Journey*, p. 123.

**Following pages:** *Parallel dune belts, majestic barriers hundreds of miles long, on their way south. They are separated by huge, flat valleys strewn with rock debris.*

ing forward and inward, and they will stubbornly retain their shape even when they come across obstacles. For example, when a barchan encounters an oasis, it threatens to surround and engulf it permanently, like the oasis of Kharga.

Wedded barchans also cling to saber dunes occasionally, as if decorating the larger mass of sand on only one slope, the windward slope. When this happens, the barchan relinquishes its usual symmetry: One of its claws will curve outward, while the other curves in tightly toward the base.

### Dune belts

When viewed from above, the northern and central regions of the Great Sea of Sand resemble the palm of a hand, with its many fingers of sand sculpted by the raging winds into great dune belts that spread along impressive corridors, in some places attaining widths of several miles. Generally, the foundation consists of hard rock that has been eroded by the wind, allowing the sands to travel quickly and unimpeded. The character of this sand is quite the opposite of that of the treacherous sands that trap their prey by implacably slowing it down.

are only found where the land is flat and the wind always comes from the same direction. The wind shapes the dune into the charming shape of a crescent moon or a horseshoe. "The individual barchan may be described as roughly … a circular dome of sand, from the leeward side of which a big bite has been taken, leaving a collapsing front in the form of a hollow semicircle."[112] This type of dune is not peculiar to Earth; satellite photos show that winds on Mars also produce this effect.

Barchans can vary enormously in size and migrate either in isolation or in small groups, their backs to the wind, their "claws" curv-

### Ripples

It is common to see fine little waves or ripples extending across the surface of vast tracts of sand that are unassailed by powerful winds, stretched out in seemingly endless curving parallel lines. They are miniature mountain ranges, known by many names, reminiscent of the ripples left by sea currents on a smooth, sandy beach at low tide. Are these provocative ripples an astonishing garden, a place of meditation on the gods, a Japanese sand garden for those who are intrigued by rakes? Or are they a dune nursery? Alas, no, for these ripples never grow up; they always remain the same size and the same shape.

### The Abu Muharek, "Father of the walking dune"

On the Mountain of the West—as valley dwellers call the limestone plateau between the valley of the Nile and the string of oases—stretches an unusually long dune. This unique belt begins north of Bahariya and spills down into the valley and oasis of Kharga through a series of steep, vertiginous passes before following the Darb el-Arbain. This seemingly impassable dune stretches over 375 miles long and some 6 miles across. The great mass of sand offers few routes that are accessible to caravans; moreover, the ground is strewn with sharp stones that cut the feet of humans and camels alike. This formidable formation is known as the Abu Muharek; it consists of one barchan dune after another and overlapping whaleback dunes, and eventually curves toward the west in a line parallel with the movement of the sand belts of the Great Sea of Sand.

## The life of a dune

### The great nomads

While a large part of the Great Sea of Sand is content to remain stationary, certain types of dunes are prompted by the wind to go exploring unknown areas. The etesian winds that blow down from the Mediterranean ensure the migration of the dunes, and their direction is predetermined: They move from north to south. While the seif dunes creep through the desert in parallel lines, the much faster barchan dunes move ahead like scouts to the south. When the dune encounters an obstacle that alters the direction of the wind—such as the great plateau of Gilf Kebir or the small springs of Gebel Uweinat, discovered by Prince Kemal el Dine around 1920—then these straight north-south lines curve clockwise toward the west. Changes in wind direction and in the dunes' migration can also be due to differences in the prevailing atmospheric conditions—air pressure, temperature, and humidity—between the northern and southern parts of the Great Sea of Sand.

As the dunes cross the border into Libya and extend into Chad, their journey nears its terminus: The dunes cease about 100 miles from the rainy regions, according to Ball, because of changes in atmospheric pressure.[113]

It is difficult to study the speed at which the dunes actually move; their independence is such that the dunes themselves tend to drive away any observers trying to measure their comings and goings. It simply is not possible to stay put in the face of a migrating sand

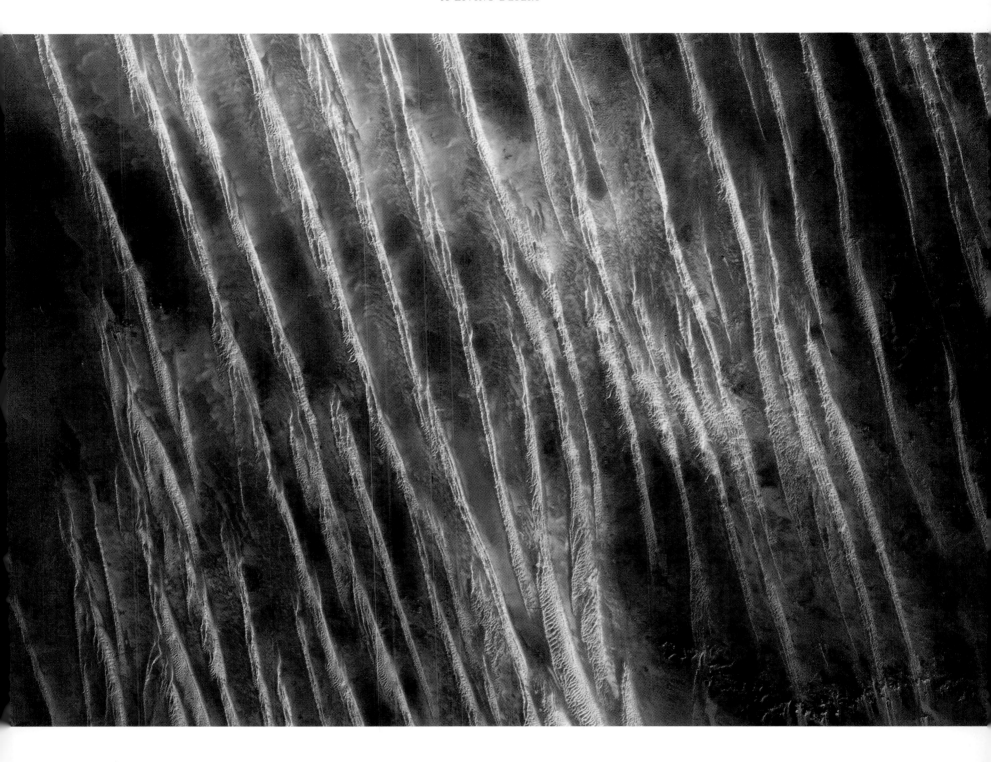

**Above:** *Satellite picture of dune belts to the south of the Great Sea of Sand and north of the Gilf Kebir. Their parallel arrangement, formed by the etesian winds, is probably unique in the entire world.*

**Right:** *Abu Muharek, the walking dune. Exceptionally long— around 375 miles—this dune separates the Nile from the chain of oases. It doubles back on itself in places, creating a sort of hollow between two lines of dunes.*

**Previous page:** *Undulating ripples next to a dune in the Great Sea of Sand.*

113. J. Ball "Problems of the Libyan Desert," p. 213, *Geographical Journal,* London July-September 1927.

*The Madman's Pass: one of the rare places where it is possible to clamber down the limestone escarpment to reach the oasis depression. The rugged slope, the soft sands, and the hostile, sharp rocks dissuade attempts at escape, but the reward lies in the sublime landscape that meets the eye.*

**Following page:** *The signature of the wind on a dune.*

114. Beadnell, *op. cit.* p. 389.
115. Ball, *op. cit.* p. 218.
116. Beadnell, *op. cit.* p. 390.
117. Bagnold, *A Further Journey*, p. 123.

dune: One only has to look at the dunes' relentless invasion of an oasis to see the damage they cause to anything in their path—roads completely covered, poles knocked over, houses buried. Still, efforts have been made to measure their progress. Beadnell spent two years measuring the movement of five barchan dunes at Kharga and estimated that "in the Libyan Desert the dunes progress steadily southwards at an average rate of 15–16 meters [ca. 50 feet] a year. The greatest movement of a barchan in twelve months amounted to 20.6 meters [ca. 67 feet], the least to 10.2 meters [ca. 33 feet]."[114]

In 1980, the Haynes expedition rediscovered one of Bagnold's camps dating back to 1930, originally set up at the foot of a barchan. By comparing the two positions, the party was able to measure the progression of the dune, which had covered the camp, then moved away again, over a distance of almost 1,300 feet!

Today the dunes are closely monitored. Though these great natural entities have for millennia managed to evade human efforts to contain or tame them, humankind has finally developed a technology from which the great dunes cannot hide. Thanks to satellites, we are able to view the topography of the Great Sea of Sand in its tiniest details and variations, and the sight is spectacular.

Now that we are able to spy on the dunes at will, we may spot the occasional anomaly of the "smoking" dune. In reality, the wind blows and carries grains of sand up to dance a ballet in the air. Ball's theory is that the grains of sand are charged with electricity when they come in contact with the air and are irresistibly attracted by the negative charge of the dune.[115]

In their longitudinal movement, the dunes retain their ability to attract the sand particles in suspension and thus maintain the corridors that separate them. This phenomenon occurs only if the wind speed reaches at least 15 miles per hour. According to studies by Beadnell, the wind blows up to 35 miles an hour during sandstorms, and the dunes may then move at an extraordinary speed of an inch to an inch and a half per hour.[116]

Not only will the dunes pick up their pace during a sandstorm, the wind in a storm may throw the grains of sand so high into the air that they are carried hundreds of miles until the storm breaks, unleashing a sudden electrical discharge. This phenomenon explains the hot sandy winds that are even known to cross the Mediterranean.

### Dune reproduction

Dunes seem to reproduce. Indeed, barchans advance faster than other dunes, and the single barchans move faster than the wedded ones, whose great mass continues to grow in inertia. The horns, or claws, of a barchan advance more quickly than the center and will sometimes catch up to the dune in front of it. This convergence of the two dunes creates an indentation like a giant navel between them; the newly formed dune continues to be affected by the wind. The wind then acts as a midwife, delivering the dune of a tiny barchan at the tip of one of the horns. When it is large enough, this offshoot detaches from the parent barchan and begins to move along its own path. "Sometimes," says Bagnold, "a little dune 20 feet or so in width

is found a few hundred yards to leeward of one of the horns of a big dune, as if some sort of reproduction is taking place."[117]

### The song of the dunes

The dunes of the desert also seem to produce mysterious sounds. Usually utter silence reigns in the dunes, and is only rarely disturbed by the sounds of a wayward bird or the rustling of a blade of wild grass determined to survive in this mineral world. But in this strange and impressive silence, every so often a plaintive song is heard by a fortunate few.

One spring evening, at the summit of a dune near Kharga, the setting sun provided a grandiose display that invited contemplation. An irregular breeze danced over the dune, brushing grains of sand off the crest in successive waves. Suddenly a harmonious combination of low- and high-pitched tones floated in the air. No one could tell where it came from. The sound seemed to grow louder as the temperature dropped. Then the wind picked up, and the unknown singer and her melody vanished in the shadows of night. Could these notes have been produced by some sort of dance of the grains of quartz sand, or by the modulation of the different-sized grains?

When Bagnold heard this plaintive, vibrating sound after a storm, he described it thus: "I climbed up to the top of a high crest .... At each step I took, a sound came out of the surface of the dune, a low growl which increased, as my feet slid downward on its steep loose flanks starting rivers of disturbed grains, into the loud vibrating hoot of the so-called 'Singing Sands'."[118]

Harding King also noted the curious song of the sand, which he heard on a plateau southwest of the Dakhla oasis. The conditions were unusual: the day had been chilly, almost cold, with a stormy sky and occasional showers, following an extremely hot week. After sunset the sky filled with lightning, and that is when his group heard it: "This was on April 19, 1909 .... The sound was very faint. There were two distinct sounds; the one somewhat resembled the sighing of the wind in telegraph wires, and the other was a deep throbbing sound that strongly reminded me of the reverberation of Big Ben ... The sound was a distinctly musical one, as opposed to mere noise."[119]

A few years later, Harding King again wrote about this phenomenon, this time offering a local explanation for the mysterious music: "The sound ... is sometimes attributed, by the natives, to the beating of drums by a class of subterranean spirits that inhabit the dunes."[120]

This phenomenon is extremely uncommon; it must demand the coincidence of various unusual atmospheric conditions, and only a careful listener will ever perceive the desert's subtle melody.

## The Gilf Kebir plateau

Gilf Kebir is located south of the Great Sea of Sand; it is a sandstone plateau, higher in the south than in the north, with an average altitude of roughly 3,000 feet. Although the dunes run aground at the base of the northern edge, they are slowly and inexorably covering it. The plateau's southern end hangs steeply over the plain at its feet, which extends to nearby Sudan. Thirteen-hundred-foot cliffs extend for about 110 miles and are practically insurmountable. The northwestern part of the Gilf Kebir borders Libya and runs parallel to a similar high plateau, called Abu Ras, and is traversed by the Wadi el Gubba. The Gilf has been furrowed with gullies by the heavy rains of the wet seasons. In the northern part, water erosion has shaped valleys that run south to north. These are called *wadis* ("valleys"); for example, *Wadi Talh* is the "Valley of the Acacias," *Wadi Abd el-*

**Previous page:**
*The smoke of departure: perhaps an indication of the dune's cruising speed?*

**Left:** *A cradle of dunes amid the perennial influence of the sands.*

**Right:**
*The song of the dunes, mysterious music of quartz.*

**118.** Bagnold, *Libyan Sands*, p. 159f.
**119.** Harding King, "Travels in the Libyan Desert," *Geographical Journal*, p. 134, vol. 39, 1912.
**120.** Harding King, *Mysteries*, p. 99f.

## Dunes of the Imagination

*What is the source of the dunes' seduction of our imaginations, their insistent presence in our escapist dreams as a prototype of aesthetic and virgin open space? Is the poetic vision of the dunes anchored in a faraway past? Some psychoanalysts, Melanie Klein in particular, have developed a hypothesis of an early life fantasy that is the foundation of humans' psychic life.[121] During breastfeeding many pleasant sensations mingle—warmth, the softness of skin, arms, breasts, smells, breath, light, feelings of plentitude, abundance and appeasement—and their repetition allows the establishment of a positive, internal reassuring object, named "good breast," as opposed to "bad breast," which is associated with unpleasant experiences.*

*The child vaguely remembers this primitive encounter: falling asleep clinging to a dozing woman who gives an impression of plentitude, symbol of the ideal maternal image. These fantasies remain ingrained in the subconscious and condition our relation to the world, familiarity or strangeness. These can recur depending on the circumstances, awakening a nostalgia for this ideal mother and this first aesthetic experience.*

*The immersion in an inordinate universe without references, such as the dunes, can reawaken in adults this diffuse memory of early experiences, with its associations of either joy or anguish: lilliputian fulfilled by innumerable and generous breasts, feminine bodies languid and reflecting the light of the setting sun; or on the contrary, terrified by a multitude of fragments of hostile and menacing bodies, or an incredible fight between giants ...*

*Escape from daily routine can lead to essentially faraway open spaces such as the Great Sea of Sand, and can take us back to ancient times, to one of the most early formative fantasies, awoken by a spectacle of inexpressible beauty, a maternal horizon.*

**Below:** *Mammisi, birthplace of dunes: a sanctuary formed by the complex of barchan dunes.*

**Following page:** *Satellite picture of the western edge of the Gilf Kebir, the pass of Aqaba and the course of the Wadi Sora, resembling a strange Martian panorama.*

121. H. Segal, *Introduction à l'oeuvre de Mélanie Klein*, Paris, 1969.
122. Almasy, *op. cit.* p. 54.

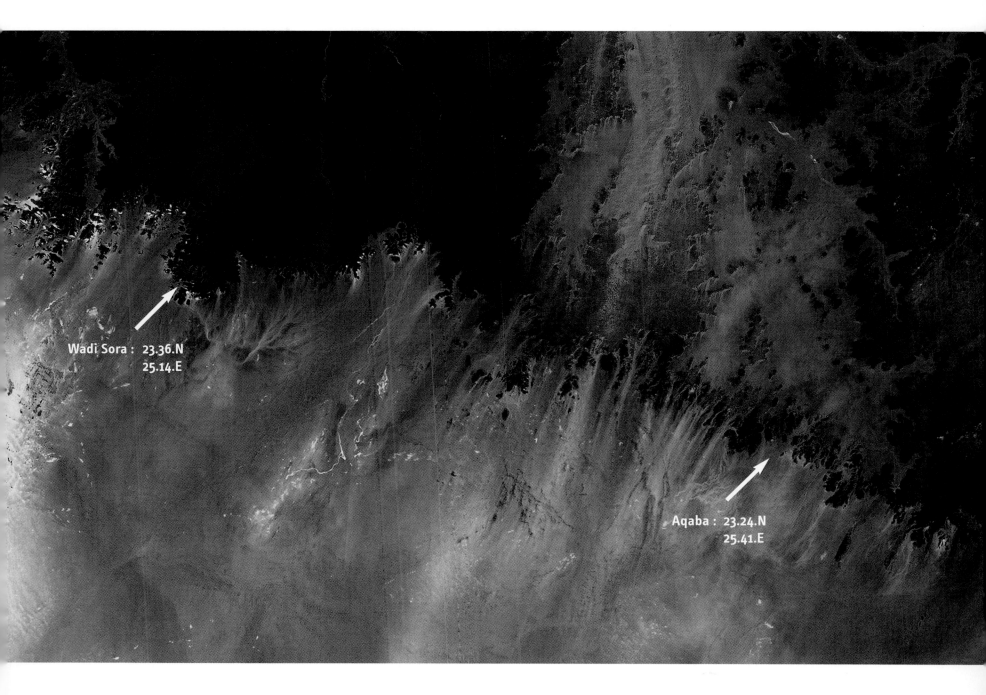

Wadi Sora : 23.36.N
25.14.E

Aqaba : 23.24.N
25.41.E

*Malik* is the "Valley of the Lost Oasis," and *Wadi Hamra* is the "Red Valley." And, of course, there is also the nameless wadi.

In the southern part of the Gilf, the river valleys run west to east: There you will find Wadi Bakht and its playa, Wadi Ard el-Akhdar with its prehistoric sites, Wadi Massa, and finally Wadi Fisaq, with its cave paintings. In the wet season, the natural drainage of most of the plateau flows toward the Nile. All of these wadis lead to dead ends and none provide access to the top of the plateau. There is a passage along the north-south face called the Aqaba corridor; this was historically a strategic defense point and it still bears land mines left by the British Army in World War II.

When the explorer Count Almasy was looking for the lost oasis of Zerzura in 1934, he described these valleys of the northern part of the Gilf: "Hamra takes its name from the uniform red color of the sand and the cliffs in this valley. Yet the pastures there are not very good; furthermore, the water holes of Wadi Hamra dry up very quickly. Wadi Abd el-Malik is named after an Arab from Kufra who

lived there a while ago and who returned to Kufra when the wadi dried up. He found white trees there. As for Wadi Talh, it is a small valley but the water spring is good; the name comes from the only trees that will grow there, the Talh trees."[122]

To the north of the wadis are traces of the great caravan route that linked Kufra in Libya to the chain of oases in Egypt. The great plateau was inhabited 5,000 years ago, but over time all of its springs have run dry and it is totally abandoned today. Unmoving in the torrid sun, buffeted by merciless winds and temperature swings that split apart the rocks, the Gilf Kebir does not seem terribly unlike the planet Mars. At first sight, it may well resemble some other planet, but on closer inspection one does find on the surface of the sand many signs of the presence of life-sustaining water, and of the people who once lived here.

The Gilf Kebir, guarding the treasures of the past, leans toward the extended fingers of the Great Sea of Sand to form the bulk of the Libyan Desert of Egypt.

# The Geology of the Gilf Kebir Plateau
## by Rushdi Saïd

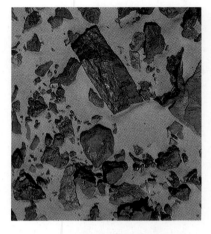

The Gilf Kebir is certainly the most striking topographic feature in the southern part of the Western Desert of Egypt. It forms a broad elliptical plateau that is suspended some 1,600 feet above the surrounding country. It consists of extremely resistant sandstone that has preserved it from erosion and kept its cliffs massive and steep. It extends in a north-south direction between latitudes 22° 40′N and 24° 40′N for a distance of more than 110 miles. A 15- to 18-mile-wide gorge separates the Gilf into a southern and a northern part.

The Gilf Kebir lies in a remote area that until recently was difficult to reach; few had dared to visit the region. It was only in 1909 that Harding King first sighted the southern region. The northern extension became known only as late as 1933, when Penderel flew northward over the western escarpment of the Gilf Kebir and discovered that it formed a distinct entity, separate from the southern part. The Gilf and its surrounding areas have since been the destination of several expeditions that remained extremely limited in number until recently because of the remote setting and harsh environment. During World War II the area became a center of activity for the Long Range Desert Group of the British Army. In trying to monitor and find ways to circumnavigate the Gilf, they completed its mapping and exploration. Later expeditions have worked out its geology, botany, and archaeology in great detail.

The top of the southern part of the Gilf forms an exceptionally flat surface that is not incised by any wadis. In contrast, the top surface of the northern part of the Gilf is deeply incised by the steep-sided wadis Hamra and Abd el-Malik, which nearly cut across its entire north-south length. These two wadis are among the most picturesque because of the presence of many trees and bushes along their courses. The monotony of the flat surface of the northern Gilf is broken by occasional dark bluish cones or flow sheets of basalt. Close to 50 exposures of these basaltic hills have been mapped, and they are approximately 38 million years old. They are therefore considerably younger than the majority of the rocks of the Gilf, which stem from the Cretaceous age (circa 140–160 million years ago).

The western escarpment of both the northern and southern Gilf forms a steep wall that is not interrupted by any wadis. It is impassable except at its southern end along the wadis el-Firaq and Wassa, through which the main caravan route and a road to Kufra and across the desert pass. The only other place cars can get through the Gilf north of Wadi el-Firaq is at the Gap, el-Aqaba, where a winding sandy wadi, in places only 30 feet wide, leads up from the western plain to the gorge that separates the southern and northern Gilf on top of the plateau. Clayton, the great explorer of this part of the desert, noticed this spot in 1931. El-Aqaba became famous during World War II when the British Army, which was patrolling the Western Desert of Egypt, mined it to deny access to the Axis agents.

The eastern scarp of the Gilf is deeply incised by steep-sided wadis that cut into the edge of the plateau, separating whole portions of it. These wadis were named by the early desert explorers and carry the meaningful Arabic names (from north to south) Mashi, Dayik ("narrow"), Maftuh ("open"), el-Bakht ("happiness" or "luck"), and Ard el-Akhdar ("green"). All these wadis have wide mouths and narrow and linearly segmented upstream portions. They commence at the scarps but have no drainage on top of the plateau, indicating that they may be relics of an older, now-defunct drainage system.

Of the eastern wadis, Wadi el-Bakht assumes special importance because of the discovery of a large neolithic settlement along its course. Approximately nine miles upstream from its mouth, a 100-foot-high sand dune had blocked its course and trapped the rains that fell on that desert during the Neolithic Wet Phase (circa 11,000–4,500 years ago), forming a lake along whose shores the herding Neolithic communities lived. Flint implements, ostrich egg shells, remains of pottery, and grinding stones provide evidence of a thriving community that lived there for at least a few thousand years.

*In a valley between two belts of dunes stands a hill of sand crowned with black stones: Qaret el-Hanesh, the "Mountain of Serpents." Bespangled with igneous quartzite mixed with multicolored jasper, it is possibly the result of a subterranean eruption.*

**Following page:** *The far edge of the Gilf Kebir plateau opening onto the plains of Libya and the Sudan.*

## Desert Plants
by Edmond Diemer

The Libyan Desert is without doubt one of the most arid places on earth: Rain, or what climatologists have in mind when they speak of "useful rainfall," is rare—that is, the kind of rain that can dampen the uppermost two or three inches of the soil.

In most deserts, even a light rainfall is enough to germinate the few seeds hidden in the soil and to turn the dunes slightly green. But in the Great Sea of Sand and in the corridors between dune belts, this does not happen; the strong winds do bring seeds from the oases, even over quite long distances, but the seeds appear not to be viable. Since plants form the very basis of the food chain, this vital cycle is interrupted; without flora, there can be no insects, neither herbivores nor carnivores … except in a few isolated pockets.

The few plants that do survive in these places have adapted to the conditions via an infinite variety of strategies. The perennials try to collect as much water as possible and, once they have obtained it, they try to store it as best they can, with a minimum of water loss. The first line of defense in this dry environment is to develop either a wide-spreading root system close to the surface or roots that penetrate deep into the soil. For example, some varieties of calligonum have roots that spread just under the surface very far from the plant, while acacia roots can reach 100 feet straight down.

To store the water, the plants' organs must act as reservoirs and the plants begin to look fleshy and succulent like cacti, which are not found in Africa. One plant family that acts in this way are the chenopods (the goosefoot family), which have globular leaves (Salsola foetida). To avoid moisture loss, plants have evolved a number of mechanisms: They reduce their upper sections that come in contact with the air, or assume a little cushionlike shape, or the form of a semicircular bush whose spherical shape provides the least surface area relative to the size of the plant.

Other plants have a more or less impermeable waxy film or a layer of furry hair covering their leaves. Some can shrink to minimize evaporation. In some, such as the ephedra, a miniature bush, leaves have been reduced to little more than invisible scales and the function of the leaves—assimilating chlorophyll for photosynthesis—has been taken over by the bush's numerous green twigs. It has been observed that many desert plants have thorns or spikes of some kind, but their role in the plants' adaptation to the desert climate is not well understood.

To guarantee that photosynthesis and the production of chlorophyll can take place properly, the plants absorb carbon dioxide from the air by means of openings called stomata. This process usually occurs during the day—when it is hot—but it cannot take place without some loss of moisture. Therefore, to reduce evaporation, the stomata of certain plants are located deep within the leaf and are often surrounded by hairs that create a microclimate to retain moisture and protect the stomata from the wind. Other plants, such as the chenopods, have developed a chlorophyll absorption system that functions better in hotter conditions, whereby the plant is able to shrink its stomata openings. Still other plants have adapted to the environment in even more sophisticated ways: Instead of absorbing carbon dioxide by day, they open their stomata in the coolness of the night so that moisture loss by evaporation is greatly reduced. These plants have what is called CAM, which stands for Crassulacean Acid Metabolism; these are the succulents and plants related to the family of cacti. They fix carbon dioxide by night in the form of malic acid which is stored in the chlorophyll assimilation cells: by day, due to the light, the malic acid decomposes and releases carbon dioxide necessary for photosynthesis, without requiring the plant to open the stomata.

"Annual plants," we are told, "… use a different strategy: they are accustomed to the brevity of the wet periods, so they accomplish their full plant cycle within a very short time. In just two weeks, a seed of Arabidopsis thaliana that is lucky enough to get a bit of rain manages to grow its plant, then flowers and seeds; the seeds will in turn lie dormant another few years waiting for a favorable environment to develop."[128] The seeds of plants that function in this manner have adapted to the dryness and can remain viable, though dormant, for very long stretches of time. One curious plant is the Rose of Jericho or Anastatica hierochuntica. This cruciferous plant grows to about eight inches and consists of stalks that lose their leaves when mature. These stems then become woody and curl up, thus protectively enclosing the seeds. As soon as some moisture is present, the twigs unfurl, releasing the seeds, which can then take advantage of the rainfall to germinate and begin the cycle again.

In the Great Sea of Sand and the corridors between the dunes, there is no longer any plant life whatsoever. Here and there one might still find dried-out grasses, a plant of Stipagrostis pungens, or a tiny ephedra bush. We found one such plant on the low slope of the western flank of a dune; it looked fairly old and owed its survival only to the great depth of its roots.

The mountainous areas of the desert tend to attract clouds and thus stimulate occasional rains, which is why the wadis and the foothills of the Gilf Kebir harbor what is left of the Libyan Desert flora. Monod, who has been exploring this desert for decades, discovered a flower that the 1999 rains should allow to develop.[129]

In the three large wadis north of the Gilf Kebir one can still find abundant Acacia tortilis, a subspecies of raddiana that used to be very common. The Acacia ehrenbergiana is much rarer; we only found one specimen in the region near the eastern face of the Gilf Kebir. Apart from acacias, the only tree still growing here is the Maerua crassifolia. In the northern part of the Gilf Kebir plateau, in a few damp niches that were deeply scored by ancient rains, a few plants have managed to survive. It is in these wadis that one can see the "greening" of the sands after a rainstorm: One year we were privileged enough to see the red sands of Wadi Hamra covered with a pale green-white down. It turned out to be tiny sprouts that would likely not survive long.

Among the species that have been observed in this region up to now—only about 50—the two most common plant families are the crucifers, of the genus Brassica (cabbages), with seven species including Shouvia thebaica, which has beautiful purple flowers and fleshy leaves that are a favorite of camels and Zilla spinosa, a thorny plant with large lilac-colored flowers, and graminace (grasses), now called poaceans, which also have about seven species.

A green shrub in the red-soiled Wadi Hamra.

An acacia, protected by long thorns.

The sand turned green after rain in the Wadi Hamra.

128. M. Bournérias, C. Bock, Le Génie végétal, p. 159, Paris, 1992.
129. T. Monod, "Contribution à l'établissement d'une florule du Gilf Kebir S-O. Egypte" p. 259-269, Bull. Mus. Natl. Hist. Natl. 4,17, 1995.

**From left to right:**

*Fagonia.*
*Colocynth.*
*Zilla spinoza.*

**From left to right:**

*Suhovia thebaica.*
*Zilla spinoza crucifera.*
*Fruits of Acacia tortilis.*

**From left to right:**

*Roses of Jericho, Anastatica
hierochunctica.*
*Ephedra.*
*Suhovia thebaica.*

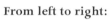

**Right:** *A weather vane in the sand.*

**169**

*The trail of a snake.*

**Following page:**
*A horned viper coiled in the sun on one of the walls of the citadel of Dush in the Kharga depression.*

**130.** T. Monod, *Les Carnets de Théodore Monod*, p. 307, Paris, 1997.

pose a real biological problem. Mantises are carnivores, so on what do [the eremiaphiles] feed? They could be cannibals. They could always eat their grandfather or son-in-law, but this does not account for the entire population. I believe they feed on insects carried by the winds that constantly blow in these places, winds that cover hundreds of kilometers from their point of origin."[130]

Snakes and scorpions are rare except in the wadis of the Gilf Kebir where the environment surrounding the plants and trees is relatively moist. They also harbor lizards and, rarely, a few mammals, mostly small mice. Several species of snake coexist here, but only their tracks are visible in the sand. One learns to recognize and distinguish the path of a colubrid from that of a viper; the most common is the horned viper. Aside from its highly poisonous fangs, it is the only reptile that has two horns protruding from its head that can lie flat or stand up straight, depending on its mood. In summer the viper burrows in the sand to avoid the heat, coming out only at night to attack with astonishing speed. In winter it warms itself on the rocks, or on the fragments of pottery in places like Abu Ballas. At Qaret el-Hanash, the "snake hill," which is strewn with colorful jasper, a mysterious smell seems to emanate from the earth itself.

*Horned Viper. In the foreground on a black background are shown a fang and one of the "horns" found above each eye. (Drawing by Bruce, from* Voyageurs Anciens, T.I. *Edouard Charton, p. 67, 1861.)*

171

*Skeleton of a viper.*

*A scorpion,* Stenodactylus petrii, *discovered under a stone.*

*A desert lizard with red spots,* Mesalina rubropunctata.

*Desert jerboa (Drawing by Bruce, from* Voyageurs Anciens, *p.67).*

Desert lizards laze in the sun and are easily approached because they apparently believe they are perfectly camouflaged. Some, such as eremia or eremia des Hamadas, have red-orange spots, harmoniously placed like carnelian pebbles on the sand. When they are not lazing about, their thin legs with long claws give them tremendous agility. Another, the zelgague, we are told, "is a tiny smooth white-skinned lizard with extremely short legs; its movements are so fast that it can actually swim in the sand like a fish in water, and just when you think you can approach it, it disappears into the ground; but it leaves a track, and if you follow it, you can easily grab one and pull it out of its hiding place."[131]

Small mammals of the gerbil family have a particularly keen sense of hearing. They are thin and easily agitated, and have developed an ability to run and jump far superior to that of their relatives in more hospitable climates. The desert jerboa (*Jaculus jaculus*) and the gerbil (*Gerbillus gerbillus*) have long hind legs and a strong, agile tail that they can use to push themselves off a surface to escape more easily from predators in exposed terrain. The small gerbil can go for long periods without drinking, thanks to its diet. Another important adaptive trait of these rodents is that their urine and feces are highly concentrated, which allows them to void themselves without giving up too much precious water. Another species, the jird, or sand mouse (*Meriones crassus*), collects food in its burrow to take advantage of the moisture found underground.[132]

The fennec, a small desert fox with pale fur (*Fennecus zerda*), prefers to feed on birds that have lost their way. This animal can be found in totally arid regions because the surface area of its large ears allows it to dispel body heat. Because these foxes are the color of sand, and because they hunt by night and occasionally at dusk, they are extremely difficult to see, but the many tracks they leave around visitors' campsites are proof of their nocturnal presence. Sometimes at sunset one can hear a strange yelping—the cry of the jackal or the plaintive cry of the hyena attracted by the camp.

Mouflon, or wild sheep, used to be very common in the Gilf Kebir, leaving tracks in the large wadis where a few acacias and occasional tufts of vegetation survive. These agile rock scree climbers are easily recognizable by their blond beards and by the tufts of wool on their front legs. They are also distinguished by their magnificently long horns, which rise above their heads, curling out and back in great spirals, reminiscent of the spiraling horns of Ammon. This peculiar animal is similar to both goats and sheep, is more or less sedentary, and survives only thanks to its climbing skill, which enables it to evade any predators by disappearing hastily up steep slopes that defy pursuers.

Most of the birds spotted in this region are migratory, and are often found dead of exhaustion on the sand—the dessicated, almost mummified remains of ducks or storks. Wagtails and other migrating passerines come to visit explorers' encampments, but are generally too tired even to drink the water they so desparately need, and end up dying, like the birds that come from the oases, blown off course by high altitude winds. Only a few white-tailed wheatears, called

*The fennec, its presence often betrayed only by its tracks.*

**Below:** *A "banded" mouflon. This species is near extinction.*

131. Daumas, *op. cit.* p. 267.
132. Vial, *op. cit.* p. 195.

*zarzur* in Arabic (*Oenanthe leucopyga*), still inhabit the Gilf Kebir and sing the plaintive ode to the lost oasis.

## A raptor turned divine: The falcon

The falcon is a rare and venerated bird in the Middle East and, once trained, is used in a highly lucrative trade. The difficulty lies in capturing one of these graceful, aloof creatures alive. On the border between Libya and Egypt, between the dunes in the vast barren corridors at the heart of the Great Sea of Sand, a schooled eye can discern the slightest movement: Such is the infallible ability of the hunter to locate the migrating falcon. The falconer uses a live chicken or pigeon as bait to trap the raptor in a kind of hoop net set at the foot of the dunes. The hunter waits patiently, without moving, until a falcon approaches. If the bird alights to devour its prey, the hunter hastily casts a net over it, ending its days at liberty, and just as quickly, covers the net with a black cloth that plunges the falcon in darkness, which quiets the captive bird. The falcon will remain covered by the black cloth for several days except at mealtimes, when it is fed wearing just a hood. Sometimes the untamed falcon's eyes may

be stitched shut to help it adjust to having a master. The bond between bird and human must be intense, and can only be brought about by close and constant contact: The bird must spend several hours a day on the tamer's arm and is fed only by the tamer. It takes several months to train a falcon successfully.

There are several subspecies of falcon, including the lanner, or *saqr hurr* in Arabic, and the *Falco biarmicus tanypterus* or *erlangeri* that flies over the Libyan Desert during its migration season in early autumn.[133] The name of this falcon comes from the Latin word *lana*, because it has dense, beautifully spotted feathers that range in color from red-brown to black on a white background, and are typically variegated and speckled. Its wingspan can reach over three feet, making it a formidable bird, able to swoop down on its prey in midflight or to pin it to the ground. Its sharp, powerful talons are bright yellow in the adult bird and are an incomparable weapon that allow it to feed on small mammals, reptiles, scorpions, though it will even eat insects when other prey is scarce. Its head is similar to most raptors: It has a reddish cap, like the Egyptian god Seth, and a greyish-blue beak so sharp that captive birds' beaks have to be filed during training so they cannot injure anyone. The falcon's huge eyes are lined with black extending down like a mustache and toward the back of

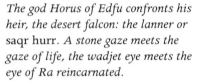

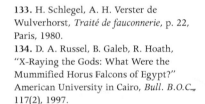

*The god Horus of Edfu confronts his heir, the desert falcon: the lanner or* saqr hurr. *A stone gaze meets the gaze of life, the wadjet eye meets the eye of Ra reincarnated.*

**133.** H. Schlegel, A. H. Verster de Wulverhorst, *Traité de fauconnerie*, p. 22, Paris, 1980.
**134.** D. A. Russel, B. Galeb, R. Hoath, "X-Raying the Gods: What Were the Mummified Horus Falcons of Egypt?" American University in Cairo, *Bull. B.O.C.*, 117(2), 1997.

**Right:** *A young falcon being trained in a corridor between dunes in the Great Sea of Sand.*

**Previous page:** *The two curved horns of a mouflon; a memorial preserved in sand.*

the head like a crown. Its disproportionately large eyes take up most of its head, and its retina give it unparalleled visual acuity, as well as the ability to zoom in visually from a distance of miles, as if it were using binoculars. Semi-darkness does not diminish the falcon's powerful eyesight, allowing it to hunt at dusk, when other animals, thinking themselves protected by the growing darkness, venture out in the desert.

The falcon's powerful vision has been celebrated since antiquity, when the bird symbolized the god Horus, as well as the *wadjet* eye— a combination of the human eye and the falcon's tear duct—a symbol of the power of Ra. The embodiment of Horus varies from total anthropomorphism to a completely animal figure, along a continuum with many variations and symbols that allude to the falcon, such as protective wings spreading out from temple pediments.

The Egyptians were highly knowledgeable about both sedentary and migratory birds of prey; they were skillful not only in taming them, but also in sacrificing and mummifying them as offerings. Radiography of hundreds of falcon mummies has enabled scientists to identify all the species that were used, as well as the tricks played to compensate when the requisite birds of prey were not available.[134] Indeed, many bird-shaped mummies have been discovered that in

fact contained a variety of other things; often shells or twigs or other animals, such as shrews and snakes, were used as filling.

## An indispensable domestic animal: The camel

The poor camel, renowned beast of burden, is not even accorded its proper name; technically, only dromedaries with their characteristic single hump, are found in Egypt. They are nonetheless erroneously called "camels," but rightly dubbed the "ships of the desert." In our imaginations, the desert, sand dunes, and camels go hand in hand: It is easy to conjure images of long lines of camels silhouetted against the crests of the dunes, immense caravans who leave their tracks on the camel paths. History tells fabulous stories of incredible journeys across the desert, of rich cargos transported by camelback, assuring trade in ancient times from one land to the next.

Yet this ubiquitous desert animal, which we like to believe we have known well for over two millennia, persistently wraps itself in an aura of mystery. Why, for instance, should it not be included in the rather thorough *Dictionary of Egyptian Civilization*, though it was honored by Napoleon in the Dromedary Regiment? Herodotus never

**Above:** *This scene of donkeys and a camel drinking from the same well recalls a passage from the Bible.*

**Following page:**
*Caravan on the* Darb el-Arbaïn, *the "40-Day Road."*

*The Dromedary Regiment in Bonaparte's army.*

once mentioned it, and it is rarely seen in hieroglyphs, pottery, and prehistoric rock painting and carving. The camel's origin and introduction into the western Egyptian Desert remain a subject of controversy. According to Beatrix Midant-Reynes, the middle-Paleolithic camel bones that were discovered at Bir Sahara indicate camels' presence in the desert much earlier than previously thought. "The discovery of fragments of a camel tibia amid pebbles clearly shaped by humans in Mousterian layers attest to the presence in ancient times of this animal that was unheard of among the Pharaonic Egyptians."[135] According to Henri Lhote, this has been confirmed by an older specimen dating back to the early Paleolithic period recently unearthed by archaeologists.[136]

The camel clearly existed in this long forgotten era, yet it seems to have disappeared and reappeared much later. "We seem to be observing the evolution of wild animals that for centuries and even millennia, harmoniously developed alongside domesticated animals such as cows and horses. Then these species disappear, most likely due to drought, and then, all of a sudden, the camel reappears."[137]

There is no doubt that there were camels in Egypt in 720 BC, when the Assyrians invaded, and again in 525 BC with Cambyses' army. We also know from Curtius Quintus that Alexander the Great was escorted on his way to Siwa by camels bearing goatskin water containers.

The domestication of wild animals is beyond question an ancient practice. According to Bernard Faye, horses were tamed as long as 6,000 years ago, cows at least 8,000 years ago, and animals in the goat family at least 10,000 years ago.[138] The domestication of the camel seems to have been more recent, since they only appeared on the Arabian peninsula 4,000 years ago, and in Egypt more recently still.[139] The Bible records their presence: "Then the Lord said to Moses, 'Go to Pharaoh, and say to him, "Thus says the Lord, the God of the Hebrews: Let my people go, so that they may worship me. For if you refuse to let them go and still hold them, the hand of the Lord will strike with a deadly pestilence your livestock in the field: the horses, the donkeys, the camels, the herds, and the flocks."'"[140]

While many of the early domesticated animals are depicted in prehistoric carvings and paintings, camels are not among them. What is more surprising, however, is that they are also absent from later artwork during periods when other evidence indicates that they were already present in the region.

Hieroglyphs from the Ptolemaic and Roman periods show hardly any camels on building walls, with the exception of a few temples in Nubia, at Kalabsha and Dakha. These carvings may have been made by nomads, who in all likelihood used camels long before the sedentary inhabitants of the Nile Valley region did. The camels' superior speed on the local terrain helped the nomads to victories over their enemies and were thus a factor in the demise of the Roman Empire, according to Peter Rowley-Conwy.[141]

Why did camels remain so little known for so long? The people of the Nile Valley did not need them, since they used donkeys or boats for transportation, and the many canals bisecting the region made the area unsuitable for camel caravans. The humid climate was also unfavorable for camels, which are vulnerable to certain insects, and camels were much more expensive than donkeys, which remained more popular and more affordable for the average person.

Camels, however, can survive in extreme conditions, particularly in the torrid desert regions such as the Libyan Desert, where they were used for a long time for both transport and in times of war. These animals are so well adapted to the desert climate that they can cover 25 to 30 miles a day carrying loads of many hundred pounds without drinking for several days. Their unusual physiological adaptations and peculiar metabolism enable them to withstand extreme conditions that are beyond the endurance of other animals. Camels are able to vary and adapt their water needs to their situation; they can lose up to 25 percent of their body water content without experiencing any ill effects due to dehydration, and, when they do find a watering hole, they can "fill up" in record time: "In the cooler season," Faye informs us, "with rich green fodder, the dromedary

needs only the water contained in its food, and can go for a month without drinking .... In the hot season, with much drier food, camels need to drink weekly."[142]

It is in its hump that the camel stores energy—not water—which allows it to withstand the extreme temperature swings that would be fatal to most mammals. Unlike humans, in sweltering heat the camel's body temperature rises in symbiosis with its environment, which allows it to retain water. At night, when the temperatures drop, its body temperature also drops, releasing the heat it has accumulated, again without water loss.

The camel has an unusual respiratory system: its nostrils collect and retain the moisture from exhaled breath, thus maintaining a moist atmosphere and limiting water loss. The camel's skin has few sweat glands, reducing the risk of dehydration. Its feet are the exception, however; here sweat glands channel some moisture when necessary to avoid overheating during long journeys. Their wide, elastic, unshod feet are better suited to sand than to rocky ground.[143]

The camel's extraordinary endurance has made it indispensable to desert travel, and images of camel caravans silhouetted against the dunes have reinforced its picturesque charm. Yet mounting a camel requires a certain skill, as became clear during Napoleon's desert campaigns, so vividly described by Vivant Denon. "A caravan included up to 1,000 or 1,100 troops and as many camels. Mounting the

camel was very pleasant: Usually a camel is slow in its movements, but in this case it lifts its hind legs quite suddenly as soon as the rider settles in the saddle, and the rider is pitched first backwards then thrust forwards, and only finds himself right side up after the fourth movement that brings the camel fully to its feet. Nobody managed to stay on after the first pitch, though each had made fun of his neighbor: we all tried again and finally set off."[144]

Today the great camel caravans are a thing of the past, leaving only their tracks in the Libyan Desert; their disappearance corresponds to that of the water and the pasture lands. The great distance between the Egyptian and the Libyan oases does not permit caravans to travel between them without at least one refueling stop. Still, a few caravans continue to use the Darb el-Arbaïn.

135. B. Midant-Reynes, *Préhistoire de l'Égypte*, p. 44, Paris, 1992.
136. H. Lhote, *Chameau et dromadaire en Afrique du Nord et au Sahara*, p. 143, Algiers, 1987.
137. Lhote, *op. cit.* p. 52.
138. B. Faye, *Guide de l'élevage du dromadaire*, p. 9, Montpellier, 1997.
139. Faye, *op. cit.* p. 9.
140. Exodus 9:1-4, Oxford New RSV.
141. P. Rowley-Conwy, "The Camel in the Nile Valley," p. 247, *The Journal of Egyptian Archeology*, vol. 74, London, 1988.
142. Faye, *op. cit.* p. 36f.
143. Faye, *op. cit.* p. 31.
144. Vivant Denon, *op. cit.* p. 289, vol. I.

# Chapter V

# An Enchanting Desert

## The desert, a burning ocean

The splendor of the desert landscape has always fascinated people, even though it is a stark, barren splendor, reduced to the essential four elements: sand rippling out toward infinity, sometimes edged by the blue waters of a mirage on the horizon, cradled by the immense vaulted sky, under the overbearing midday sun whose spectacular sunrises and flaming sunsets captivate us.

The exhilarating freedom you experience in the desert is akin to the feeling of sailors surrendering to the wind and the sea once the anchor is lifted and all signs of civilization recede with the land. The ocean is often used as a metaphor for the desert and the dunes, whose ever-shifting relief even resembles waves. This vast landscape may also make us feel absurdly insignificant, like a Lilliputian lost in a gigantic, unmoving natural world, where one feels lost as Guy de Maupassant describes: "You know the uniform sand, the sand coming straight out of the endless beaches of the ocean. Well then! Imagine the ocean itself turned into sand in the middle of a hurricane; imagine this silent storm made of unmoving waves of yellow dust. The waves are as high as mountains, uneven, different, lifted like unloosed cascades but even larger and striped like moiré silk."[145]

Extremes prompt strong reactions, and the absence of landmarks elicits unbearable anguish. Nature becomes threatening: The wide open spaces are devoid of people, the sand becomes an ocean of fire, and thirsty people begin to rave. As Jules Verne put it: "Thirst and unceasing contemplation of the desert tires the soul; there wasn't a single landmark in the terrain, not a hillock of sand, not a pebble to catch the eye. This unbearable flatness made one feel sick with an indefinable malaise, a desert sickness. The impassible dry blueness of the sky and the vast yellowness of the sand eventually grew frightening. In this burning atmosphere, the heat became vibrant and visible, like the air over an incandescent flame; the soul gives way to despair at seeing such huge calmness, and sees no reason for this state of things to cease, since immenseness is a sort of eternity."[146]

The sun becomes a persecutor and the body suffers terrible assaults, with no possible protection, no escape, no end to the infernal suffering in sight; meanwhile the fear of burning forever like someone damned to hell only increases. "Now it is the enemy," Monod writes, "a cruel god, merciless, creator of this demonic blazing fire, and of this terrible thirst that scorches and blisters the tender flesh, its eternal threat hanging over the back of our heads, that parches our throats, shrivels our lips to a crevassed mess, makes our eyes ache and the ground unbearable to touch with our feet, he's the one who chars the dead lands of the desert and who, under the metallic colorless sky, sends down flames with its vertical beams."[147]

The climatic conditions of the Egyptian Desert have always been reputed to be intolerable: heat, thirst, fatigue, and disorientation all exacerbate the feeling of panic in the hostile world that fast becomes a trap from which there is no escape. Even the sand becomes heavy, moving, stymieing attempts to walk across it, thwarting progress, and prohibiting escape. "One has to fight not only against ardor and the dryness of this land," said Curtius Quintus, "but also against the extreme tenacity of the sand, which is thick and moves beneath one's each step, allowing only very difficult progress."[148]

Where the sun is intense enough to split even rocks, people cannot cope long, especially without water. Saint-Exupéry, whose plane crashed in the Libyan Desert in 1935, knew the precariousness of survival in this realm: "I seem to recall about the Libyan Desert… that life just evaporated like steam. The Bedouins, travelers, colonial officers alike all taught us that we could only last 19 hours without drinking. After 20 hours, one's eyes fill with light and it is the beginning of the end: Thirst overcomes you at lightning speed."[149]

One may certainly die of thirst in the desert, but another real and very likely danger is *khamsin*, the sandstorm, an event every bit as terrifying as its marine counterpart. The feeling of suffocation in the midst of a sandstorm is overwhelming; the sand works its insidious way into every orifice—openings, it seems, only camels can close in self-defense. Vivant Denon described his survival of a sandstorm:

*"A man upright, a small grain in the waves of sand." (Hawad, Caravanes de la Soif)*

**Right:** *A narrow bottleneck that allows a glimpse of the Wadi Abd el-Malik from the plateau of Gilf Kebir.*

145. G. de Maupassant, *Contes et nouvelles*, p. 799, Paris, 1960.
146. J. Verne, *Cinq Semaines en ballon*, p. 160f., Paris, 1939.
147. Monod, *Méharées*, p. 18f.
148. Curtius Quintus, quoted by Leclant, *Per Africae Sitientia*, p. 201.
149. A. de Saint-Exupéry, *Terre des hommes*, p. 238, Paris, 1950.

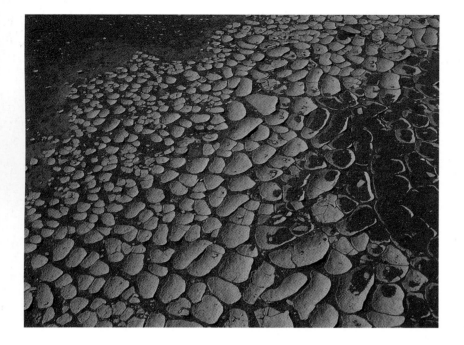

"The only light came from a reddish glow in the gloom, our eyes were ripped and torn at, our nostrils blocked, our throats could not moisten what our breathing made us absorb in dust; we were lost from each other as well as from our road …. In these moments we understood clearly what a nightmare it must be for someone to be caught by surprise in the desert by such a phenomenon."[150] As if the experience of the sandstorm itself were not enough, in its aftermath, all tracks have disappeared in the clouds of sand and the road has been erased, making one feel utterly and permanently lost.

The seemingly hostile convergence of the four elements—the treacherous shifting ground, the unbreathable air, the burning sun, and the dearth of water—threaten the life of those who lose their way, who are sure to know they have been damned by the gods.

## A place haunted by legends

The time and space of the desert create inhuman dimensions, an unbearable emptiness; but since nature abhors a vacuum, humans have always repopulated the void with imaginary creatures matching the pervasive disproportion. Here lurk temptation, bad *jinns*, and other gloomy creatures. The desert has traditionally been a refuge for enemies, invaders, and monsters. The latter abound in stories told by the Christian recluses such as St. Anthony, who describe how they were haunted by temptations; but these are invariably internal, or metaphorical, monsters, hallucinations brought on by the sleep deprivation and hunger requisite on the path to sainthood. The desert is a place of trials, where the individual faces the enemies within, and struggles against personal demons.

But there are traditional tales of more ambiguous monsters: half-women, half-animal carnivores ready to consume the careless traveler. According to the legend told by the early Christian patriarch, St. John Chrysostom: "They thought to see a woman lying on a dune, the lower half of her body covered in an animal skin, in the fashion of Libyan women, with chest and breasts uncovered, her neck tilted

**Left and following page:**
*"The soil's surface like a skinned corpse, leaving the bare bones polished by the wind, wrinkled shreds of skin, soil reduced to a thin film of salt …" (Jacques Lacarrière,* La poussière du monde *[The Dust of the World])*

---

150. Vivant Denon, *op. cit*. vol. I, p. 285f.

**Above:** *The sun and the wind reign as absolute rulers over the dry mountains and plain.*

**Left:** *Trees charred by the implacable, scorching sun.*

**Following page:** *Sand blown about in the strong desert wind.*

151. St. John Chrysostom, quoted by Leclant, *Per Africae Sitientia*, p. 224.

back. They supposed that a courtesan had reached this place before their herds. Two quite young fellows were so struck by her beauty that they went ahead and one was in such a hurry that he passed the other; the monster dragged him to a hollow in the sand and devoured him. The other had kept advancing until he saw what happened and screamed; thus the other travelers came to help him. The monster rushed at him, snake part forwards, killed him, and ran off whistling. The travelers found the broken corpse already rotting. The Libyans who were guiding the caravan allowed no one to touch the body, or else all would die."[151]

In the time of the Pharaohs, the desert had an evil reputation. It represented ultimate chaos—as opposed to the more organized life of the Nile Valley, the cradle of civilization—and harbored only dead people, convicts, and the warrior gods. Although the martial deities protected against invaders, they were themselves violent and destructive—among them the lioness goddess Sekhmet or the gods Seth and Ha. While Bastet, the cat goddess, personified the beneficial and joyful aspects of the sun's eye, Sekhmet's red eyes represented the sun's more destructive nature. Sekhmet was sent by the gods to punish humans and, crazed by the smell of blood, she wanted to destroy them all. But the people set out beer tinted red with ochre to

look like blood so that Sekhmet would get drunk on this and in her humiliation exile herself in the desert. According to the myth, she was "so inflamed with anger that her mane was literally in flames, her eyes burned, and her back glowed red." It was only once she returned to the Nile Valley that the goddess of the desert calmed down and allowed Bastet to predominate, bringing the benefits of sun to the people there.

Seth was the red-haired god who murdered his brother Osiris and personified violence. After he was defeated in combat against Horus, the gods finally exiled him to the Western Desert, where only his hot breath still haunts the red sands.

The god Ha did not personify the desert, but it was his duty to watch over the roads that crossed the Western Desert.

In ancient times the desert was haunted by all these violent, killing gods. Even today the land remains marked by a kind of taboo, because the infinite space and the lack of retreats give rise to terrible anguish and vertigo, hallucinations and illness, … or even inebriation and euphoria!

*Rocks that have been carved into layers by the wind, giving rise to monsters cut from stone.*

## Exile and renaissance

*They exiled old men and bishops to deserts, wild and terrible places.*[152]

Because the desert made access, orientation, survival, and escape difficult or nearly impossible, it was early on recognized as an ideal place of exile, and common criminals and political undesirables were sent there already in ancient times. Attempts to escape inevitably led to a horrible death, and so were rare; "imprisonment" on this desert island was permanent.

With the advent of Christianization, the desert remained useful as a place of exile, but with a slightly different significance. While some individuals were banished to the desert for political purposes, others went into self-imposed exile. Important people who disagreed with the authorities, such as Athanasius or Nestorius, managed to transform their imposed isolation in the Kharga oasis into a productive time: Exile gave new energy to these ideological outlaws, who attracted disciples, taught, and wrote texts that would endure for centuries, like Athanasius' *Life of Saint Anthony*. Christians began to seek voluntary seclusion in the Egyptian Desert shortly after the death of Jesus Christ. The first such exile was St. Anthony, whose lead was followed by several hermits, both men and women. For these exiles, the desert became a place to be tested, as Christ had been, and was a privileged route toward sainthood.

Today, exile in the desert is voluntary, organized, temporary, and recreational. We shrug off everyday worries and restrictions to experience a simpler way of life, only to meet other complications along the way. Still, an expedition to the Egyptian Desert arouses feelings we may not readily experience in any other place. Here, where nature is still unspoiled and much like it was at the dawn of the universe, where the world has not yet encroached too far, there is also a possibility to retrace the steps of our distant ancestors and meditate on nature's works of art.

Colored draperies cover the foot of
the mountain, variegated sandstone
meanders like a stream issuing from
a spring.

152. Athanasius, quoted by Leclant, *Per
Africae Sitientia*, p. 207.

**Above:** *A hostile universe.*

**Top:** *A desert necropolis guarding its tombs.*

## A desert necropolis, the bridge to the next world

Because the desert was considered devoid of life, it was traditionally reserved for the dead. The dry air naturally preserved bodies; people noticed that a corpse buried in sand remained relatively well preserved, which led to experimentation with mummification. Geographical borders were used to distinguish the realm of the living from that of the dead: In the Nile Valley, the living claimed the arable land, and in the oases gravesites were placed at a distance from dwellings. The desert was where the dead could rest in peace while waiting for entry into the next life. The isolation of the burial sites also protected the living from an inopportune return of the deceased, allowing the living to carry on uninhibited. At Siwa, the hill of the dead, *Jabal al-Mawta*, is located outside the city; the same is true at Bahariya and at Kharga, where the great necropolis of Bagawat lies.

The "desert of the western mountain," home of the dead, was a place of mystery and hope: where the god Ra disappeared, where the battle against demons began, and where night offered regeneration before the rebirth of morning. The desert was an aptly chosen place for the dead to follow the example of the gods and await eternity.

The goddess Sekhmet, lioness and harbinger of divine wrath; temple of Deir el-Haggar, Dakhla oasis.

Seth, the traditional god of borders and the desert, shown here with the features of Horus, spears the serpent Apopis on an interior wall of the temple of Hibis.

The god Ha, protector of the Western Desert; tomb of Bannentiu in Bahariya.

# The Gods of the Libyan Desert
## by Professor Nicolas Grimal

When he described Egypt as "the gift of the Nile," Herodotus was merely stating the obvious: Water brings life and thus gives birth to civilization. The gods of ancient Egypt were like people. They lived in a valley, and, when they left it, it was to settle in an environment that they had carefully thought up and built to resemble that valley. It is estimated that less than 3 percent of the Egyptian population lived in desert regions at the end of the 19th century. This number is probably quite similar today, despite the development of the "New Valley," which largely compensates for the country's dramatic increase in population. Even if we suppose that the population will one day be able to live in newly cultivated areas, a civilization that flourishes in an irrigated desert will still be one of the valley.

We do not know enough about the nomadic cultures that traveled this desert in the Pharaonic period to say much about the ancient Bedouins' pantheon of gods. We only know what the Egyptian monuments convey to us, which is that the culture of the communities settled in the oases and around the watering springs near the valley.

When the ancient Egyptians settled in the oases, they simply transplanted their culture and adapted it to an environment that they attempted to make as similar as possible to what they had left behind. One example is the tale of a branch canal of the Nile that was meant to allow the sacred boat of the god to reach the doors of his temple; this is told at the Hibis temple in Kharga. Yet the Nile was over 125 miles away as the crow flies. The temple itself is dedicated to the god Ammon, who ruled over the oasis just as he ruled over Thebes, with his wife and son by his side. One can safely presume, based on the funerary and worship items found in the archaeological digs in the oases, that there was not much difference between the beliefs of a peasant in the oasis and those of her or his cousin in the valley.

Does that mean that there was no pantheon that belonged exclusively to the arid desert regions? Not exactly. Several gods were recognized as having a certain "specialization," which naturally became the object of a localized worship. For example, the goddess Hathor played a pivotal role in the Sinai, and the gods devoted to protection of borders and deserts were more present in the oases than in the Nile Valley. Sekhmet, the lioness messenger of divine wrath, naturally haunted the roads across the Western Desert. At the beginning of the second millennium before Christ, the god Ha, who was originally a god of fertility associated with Min and Ammon, came to be associated with the protection of the Western Desert and the Lib-

yan region in general. In this part of the world, he played essentially the same role that Soped plays in the east and Dedoun in the south.

Seth, traditional god of the desert and remote places, came to play an important role that led to certain aspects of his iconography that resemble Horus fighting: This explains why his extraordinary image in the shape of Horus is found only in the temple of Hibis, and only in Kharga. There he stands upright, throwing a spear into the body of the snake Apopis, in a position that echoes (or presages) the iconography of Saint George slaying the dragon, but really is a direct reference to the depiction of the god Ha, who is also shown handling a spear in the tomb of Bannentin at Bahariya.

After Alexander the Great conquered the region, the inhabitants of the subdesert zones developed worship rituals that were particular to the gods of the Greek pantheon, associated with or assimilated to more or less military figures. Thus, Heracles played an important role in the Bahariya oasis—in fact, across the entire caravan region that linked the Coptic area to the Hellenistic settlements along the Mediterranean coast—like Pan in the Eastern Desert. He was revered in the form of a falcon-headed god, in the temple that Alexander built at the end of the Siwa road. It is probably his resemblance to Ammon that allowed him to be likened to Khonsu in this temple and at Bawiti.

Ammon himself, the god of Siwa, is a good example of syncretism or, more accurately, of adaptation to a different cultural context. He was transplanted to Cyrene in the 6th century BC where he took on the look of a bearded Zeus with spiral ram horns for ears, like Ammon, and was likened to Apollo. His oracle was among the most important ones in ancient Greece, and when Alexander came to ask the oracle at the temple of Siwa for confirmation of his power, he was not visiting an Egyptian god, but a god that he considered his own.

Zeus-Ammon, who later become Jupiter-Ammon, or in Cyprus and North Africa Baal-Ammon, came to be closely linked to imperial power in the Roman era. For similar political reasons, in Egypt he developed close ties to another ptolemaic creation, Serapis and the Isiac environment, in combination with the omnipresent Medusa that came directly from Greek mythology.

We are not able to understand fully the cultural depths indigenous to the desert, yet the religious developments prior to the Arabs' conquering of Egypt indicate their importance fairly clearly, essentially as a road of communication and as a place that was appropriated, though it was traditionally under the control of Egypt.

# Chapter VI

# A Desert with Extraterrestrial Treasures in the Sand

We know that the desert carefully preserves tracks left by past travelers; it also preserves gifts from the skies and the earth. Objects may lie on the surface of the sand where they fell for thousands of years, though they are susceptible to erosion. Still, a discerning eye may catch sight of these treasures thanks to the contrast cast on them by the desert light.

## Fulgurites

When the clear blue sky that normally prevails over the golden sands of the desert gives way to clouds, the storms that arise can be brilliant, with thunder and lightning that leaves scars on the ground. When these arrows of fire strike most regions, they can level a house or a tree, but here, where the earth is barren, lightning penetrates the sand itself, with nothing else to ground it. The temperature of lightning can be as high as several thousand degrees. It causes a kind of instantaneous vitrification along the path of impact, creating something like a glass tube, smooth on the inside, but the outer surface is a composite of microscopic grains of quartz, rough like bark, yet fragile like glass.

These tubes left by the lightning are called fulgurites, from the Latin word for lightning, *fulgur*. Fulgurites may penetrate many feet down into the dunes and only become visible when the sands shift and foreign bodies are either unearthed or pushed up to the surface. Others are found lying on the sand or sticking straight up, revealing the slightly different shades of gray on their exterior surface. "We can come across a tube sticking out of the sand," recounts Diemer, "the result of lightning striking the dune. If we dig carefully we can uncover the buried part of the fulgurite, which is usually still in one piece; we noticed that the part of the fulgurite that is exposed and the pieces spread around on the sand had taken on a darker shade of grey, while the buried part was lighter and very fragile."[153]

As movement in the dunes brings the fulgurite to the surface, pieces of it break off and scatter around the original point of impact like small branches, forming a circle, more or less, that is visible from a distance. The sand that has been brought to the surface around the fulgurite is reddish, most likely due to oxidation of its iron content.

Although fulgurites are rare in the desert, they seem to occur in clusters within clearly defined areas, which suggests that lightning tends not to strike just anywhere, but in zones with a particular microclimate. The impact points tend to be on the lower slopes of dunes and in the interdune corridors, where there is a slight amount of humidity.

No effective means of determining the age of fulgurites has yet been developed, so we are as yet unable to distinguish a prehistoric sample from one of more recent origin.

## Meteors and meteorites

The earth is full of meteorites weighing anywhere from milligrams to millions of tons (Meteor Crater, near Winslow, Arizona, which fell an estimated 50,000 years ago; the largest intact meteorite on earth is the 60-ton Hoba West in Namibia). These are fragments from the asteroid belts orbiting the sun between Mars and Jupiter. The traces of their journey through the atmosphere are preserved on their surface in a crust formed by fusion.

While meteorites may fall anywhere on earth, they are more likely to fall in some regions than in others—or, at least, they are easier to detect when they land on glacial ice caps or desert sands. Some scientists try to record the trajectory of meteorites known to be fall-

**Above, right, and following pages:** *Layer of fulgurites on the slopes of a dune; vitrified traces of lightning, petrified thunderbolts preserved by the sand.*

---

153. E. Diemer, "Observations regarding the Saharan fulgurites and recalling the principal characteristics of the fulgurites in general," p. 3f., *Conference on "Lighting and Mountains,"* Chamonix, 6-8 June 1994.

*Detail of a fulgurite still standing in the ground, its base oxidized.*

ing toward earth and attempt to pinpoint the likely impact site so that they can retrieve it. Like any direct evidence from elsewhere in the solar system, it is hoped that these rocks can help us understand the makeup of the planets.

Though generally meteorites stand out against the light color of the desert sand and can be easily distinguished from terrestial rocks, it is still possible for even an expert eye to be fooled. It is not uncommon for any of us to pick up a rock in delight, thinking it is a meteorite, only to fling it down again in disappointment. Morning light is advantageous for distinguishing meteorites because its harshness enhances their revealing contrasts.

Meteorite expert Alain Carion offers the following caveat about meteorite hunting: First, one must beware of snakes and scorpions, for they do not like to be disturbed. You have to dig away the sand around these rocks, which you can recognize by certain distinguishing characteristics: "... it is often interesting to turn over rocks that have been half-buried in sand because their surface is eroded and polished by the wind, but the structure of the hidden side may look like a shield, marked by leakage lines or regmaglyptes that are typical of certain meteorites."[154]

Indeed, when a meteorite enters the earth's atmosphere, the side facing the earth is subjected to the strongest fusion and forms a fusion crust called a shield. With the fusion occurring at high velocity, droplets of molten rock flow out from the shield onto the rock's surface—these are the so-called leakage lines. More rarely, some meteorites have small abrasion pits caused by fusion as the meteorite passes through the atmosphere, called regmaglyptes.

Some meteorites are magnetic and it is easy to be fooled into thinking any rock that attracts a magnet must be a meteorite. Carion recommends using a compass to test the authenticity of a rock of extraterrestrial origin: "If the needle of the compass follows where you turn, then the rock contains negatively charged iron or it is magnetic, which is highly unusual for an earth rock."[155]

Of course, not all meteorites are magnetic, so the compass test is only useful for certain types, namely the siderites, or irons, composed chiefly of nickel and iron; and the siderolites, a composite of metal and stone. For aerolites, or stony meteorites, only laboratory tests can distinguish between a meteorite and a plain earth rock.

The unusually pure air of the desert allows an exceptional view of the sky and allows us to observe shooting stars—that is, meteor showers—at certain times of the year. Unlike meteorites, which actually fall to the earth, meteors consist of dust or microscopic particles that pass through the earth's atmosphere, which ionizes their gases and produces a luminous effect. For example, when a comet passes close to earth, what we call its tail is in fact gases that appear as an explosion of light emanating from the body of the comet. In November 1998, the swarm of shooting stars called the Leonids (because they appear in the constellation Leo) painted bright-colored stripes across the sky a few hours before dawn. When the moon rose on the horizon, the sun behind it, the colors grew even more radiant. Harding King was fascinated by shooting stars and tells us of the spiritual interpretation of indigenous people: "Shooting stars, which in the desert often blaze out with a brilliance difficult for dwellers of a misty climate like England to conceive of, are believed by Moslems to be arrows shot by the angels to drive away evil spirits when they steal up to eavesdrop at the gate of heaven."[156]

*Piece of a large meteorite that fell into the Great Sea of Sand. The rusty color of its surface is a result of its burning upon entering the earth's atmosphere.*

## The enigma of Libyan glass

The trained eye, practiced in the search for meteorites, may suddenly come across a strange pebble shining in the sun whose unusual light color stands out against the darker colors of the rocks around it. It will be more or less dark green, sometimes translucent and occasionally even stunningly transparent, utterly unlike the sand surrounding it. This color tempts us to believe that we are looking at water, yet remember, we are in the Great Sea of Sand. Some specimens even contain bubbles or tiny white beads. Their surface appears to be polished and sculpted, though by what kind of agent: wind, water, or human hands?

What is the origin of these glass rocks? Were they abandoned, discarded, or forgotten by some primitive craftsman? The similarity of this Libyan glass to man-made objects has been pointed out by Fulgence Fresnel, who observed: "the current sultan [promised] a fabulous reward to the khabir of the caravan who had just arrived from Benghazi in 1846, el Hadj Huceyn … if he managed to cross the Libyan Desert between the oasis of Koufarah (or Kebabo) and one of the Egyptian oases. This khabir told me he had seen the traces of an ancient route east of the first oasis, which he had explored for two or three days and where he had found large quantities of fragments of glass, an obvious sign that it had been inhabited in ancient times."[157]

It was not until 1932 that Major Clayton, while conducting topographical surveys in the Libyan Desert, discovered an area covered with pieces of glass. Clayton inventoried them and collected a few samples of what has since been known as Libyan glass, or Libyan desert glass. This kind of glass, found nowhere else on earth, continues to intrigue scientists. Several conflicting theories have been proposed to account for it, but none has been proven.

There are two basic schools of thought: One school holds that the glass was formed slowly under normal temperature and pressure conditions; the other maintains that there must have been some kind of shock or impact whose spiking high temperature triggered a process of vitrification. Although the former theory has gathered few supporters, the latter is also unsatisfying because it raises at least as many questions as it answers; it begs the question, what kind of shock? Was it volcanic? Or was it extraterrestrial, as the currently prevailing explanation maintains? But is it possible for an object from space to encounter a high enough temperature to form glass? And, also, why would it appear here and nowhere else, when we know that every part of the earth is bombarded by objects from space? Could it have been due to some exceptionally rare phenomenon, such as a very close encounter with a comet that would create in its wake the necessary conditions to form glass out of the desert minerals? This seems a plausible explanation. One thing is certain: Scientists have succeeded in dating the Libyan glass; it has been determined that it originated 29 million years ago.

Among the many different-sized rough fragments of glass, some were carved by people during the Neolithic period, who made a variety of miscellaneous cutting instruments, blades, scrapers, arrowheads, needles, jewelry, amulets, and cult objects. Prehistoric humans had clearly noticed the quality, transparency, and beauty of this unique substance buried in the desert. We do not know, however, whether the ancient Egyptians were aware of this precious glass. One

154. A. Carion, *Les Météorites et leurs impacts*, p. 181, Paris, 1997.
155. Carion, *op. cit*. p. 181.
156. Harding King, *Mysteries*, p. 119.
157. F. Fresnel, "Memoir of Mr. Fulgence Fresnel on the Waday," p. 82f., *Bulletin de la Société de géographie*, vol. 13, 1850.

**Right:** *Libyan glass with a hole in it, probably used as an amulet; it resembles a face in profile.*

**Bottom right:** *A pectoral that once belonged to Tutankhamun with a solar scarab of Libyan glass set at its center; its body merges into that of a falcon with spread wings.*

**Previous page, left:** *Uncut fragments of Libyan glass, both transparent and opaque, found on the ground or sometimes partly buried in it. The exposed surfaces have been polished by the fine particles of sand carried by the wind, while the parts buried in the ground retain a rough appearance.*

**Previous page, top right:** *A tool of Libyan glass, 2 inches long.*

**Previous page, bottom right:** *Small tools and knife blades of Libyan glass, 1¼–2⅓ inches long.*

recent study demonstrates that a Pharaoh had the rare privilege of possessing a single piece of this glass, set in a funeral necklace.[158] Tutankhamun wore a chest ornament featuring a magnificent greenish-yellow scarab beetle in the center, its body blending into a falcon with outspread wings.[159] For many years this scarab was believed to be chalcedony, a translucent quartz, but laboratory tests have now established that it is in fact Libyan glass. Further studies are being performed on various gems and ancient artifacts of the Pharaohs', such as the five rings made of stone, one of which might be of the same origin; the results are not yet known.

**158.** V. de Michele, "'The Libyan Desert Glass' Scareb in Tutankhamun's Pectoralin," p.107ff., *Sahara*, vol. 10, 1998.

**159.** The scarab, a common insect more often known as a dung beetle, pushes a ball of rubbish that contains its eggs. The Egyptians called the scarab kheper, associating it with ideas of existence and development by using the same hieroglyph for all three. The scarab is also linked by homophony to khepri, the rising sun, a morning sign of the sun god, who becomes Re at sunrise and Atum at sunset. The scarab embodies the gift of regeneration and takes on the task of pushing the solar ball during the night so that it will be reborn in the morning. Used as a seal or protective charm, the scarab appears in many paintings and bas-reliefs. Cf. Yoyotte, *Dictionnaire*, p. 259.

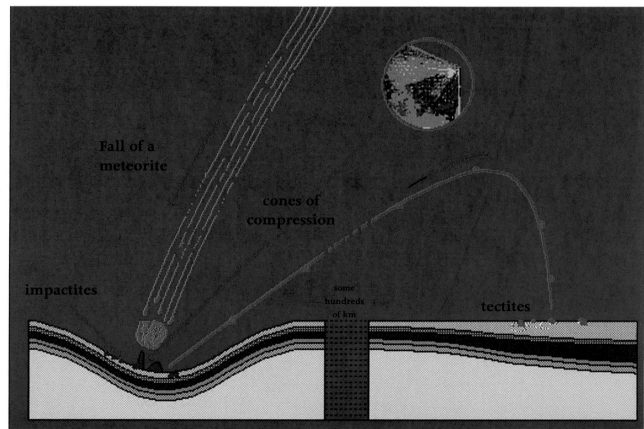

**Above:** *One hypothesis to explain the origin of this unique, 29-million-year old glass is that it resulted from the impact of the head of a comet.*

**Left:** *Diagram showing the impact of a meteor (Diemer).*

160. R. A. Weeks, J. R. Underwood, R. Giegengack, "Libyan Desert Glass: A Review," *Journ. Non-Cryst Solids*, 1984.

# Libyan glass: An impactite?

by Edmond Diemer

*Ever since Patrick Clayton rediscovered Libyan glass in December 1932, more than 170 publications have mentioned this glass and 90 percent of them are scientific studies examining its composition and origin and comparing it with other natural glass. Theodore Monod of the Muséum national d'histoire naturelle (Museum of natural history) was the first French scientist to take up the question. He visited the site many times, and we accompanied him on six of those expeditions. We encouraged French scientists to study the glass and several papers have been published about it.*

*The glass is located in the Great Sea of Sand in the Libyan Desert, spread over an oval area about 80 miles long north to south, and approximately 30 miles wide from east to west. The area appears to be centered around 25° 30′ N and 25° 30′ E, not far from where the dune ranges—generally oriented NNW–SSE—cease on the border of the sandstone plateau of the Gilf Kebir. The glass pieces lay spread out on the sand in the 2- to 3-mile-wide corridors between the linear dune ranges. Clayton was the first person to map the site.*

*The dimensions of the pieces of glass are quite varied. The smaller pieces measure 1 to 1½ inches and are found among pieces of quartzite strewn on the sand in the perfectly flat dune corridors. The larger pieces range from 2½ to 4 inches and are more or less buried; the tip that is above ground has been polished by the wind and so is shiny and soft to the touch, while the buried part is unpolished and feels grainy, probably owing to erosion by humidity. The moisture in the sand is, of course, very slight, but over millions of years it can have an effect on stones.*

*The smaller pieces of glass found on the surface have smoother, rounded edges, which indicates that they may have been carried by water, while the buried pieces are much sharper. The largest pieces found have been completely buried; the single largest ever found weighed just over 57 pounds and was donated to the French National Museum of Natural History.*

*Libyan glass has a more or less transparent yellow to light green color; some samples have air bubbles that give them a whitish cast, and when there are many air bubbles the glass looks opaque. Among the most typical and readily visible interior structures are white spherules that turn out to be cristobalite—a kind of quartz—and brown streaks called schlieren. It should be noted that the schlieren are often stratified, thus showing a fluid composition; the same can be said of the air bubbles, which line up in a parallel formation and are often spread out lengthwise along the stratifications. The schlieren, which are readily visible to the naked eye, contain minute quantities of trace elements—often on the order of a few parts per billion—that can only be identified by means of advanced techniques.*

*The glass has a hardness of 6, which is identical to normal glass. Its density is 2.2, which is slightly lighter than normal glass, and over 98 percent of it is silicon dioxide; the other 2 percent includes aluminum oxide, iron oxides, and titanium, plus a wide variety of trace elements whose presence and manner of distribution within the glass appear to be critical factors in the scientific efforts to determine its origin.*

*This glass contains a much higher proportion of silica than all other known types of natural glass—such as volcanic obsidian whose silica content is just over 75 percent. In addition to the air bubbles and cristobalite mentioned above, there are other constituents in the glass that are visible to the naked eye, or to an optical or an electronic microscope, and these seem to be of biological origin.*

*The seemingly biological constituents have convinced some scientists that this glass formed as the result of the solidification of a silica gel, which would have occurred at normal temperatures, allowing organisms present in the water to be enveloped and preserved. More recent analyses, however, have presented facts that are incompatible with this explanation involving normal temperatures. In particular, studies of the arrangement of the silica tetrahedrons and their behavior under infrared radiography do not lend support to the low-temperature theory. In one study, a zircon underwent an in-situ transformation into a similar composite called baddeleyite, which indicates that there had to be a temperature of over 3,000 °F (1,676 °C).*

*The presence of stishovite, another type of quartz crystal, proves that the glass must have undergone a shock of over 20,000 bars. The iridium content, which is considerably higher than that of terrestrial rocks, suggests that material from space penetrated this glass. The relative content of a number of metals—including iron, chromium, cobalt, iridium, and nickel—is quite unlike the relative content found in the earth's crust, yet it does correspond to levels found in meteorites.*

*In view of all these facts, it seems logical to conclude that this glass was formed either upon impact of a meteorite or the nucleus of a comet, or upon their explosion at a very low altitude above the earth. Such an event would have caused the rock to melt, and thus turn into glass. There are many places on earth where there is evidence of events of this kind; 130 have been identified as meteorite impact craters. Many such craters have disappeared due to erosion and age, including the meteorite crater at Rochechouart in France, which is 200 million years old.*

*To understand the many consequences of such collisions, let us consider the Ries crater near Nördlingen, Germany, between Stuttgart and Munich, because it demonstrates all aspects of this phenomenon. The crater is 15 million years old and has a diameter of 15½ miles. One can see the crater clearly from the beautiful medieval town of Nördlingen, which sits approximately at the crater's center. When the meteorite hit, the rock shattered and melted. Shattercones show fracture lines from the tip of the cone, which usually indicates the direction from which the meteorite came. On the ground around the crater, melted rock was transformed to glass. This glass is called impactite and was used to build many of the buildings in Nördlingen (the same is true in Rochechouart). Finally, a few smaller pieces of melted rock were flung high up into the atmosphere and the stratosphere and came down several hundred miles away from the point of impact. As they fell back down through the atmosphere, they melted a second time; taking on an aerodynamic shape. These are called tectites. All of these artifacts can be found at the Ries crater; the tectites created by this collision are called moldavites and can be found 200–300 miles east of Nördlingen, in Bohemia.*

*If, indeed, the same phenomenon were responsible for Libyan glass, then these pieces in the desert would be impactites.*

*The next step is to determine the date of the collision; this can be done using some of the many carbon-dating methods. Several independent laboratories have come up with the same results, which show that the glass is 28.5— 29.5 ± 0.4 million years old. The impact, thus, dates back to the Tertiary (Oligocene) Period, and it is known that, since that time, erosion has lowered the ground level by about 1,000 feet, which explains why the original glass rock and the signs of the crater have disappeared.*

*How much glass was created here? An American team tried to determine the exact quantity in 1984.[160] By estimating the amount currently on site, and the probable amount lost to erosion, they calculated that there must have been a mass of about 14 million tons. If we take into account this figure and the distribution of cristobalite spherules, which indicate the cooling process of the melted mass, we can imagine the following scenario: The nucleus of a comet or a meteorite hit the Nubian sandstone at a speed of 20 to 30 miles per second. The shock wave caused the temperature to reach over 3,600 °F (ca. 2000 °C). The crater had a diameter of almost 2 miles; the ground inside the crater was flat and had a central cone. It contained a lake of melted matter about three feet deep. The walls must have collapsed back on this melted mass, slowing down the cooling process. Erosion due to water progressively removed the 1,000 to 1,300 feet of sediment that covered the Nubian sandstone, and also dislocated the mass of glass, made up of sandstone and Nubian quartzite. The water then carried the pieces of glass to rivers, depositing them on the ground as we see it today.*

*If this scenario seems coherent, let us not forget that the characteristics of the crater and of the projectile are based on the estimated quantity of glass formed on impact; this is, therefore, only an educated guess.*

*Finally, this scenario does not take into account several considerations. According to this theory, we should have found samples made of both glass and wall fragments showing the transition from the mass of melted glass and the walls of the crater. But we haven't. As for how the glass was carried, although many of the small pieces were clearly shaped by water, most of the larger buried pieces seem not to have been carried far from the impact epicenter.*

*To some extent, then, Libyan glass remains a mystery, and unlike any other known impactites on earth.*

# Chapter VII

# A Desert Marked by Prehistoric Humans

## Climatic conditions reversed over the years

The Libyan Desert is extremely arid, receiving less than a quarter of an inch of rainfall per year. Yet throughout the region are signs of human habitation that could only have been made possible by a more favorable climate. Today it is completely uninhabited and was only truly explored in the archaeological sense during the 20th century, when the primarily cartographic or military expeditions brought to light important prehistoric sites. It is extremely difficult, however, for even archaeologists and paleoclimatologists to work in such inhospitable conditions, and they must limit the amount of time they spend on site. The absence of any place where they could restock their supplies of water and food obliges any party to carry everything they anticipate they will need, which requires minutely detailed planning and a heavy load of food, water, fuel, and equipment. This, of course, must be limited to the barest essentials and research equipment such as microscopes, cameras, measuring instruments, as well as spare tires, diesel filters, and other such items, all of which often malfunction if sand gets inside them (which it inevitably does).

Still, the archaeological digs that have been conducted have revealed a long succession of highly contrasting dry and wet periods that completely upset living conditions.

Long ago, and in various periods, humans were able to live in this region; the extent of their migration depended on the overall weather patterns and on their own ability to adapt to more extreme climatic conditions. The oldest known civilization in ancient Egypt dates back to the Paleolithic Age; the presence of *Homo erectus* is indicated by the discovery of certain tools dated to approximately 300,000 BC. One famous example is the two-sided, almond-shaped Acheulean flint with a rounded edge that improved on the pebble culture dating to the beginning of this period. These tools, made of flint, quartzite or sandstone, are typified by their large oval shape, their weight, and their ease of handling. They can be found in many sites beyond the oases, for example, in the Gilf Kebir, in the Great Sea of Sand, and in the Nile Valley.

According to Midant-Reynes, an archaeological dig at Dakhla near Balat uncovered two fossil shafts containing thousands of artifacts, including scrapers and awls and a large proportion of Acheulean tools.[161]

These stone tools attest to a period when humans survived by hunting large and small game and gathering wild plants. They traveled great distances across the savanna, and already used fire.

During dry periods, these populations took refuge in the valleys where their tool-making technology evolved and diversified by adapting the various materials available to different purposes. Approximately 150,000 years ago, *Homo sapiens* began to make lighter and more specialized tools, which improved upon but did not quite supersede the Acheulean implements. Eventually the newer tools showed evidence of the Levallois technique, developed in the Acheulean period and in full use in the Mousterian period, 70,000–35,000 years ago. Midant-Reynes explains that the Levallois cutting technique "was a methodical way of chiseling off centripetal chips around the entire surface of the stone until a final blow culminated in a particular shape of tool: This final blow is called the Levallois blow."[162] It is not uncommon in the desert to come across many rock chiseling sites near places where the appropriate materials were found; the sites themselves are indicators of the population migrations.

During the Upper Paleolithic Age, about 33,000 years ago, a new era began with the appearance of blades; this kind of tool saved on raw materials and allowed toolmakers to refine their production techniques. The microlith, a tiny flint tool often set into a haft made of bone or wood, is the trademark of *Homo sapiens sapiens*, who fashioned chisels, arrowheads, scrapers, awls, axes, and even small needles, often in geometric shapes. Some chips were finely chiseled and fitted onto a wooden handle to make harpoons and sickles. These tools indicate a vital evolution, further illustrated by the introduction of food-storage methods and by the oldest known tomb, dating back to 30,000 years ago, found at Nazlet Khater by the team of P. Vermeersch.[163]

During the Neolithic period, alternating wet and dry cycles continued, but began to differentiate from north to south. When drought

*A small mound unobtrusively marks a prehistoric site. The ground littered with rock splinters preserves the memory of the presence of humans.*

**Right:** *A tool used by* Homo sapiens*: a large, heavy flint, well-adapted to the shape of the hand and with very sharp edges.*

161. Midant-Reynes, *Préhistoire*, p. 36.
162. Midant-Reynes, *Préhistoire*, p. 33.
163. Midant-Reynes, *Préhistoire*, p. 17f.

*A nucleus of uncut flint accompanied by its gangue.*

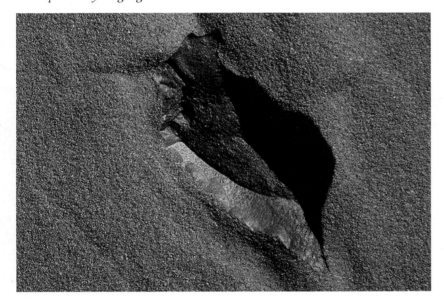

*A Paleolithic tool fashioned using the Levallois technique. The mottled point has a denticulate edge.*

*Flint blades made with the Levallois technique, 1½–2¼ inches long.*

**Right:** *An ovoid concretion still set in the marble that created it.*

affected the desert region, its inhabitants took refuge in the Nile Valley. When a rainy period returned, the people established new sites that actually have yielded more artifacts, revealing even more detail about life in those distant times than the Nile Valley cultures, which were often destroyed by floods. These were nomadic hunters and so-called playa cultures (see page 203). Beginning around 9,000 BC, the last wet climate cycle lasted until around 3,200 BC.

## Nomadic hunters

The hunting culture of the nomads that followed the playa culture is less well known to us, and no clear link between the two can be established. These mostly nomadic peoples lived by hunting and by gathering wild plants and fruits; they moved frequently but could always return to a previous site if conditions permitted. Their encampments were light and simple so that they could pack and move out quickly; their communities were unstable and limited in number. This hunting culture eventually developed into a prepastoral culture, similar to pockets still found in the Sahara today.

Dogs were the first domesticated animals; they were trained for hunting and buried next to their master. They were of invaluable help in capturing first wild cattle in the Nile Valley, and later wild goats and sheep. A study of wildlife from that period has determined that only hares and gazelles were able to survive without a regular source of drinking water due to their ability to absorb the dew off plants at dawn. By contrast, many of the bovine bones found could only have originated through the transhumance of these domesticated animals as they were herded along to find pastures in remote regions. It is most likely that the hunters domesticated the wild animals, since they had the best knowledge of animal behavior: "hunters, who lived in close symbiosis with wild animal herds, were in a position to know the habits of these animals, and thus to experiment with them, either accidentally or on purpose. These would have been the first steps that led to domestication."[164]

A prehistoric cave created by river action on variegated sandstone near one of the Mud Pan sites. The cave is now inhabited by foxes, and has been dubbed "Fox Village."

164. J. Leclant, P. Huard, "The culture of the hunters in the Nile and Sahara," p. 491, *Mémoires du Centre de recherches anthropologiques, préhistoriques et ethnographiques*, 29,2, Algier, 1977.

A workshop for
making tools:
the seat that the
craftsman used for
support while
fashioning stones,
surrounded by
rejects.

**165.** F. Peel, "The Tibu
People and the Libyan
Desert," p. 73-87,
*Geographic Journal*,
London, 1942.

Animals were shackled to stones to hold them captive in a grazing area. The hobble stones that can be seen today are easily distinguished by the well-worn notch where the rope was tied. There are also engravings of these animals in many of the wadis where they drank water, which establishes their presence in this period. This civilization did not make pottery, but continued to use hunting traps and carved stone utensils and weapons. They ate wild game—giraffe, ostrich, elephant, and occasionally hippopotamus and other large game—but only drank the milk and the blood of their domestic animals, just as some Masai tribes in Tanzania and Kenya still do today.

## The Tibu nomads

From the earliest known times, some nomadic ethnic groups moved great distances to find food and water for their herds, and also to gain access to the goods of more settled civilizations. The nomads came mostly came from remote areas of southern Libya and northern Chad, and some of them still exist. They were called *Guraans*, a generic term for many different tribes, and often raided the settlements in the playas. The best-known and longest-lived of the tribes who reigned over the desert were the Tibu.[165] The name itself means "men of the rocks," a name the Arabs used for the people of Tibesti.

The Tibu way of life changed little over the centuries, and so the explorers of the early 20th century, who encountered the last surviving members of the tribe, were able to record something of their customs and lifestyle. They lived in very light huts that were easy to dismantle, pack, and carry. They knew the distances between all the watering holes in the desert, which allowed them to travel and, if need be, disappear into hiding when the victims of their raids tried to retaliate. They were skilled craftsmen and knew how to make light, durable baskets, as well as a kind of rustic pottery that could survive travel. They also built a kind of monument of stones laid out in a circle on the ground, though it remains unclear if these were monuments or burials sites, or simply encampments.

## The civilization of the playas

During wet periods in the ancient Neolithic, the Great Sea of Sand had a completely different landscape: The ground was covered in vegetation that grew around a series of lakes fed by rivers and received heavy seasonal rains of up to 20 inches per year (100 times what it is today). There were many springs with abundant water sources, creating widespread habitat around lagoons filled with layers of silt, clay, and fertile mud that allowed a variety of flora and fauna to flourish. It was a golden age for native cattle, gazelles, ostriches, and fish, especially perch. These typical prehistoric sites of habitation in low-lying areas near water were called playas. The most famous is Nabta Playa, which is about 60 miles west of the Nile on the same latitude as Abu Simbel. Nabta Playa has many valuable vestiges of human occupation and,

*Stone hobbles worn down by the rope holding the captive animals; a rock carving shows the technique used.*

**203**

**Above and pages 208–209:**
*Typical landscapes of the civilization of the playas at the foot of sandstone massifs. The once very fertile floor of the depressions is still covered with dry, variously colored loam. This is where the very first farmers settled.*

**Left and following page:** *The civilization of the playas: Saddle querns, their flat stone beds worn by the stone—here spherical— used to crush or grind both wild and cultivated grains.*

166. J. Kérisel, *Le Nil: l'Espoir et la Colère*, p. 42, Paris, 1999.
167. F. Wendorf, R. Schilde, "Les Débuts du Pastoralisme," p. 440, *La Recherche*, vol. 220, April 1990.
168. Wendorf, Schilde, *op. cit.* p. 442.

according to Jean Kerisel, was also a place of worship.[166] Other sites further away from the Nile Valley are dispersed throughout the region and include Bir Sahara, Bir Kiseiba, and Bir Tarfawi. We know of three successive periods when these sites were clearly used, interspersed with periods of exodus due to dry cycles, and each successive civilization shows the evolution of the culture and habitat.

People became more and more settled around the playas as these sites became the seasonal gathering place where tribes could find a watering hole, pastures, and forest. As hunting, fishing, and animal husbandry activities became more centered on the playas, people began to apply their knowledge of wild grains to the deliberate cultivation of barley and later wheat. This is demonstrated by findings of minute bits of grains found on some tools, and mill stones worn down by intense usage. The periphery of the playas was still moist when the waters receded, providing fertile ground for these early farmers, who began to store the harvested grain in large silos. According to Fred Wendorf and Romuald Schild,[167] recent archaeological digs at Nabta have established that there were two wells, one of which was deep enough to reach the water table even in dry periods thanks to an interior set of steps, and it was located near the huts and stores. Other signs of long-term habita-

tion were found, including a fireplace protected by a vertical semi-circle of stones set into the ground to shelter the fire from the dominant wind. Other, simpler encampments on the surrounding hilltops sheltered shepherds during high-water periods.

The earliest, rudimentary pottery was found here—a kind of reddish-brown clay that was clearly baked but undecorated and used to store food and other provisions, as well as ostrich eggs. Wendorf writes that tasks were distributed among people, hierarchies were established, and labor became more specialized, following the rhythm of the seasons; most likely, people gathered during the rainy flood season.[168]

Evidence suggests that humans were present just as early around the oases, insofar as travel was easier thanks to the plentiful watering holes in that period. Jewelry and other kinds of ornaments made of seashells from the Red Sea found in tombs indicate that some active form of trade was already established in that era.

**Left:** *Rock carvings dating from between 8000 and 5000 BC in the Djara cave first described by Rohlfs. They are on a limestone column near the entrance as signs of welcome, and depict bovids, ostriches, antelopes, and other animals.*

**Right and pages 212–213:** *A stone portal providing access to a yardang landscape, a national park with ancient "seals" left stranded by the withdrawal of the sea, and watching for its return.*

172. R. Kuper, *Between the Oases*, p. 81.

## Vestiges of prehistory

### Djara, Rohlfs' cave

The Djara cave, located near the huge Abu Muharek sand dune, was first described by the explorer Rohlfs in 1875, but was then forgotten until Bergmann rediscovered it in 1989 during one of his annual winter camel expeditions. Kuper has since supervised systematic archaeological digs while taking great care to protect this unique site.

The entrance to the cave is quite low, on otherwise unremarkable flat ground, and gives no hint of the spectacle that awaits you inside. In order to explore the cave, you must first crawl between the sharp fangs of the gaping limestone jaws at its entrance, trying to avoid stirring up the powdery sand, and end up sliding down a slope on your back. As the cloud of sand dust settles, the breathtaking architecture of this pillared underground hall comes into view. Seemingly draped stalactites meet up with striped or glistening stalagmites, some of which are even encrusted with crystals, forming impressive columns. Some have already collapsed and others appear to be on the verge. This mysterious world seems to be inhabited by an ineffable presence for which one cannot help but search. There is no water here, though there are signs that it was once abundant, even quite recently. Today it is completely dry, with mere traces of parched silt strewn on the ground. At one end of the cave, daylight illuminates the avalanche of sand that obstructs the entrance and presages the visitor's difficult journey back out of the cave. Near the cave exit, on the right, there is a pillar half-buried in the sand, covered with paintings of animals: cows, ostriches, antelopes ... This was clearly a refuge for Neolithic people between 8000 and 5500 BC, and they left their mark on several walls.

Their former presence is also manifest outside the cave, where a water hole allowed them to set up a large flint-tool carving site, making use of the flint that is abundant in the region. Explorers have tried, without success, to find other such carving sites in this area. Djara is thus one of the most important sites of desert civilization, as Kuper affirms: "With [its] specific composition of its spectrum of artifacts and its geographical position between the oases and the Nile, the site of Djara appears to be able to make an essential contribution to the cultural and chronological relationship between the Sahara and the Nile Valley."[172]

### Mud Pans and lakefront dwellings

The term "Mud Pan" designates several immense bowl-shaped areas filled with silt situated between the string of oases and the Gilf Kebir. In such places, when the sea retreated, it left behind some of its fauna, for example, a few sirenians and cetaceans fossilized in the playa sediment. These seabed deposits composed of materials with varying degrees of hardness gave rise to something called *yardangs*— compacted, hardened sandstone "seals" sculpted by wind erosion, always facing the prevailing wind, creating the illusion of a still herd waiting for the sea to return.

These areas were particularly fertile. Petrified wood found here indicates that they were covered with forests that must have attracted Paleolithic and then Neolithic peoples. They likely built only simple villages of a few homes on the nearby hilltops. The domiciles were set

**Above:** *Between light and shadow, the prehistoric artist has used the structure of the rock to bring the body of a giraffe into relief.*

**Right:** *Young addax suckling.*

**Previous page:** *An elegant silhouette of a nude woman, long-limbed but headless, as is often seen in rock carvings; this demonstrates the importance of the female body as a symbol of fertility.*

horns, seems to be caught in a circle, perhaps symbolizing a trap, a lasso, or a pen, or maybe just the hunter's desire to capture it. Near it is a young addax suckling at its mother's teats, which appears unconcerned by the spotted hyena nearby. Something that resembles a hop-scotch outline is drawn on the ground: a grid of rectangles, some with crosses in them, but their meaning remains unclear. Finally, there is a beautiful outline of a surprisingly long-legged and slim naked woman, whose head, however, has disappeared.

Other rock paintings of various fauna can be seen on several hillsides of these hills between the Mud Pans and Abu Ballas. There are, in all, many fine examples of rock art types and techniques, including carving, brushstrokes, dots, polishing, and stylized animals always drawn in profile.

Not far from the twin hills of Abu Ballas, at the foot of the escarpment, is one of the world's most spectacular and haunting desert landscapes: an immense playa where purplish-red yardangs seemingly float on pastel blue-green and yellow-grey waves of silt. Dated to 8000 BC, these sites have yielded many tools, including grinding stones and other grain-related objects.

### Wadi Hamra: Acacias and rock paintings

Wadi Hamra, the red valley, cuts deeply into the northwestern part of the Gilf Kebir, on a north-south axis. It is accessible only from the Great Sea of Sand and its narrow entrance penetrates several miles into the Gilf. The valley snakes along between two cliffs that reach up more than 300 feet, and wide open spaces alternate with narrow gorges until it reaches the confluence of two ancient branches of the wadi. The

remains of many fire pits show that the promontory that separates the two valleys must have been a paradise of sorts for prehistoric people, with its extraordinary flora and fauna. Abundant vegetation still lies hidden on the wadi floor today, though some species, such as the *Acacia tortilis raddiana*, prefer the cliffs, where the reptiles stake out their prey.

This site was discovered by plane when Count Almasy organized an expedition to look for the legendary Zerzura oasis in 1932. Many other explorers, including Clayton and later Frobenius and Rhotert, subsequently inventoried the wadi. More recently, Giancarlo Negro, Wally Lama, and Louis Carion have added to our awareness of the valley with discoveries of additional rock paintings.

The drawings and carvings found here reveal the evolution of rock painting techniques, and of life in the valley. These sites were inhabited over very long periods, starting in about 6500 BC. For example, some sketches that include carved dots are next to utterly realistic paintings of herds, while there are a few drawings that suggest an almost comic allusive style: two irresistibly cute giraffes look like they popped straight out of a cartoon. Representations of humans are rare, but those that do exist are very interesting: One painting depicts a man standing up on the tail of a cow, and another holding a bow, standing on the back of an addax; another shows a man surrounded by his pack of dogs. Several flat rocks show deep vertical notches; the meaning of these is unknown. Some are V-shaped while others are U-shaped. It has been hypothesized that the V-shaped notch was where they sharpened cutting tools and the U-shaped notch was a kind of trench for polishing stones or ostrich eggs to their typical small disc shape, which would then be used like beads in jewelry.

*Rock carvings at the Wadi Hamra:
A herdsman watches over his ostrich
herd, aided by his dogs.*

*Various carvings of giraffes:
excellent game, but difficult to catch.*

*Young giraffes watched over by their
mother; ostrich.*

The drawings were mostly of wild animals: gazelles, addax, oryx, bulls, wild sheep, ostriches, rhinoceroses, and above all (literally), giraffes, whose plentiful meat made it the game of choice, even though they are fast and difficult to catch. At the time, the climate particularly favored giraffes, whose survival depends on the availability of abundant water. Giraffes were probably the first animal to disappear from the desert during a shift to an arid period; indeed, Gautier and Negro observed that when annual rainfall dropped below 4 inches, around 6000 BC, giraffes disappeared from the rock paintings in the Gilf Kebir.[176]

Unfortunately, the combination of erosion and patina on the paintings has erased some of the oldest drawings, and their outlines now blend with the rock surface. Sometimes falling rocks and landslides will bury some of the paintings, or fragments are knocked askew such that some of the animals' bodies are preserved but their heads are upside down. It is reasonable to suppose that there are many more rock drawings yet to be discovered.

### Wadi Firaq: The cave of Magharat el-Kantara

In the southeastern and center parts of the Gilf Kebir, at the far end of the Wadi Firaq, where land mines from past wars are still a problem, there is a cave nestled in the summit of a hill. The site was discovered by accident in 1935 when the Englishman Kennedy Shaw was exploring this unknown part of the plateau. The cave faces east, and in winter the rays of light from the rising sun sweep briefly across the magnificent cave paintings decorating the upper part of the overhang. The nearly 50-foot-wide entrance to the cave lets in plenty of light for admiring the herd of a dozen steer, all but one shown in profile facing to the right. The scene highlights the diversity of the animals, depicting cows, bulls, a calf, and all in many different shades of creamy white, light and dark ochre, plain and speckled. Their elegant horns, either splayed out or pointing forward, suggest two different species of cattle. Some of the cows wear several collars and are easily recognizable by the udders near their hind legs. Gautier and Negro used samples taken by Shaw and analyzed by Jordan to determine the exact composition of the pigments used for the base paint and for the colors: "For the red color they used iron oxides (hematite), aluminum, and silica from burned sandstone, for white they used magnesium, a little aluminum, and silica … this paint is certainly made of white clay."[177]

It is surprising that these paints were able to stay so vivid, given the lack of any organic element to act as fixative. It is possible that the paintings were covered by a layer of sand that protected them from the erosion that damaged the right-hand side of the cave, where only a faint picture of a giraffe and a few groups of people and animals can still be detected. Three human couples seem to be occupied with different tasks: Two hunters wearing headdresses look like they are running after one another on short legs, the second holding a bow; two people with grotesque expressions face each other, one, with an enormous belly, leans over the smaller figure; and there is a couple typical of the period, the man standing, wearing a large light-colored apron, his back turned to a woman who sits in a round hut

*Wadi Firaq: Entrance to the el-Kantara cave, and a view of the paintings in it. These are difficult to date, but were probably done between 7000 and 5000 BC; they are typical of the art of these Saharan herdsmen.*

176. Y. Gauthier, G. Negro, ''Magharet el-Kantara (Shaw's Cave) revisité: art rupestre du sud du Gilf-Kebir,'' p. 130, *Sahara*, 9, 1997.
177. Gauthier, Negro, *op. cit.* p. 125.

*Detail from a picture of a herd of bovines wearing collars and gathered around the bull.*

**Below:** *Woman seated in her hut at the foot of a man dressed in a long loincloth.*

*A fight between strange horned animals.*

*A herdsman running after his herd.*

where household utensils hang from the ceiling. Finally, there are two rather odd-looking animals of an indeterminate species.

These paintings were done during different periods and are difficult to date exactly, although the subjects and the workmanship seem typical of the Saharan pastoral painters from 7000–5000 BC.

### The mysterious human paintings of Wadi Sora

Deep in the heart of the Libyan Desert, at the far edge of Egypt near Libya and Sudan, several hundred miles from the Nile Valley, is hidden the most remote, most inaccessible cave drawing site yet found, at the foot of the Gilf Kebir. The most direct route to reach it is across the Aqaba Pass that divides the Gilf Kebir plateau, but this pass, like the Wadi Fisaq, is still littered with land mines, making it for all intents and purposes impassible. There is another, safer path that goes around the plateau to the south, but it is a long, arduous journey via Eight Bells. Along the way is a monument erected by Count Almasy in honor of Prince Kemal el Dine, and then the route heads northwest along the escarpment. The length of the journey depends on how often the traveler finds the path completely covered by sand under the burning sun …

In 1933, while searching for the rock paintings of giraffes mentioned by Clayton, Almasy became intrigued by a large bow-shaped wadi carved into the ground at the foot of the Gilf escarpment, whose ancient path was lined with rocks that had fallen from the cliffs. On the eastern bank, he discovered several caves, two of which held the most beautiful rock paintings ever found in the Libyan Desert. This is the Wadi Sora.

One of these caves could be called the "Archers' Cave," because it shows a group of elongated male and female hunters armed with bows and arrows, at a campsite, their bodies in extraordinary positions. The women's flat chests contrast sharply with their ample hips. Nearby is a rustic country scene of a herd of cattle and a man drinking milk directly from a cow's udder, to the dismay of a calf that the man has displaced. The two themes clearly show the two ways of life: hunter-gatherers and pastoral peoples living side by side.

The other cave, known as the "Swimmers' Cave," contains a painting of many people who seem to be floating weightlessly all over the wall, each doing something different. This discombobulated picture is disturbing to look at and hard to interpret. The collage-like composition seems more random than organized and must have been painted during different periods. There are a few greenish-yellow figures and animals that probably date back to an earlier period than the other drawings, since the latter, ochre-colored images partly cover them. Some of the figures seem to have incorporated the texture of the rock wall into the picture, thus attaining an almost three-dimensional feeling of movement. Others are painted in niches in the wall, giving the scenes a sense of intimacy; for example, one scene of three people sitting facing each other in invocation feels quite personal and private. There are tapered bodies sketched in dancing movements and more robust, unmoving figures decked out in harnesses and bracelets. But then there are the life-sized hands—what

*Wadi Sora in the southern Libyan Desert on the western edge of the Gilf Kebir; view of the site with its two caves containing paintings.*

*The Archers' Cave: a group of hunters.*

*Detail: A man drinking from the udder of a cow, while a calf waits its turn.*

Procession.

Trance scene.

Group of hunters, either tattooed or
wearing bracelets, enlivened by the motion
of waves at their feet.

"Negative imprint" of a hand
containing a mysterious symbol.

178. Cf. Lindner, *Chasses préhistoriques*, quoted by Allequ, *Encyclopedia Universalis*, vol. X, p. 299, taken from Leclant, *op. cit.* p. 527.
179. B. Midant-Reynes, "La Taille des couteaux de silex du type Gebel el-Arak et la dénomination du silex en égyptien," p. 263, Poznan, 1993.
180. Narmer's palette illustrates the unification of Upper and Lower Egypt under the reign of the first Pharaoh, Ménès or Narmer. Two swimmers are the main focus, the origin of which is unknown, just like the ones of Wadi Sora!
181. *Histoire de l'Égypte ancienne*, p. 49, Paris, 1988.

could they be entreating or dispelling? One hand is in negative with its palm filled by a scene of dancing hunters in animal-skin belts like those found in the Sahara. Some of the human figures dispered in the painting are in strange poses, like swimmers or divers carried on sometimes clashing currents. They seem to be from yet another era, since they include three different colors—the older ones in white, then some in greenish-yellow, and even more recent ones in ochre.

These poses have not been found anywhere else and remain a mystery. Were they simply swimmers splashing during the period when the wadis overflowed with water? Were they drowned bodies with swollen bellies, passing from life to death, or does the seemingly upward travel of the figures indicate images of rebirth into another life? Was this cave a place of worship where ceremonies and initiation rituals were conducted? Were these bodies in levitation or adoration? Were the artists themselves in a trance so that the paintings illustrate the different states of consciousness they experienced during the rites of passage?

To enter into a trance, one turns inward, as if into a swirling vortex, like the nearby water, and this vortex overtakes the conscious mind, creating an upward spiral, an image symbolizing the link between humans and a superior being whose oracles were then transmitted to the uninitiated. Was this cave one of the oldest places of worship for amazons and hunters seeking the protection of their god? After all, "the magic of hunting was the oldest expression of religious sentiments."[178]

The civilization of the Nile would have been born when the hunter-gatherers joined together with the pastoral nomads, bringing their knowledge of animals, domestication, agriculture, handicrafts, and their religion. Moreover, they probably left these places as they grew arid and hostile toward the end of the fourth millennium BC, which is when Narmer, the first Pharaoh of the First Dynasty, began to unite Egypt.

A flint knife found at Gebel el-Arak dates to this critical period and seems to be illustrative of this sharing of material and spiritual

*"Swimmers' Cave": figures painted in various attitudes in successive epochs;*
*the negative imprint of a hand can been seen on the right.*

knowledge. Flint was the stone of choice of prehistoric peoples and is usually represented in hieroglyphs found in the Pyramid Texts designating a tool sacred to the Pharaohs—"The knife used by kings and gods for fighting the demons from beyond."[179] The art of carving flintstones was perfected in this period, but the knife found at Gebel el-Arak was a funerary object; it was not a tool for everyday usage or for display. The handle, carved from a hippopotamus tooth, shows a desert hunting scene, dogs with collars, and gazelles under the protection of the master of animals, the god of hunters; violence is sublimated, permitted only to god and the Pharaoh, sole holders of power, who used their power to maintain order: "These fantastic compositions become symbols of the power of animals that humans must master if they are to organize the cosmos. The warrior shown on the Gebel el-Arak knife handle is pushing back two wild animals using only the strength of his two arms, whereas the monsters on Narmer's palette[180] are held captive, yoked together at the neck. Any representation of humans on the palettes shows this establishing of order in creation."[181]

Both the hunters and the pastoral figures depicted are performing rituals involving both wild and domesticated animals, rituals to protect themselves from danger or from divine retribution, or from other animals. The aim was to secure the animals' benevolence and to appropriate their power by eating their flesh, milk, or blood. In addition to carvings and paintings, animals were also represented as totems: The chosen animal was perched on a pole erected to identify and unify primitive clans, helping them to face conflicts and gain victory. Animal worship was absorbed, developed, and enriched by the Egyptians, who even turned them into all-powerful gods: The power of the Pharaoh was embodied in Horus, the falcon god, while other gods assumed various shapes, such as Sekhmet, the lioness goddess, Anubis, the dog god, or Ammon, the ram god. Each had its own power and character, which determined how they were worshipped in the temples dedicated to them. The presence and representation of these animals, as it was both sublimated and deified in Egyptian art, have their roots in the hunter-gatherer and pastoral cultures that permeated the heart of the desert.

# List of the major Pharaohs

## EARLY DYNASTIC PERIOD: 3150–2700 BC

| Several kings, including Scorpion and Narmer | **1st Dynasty** Aha-Menes Djer Wadji | Dewen Adjib Semerkhet Qa'a | **2nd Dynasty** Hetepsekhemui Nebre Ninetjer | Wenegnebti Sened Peribsen Sekhemib | Khasekhemui |

## OLD KINGDOM: 2700–2190 BC

| **3rd Dynasty** Nebka Djoser Sekhemkhet Khâba Mesokhris Huni | **4th Dynasty** Snefru Cheops Djedefre Chephren Bikheris | Mycerinus Shepseskaf  **5th Dynasty** Userkaf Sahure Neferirkare | Shepseskare Reneferef Niuserre Menkauhor Djedkare Unas | **6th Dynasty** Teti Userkare Pepy I Merenre I Pepy II | Merenre II Nitocris |

## FIRST INTERMEDIATE PERIOD: 2140–2022 BC, 7TH–11TH THEBAN DYNASTIES

## MIDDLE KINGDOM: 2022–1674 BC

| **11th Dynasty** Mentuhotep II Mentuhotep III | Montuhotep IV | **12th dynastie** Amenemhat I Sesostris I | Amenemhat II Sesostris II Sesostris III | Amenemhat III Amenemhat IV Nefrusobek |

## SECOND INTERMEDIATE PERIOD: 1674–1553 BC, 13TH–17TH DYNASTIES

## NEW KINGDOM: 1553–1069 BC

| **18th Dynasty** Ahmose I Amenhotep I Thutmosis I Thutmosis II Hatshepsut | Thutmosis III Amenhotep II Thutmosis IV Amenhotep III Amenhotep IV Akhenaten | Smenkhkare Tutankhatun Tutankhamun Ay Horemheb | **19th Dynasty** Rameses I Sety I Rameses II Merenptah Amenmesse | Sety II Siptah Tausret  **20th Dynasty** Sethnakht | Rameses III Rameses IV Rameses V Rameses VI Rameses VII Rameses VIII | Rameses IX Rameses X Rameses XI |

## THIRD INTERMEDIATE PERIOD: 1069–664 BC

| **21st Dynasty** Smendes Amenemnesut Psusennes I Amenemope Osorkon the Elder | Siamun Psusennes II  **22nd Dynasty** Sheshonk I Osorkon I | Sheshonk II Takelot I Harsiese Osorkon II Takelot II Sheshonk III | Pimay Sheshonk V  **23rd Dynasty** Pedubastis I Osorkon III | Takelot III Rudamun  **24th Dynasty** Tefnakht Bikharis | **25th Dynasty** Piy Shabaqo Shabitqo Taharqo Tanutamani |

## LATE PERIOD: 664–332 BC

| **26th Dynasty** Nekau I Psamtek I Nekau II Psamtek II Apries | Amasis (Ahmose II) Psamtek III  **27th Dynasty** Cambyses II Darius I | Xerxes Artaxerxes Darius II Artaxerxes II | **28th Dynasty** Amyrtaios  **29th Dynasty** Nepherites I Psammuthis | Achoris (Hakor) Nepherites II  **30th Dynasty** Nectanebo I Teos | Nectanebo II |

## PTOLEMAIC ERA: 332–30 BC

| Alexander the Great Philip Arrhidaeus | Alexander IV Ptolemy I Soter → | Ptolemy XIII Cleopatra | Ptolemy XIV Ptolemy XV Caesarion |

## ROMAN ERA: 30 BC–395 AD

| Augustus Tiberius Caligula | Claudius Nero Galba | Otho Vitellius Vespasian | Titus Domitian Nerva | Trajan Hadrian Antoninus Pius | Marcus Aurelius Constantine Theodosius the Great |

## BYZANTINE ERA: 395–642 AD / ARAB CONQUEST: 642 AD

Based on Nicolas Grimal,
*Histoire de l'Égypte ancienne*,
Fayard, Paris, 1988.

# Conclusion

*I have always loved the desert. You sit on a sand dune.*
*You see nothing. You hear nothing. And yet, something*
*radiates, vibrates in the silence…*
*What makes the desert beautiful, said the Little Prince,*
*is that it hides a well somewhere…*[182]

Water in Egypt takes on different forms: the royal river that flows on the surface, and water hidden in the depths. Swelled with rain that falls in faraway lands, the royal river, free and visible, gives life; but is confined to its own valley, even during its occasional tantrums. It cannot water the string of oases, and is thwarted by the land surrounding it. The underground water was stored deep inside the earth in some distant, long-forgotten time when the climate was rainy. This water flows deep, becomes fossilized, is held captive, hidden; and yet it brings life and the possibility of survival to the oases.

Another Egypt—that of the oases—was a refuge in prehistoric times, when drought forced pastoral nomads and their herds from the desert. When the rains returned, they also returned to the mountains. Later, in the predynastic period, the dry cycle that continues today settled in: The oases became a permanent home for those who had to abandon their nomadic lifestyle. They brought with them their desert culture, their knowledge of animals and wild plants they had domesticated and cultivated in the semi-arid zones, their stone tools and crafts, their carving and painting. Their integration gave rise to the oasis culture and traditions.

Once a gathering spot for caravans and a place of refuge or exile, the oases have become a place of immigration: They now attract Nile Valley residents who see their vital resources dwindle in the face of overpopulation, rather than drought. The oases were settled by people fleeing desertification and now they draw those whom the floods of the Nile Valley can no longer support.

The inhabitants of the oases have developed extensive irrigation systems to hold back the encroaching desert and extend the arable land, but this effort is water- and labor-intensive. Demographic expansion in the oases implies an increase in water consumption, and the existing natural springs and hand-built wells are no longer adequate to the task. Life-giving water must now be tapped from the deeper water tables, yet that cannot be replenished. Water, like oil, iron, or coal, is a natural resource whose supply, although considerable, is nonetheless limited. Such nonrenewable resources may have a great future, but they are not inexhaustible, and it is a wonder they have lasted this long. Yet, thanks to the miraculous element that is water, life continues to develop in this other Egypt founded in the desert civilization.

As Monod has expressed it, "this is a devilishly interesting desert."

182. Saint-Exupéry, *The Little Prince*, San Diego, 1968.

# The Explorers of the Western Desert of Egypt During and Between the Two World Wars

## by Peter H. Clayton

Exploration of the Western Desert of Egypt was initiated by the need to combat the Senussi invasion from Cyrenaica in 1916. The operations of the Light Car Patrols (LCPs) using Ford Model "T" cars and the Duke of Westminster's Rolls-Royce armoured cars and tenders led to accurate the survey of many locations in the North West Desert by Dr. John Ball of the Egyptian Geological Survey (EGS), which had been set up in 1896 for the exploration of mineral resources throughout the land of Egypt.

In 1918 Dr. Ball and Captain C. H. Wilson, Pembroke Yeomanry, went from Dakhla around the south eastern edge of the Great Sea of Sand using the LCP's Ford "T"s and discovered Pottery Hill (Abu Ballas).

After the war the Frontiers District Administrations (FDA) was created to administer and police the Districts away from the Nile Valley, such as Siwa and the Central Oases. The FDA, in addition to its superb Camel Corps, took over the tasks of the LCP when British troops were withdrawn to the Nile.

Colonel de Lancey Forth, the Commander of the FDA Camel Corps, went in 1921 with Colonel McDonnel, then Governor of the Western Desert, 100 miles into the Sands south of Siwa. In 1924, with Captain Hatton of the FDA, they penetrated another 100 miles southwards. Forth also explored the country west of the Dakhla-Abu Mingar Escarpment in 1922, but his guide got lost so they returned to Abu Mingar.

Prince Kemal el Dine's first motor expedition in 1923 with Dr. Ball, into the South West Desert, revisited Abu Ballas. They used six FDA standard two-gear Ford "T" pick-ups and the Prince's three Citroën half-tracks. Major Jarvis, the Governor of Kharga and Dakhla Oases, and Lieutenant Fairman of the FDA had set up two dumps on the prospective route beyond Dakhla using these vehicles. The Desert Survey Department (DSD) was formed that year under Dr. Ball, specifically to map the deserts and Major Patrick Clayton was invited to transfer from the EGS (Egyptian Geological Section) for this task.

In 1924 Prince Kemal el Dine and Dr. Ball reached Regenfeld; their narrow twin tyre marks on stretches of gravel are still distinct. In 1925 and 1926 they got to Uweinat on a different route each time and identified and named the Gilf Kebir.

In 1926 the DSD bought three Ford Model "T"s for the Inspectors, cars for Mr. Murray and Mr. Walpole and a truck for Mr. Clayton, all with Ruckstall two-speed axles. Mr. Clayton and Lieutenant Fairman of the FDA made a preliminary reconnaissance of the Western Frontier prior to the Anglo-Italian Frontier Demarcation expedition in 1927. Using oversize tyres, the DSD truck and a FDA "Sand Car" reached 350 kilometres south from Sollum on the coast into the Great Sea of Sand on the 25th Meridian. This was a major achievement but showed the limitations of the Model "T" in sand. The FDA "Sand Cars" were Ford "T" long wheel base trucks with an additional central axle with wheels and chain tracks.

Mr. and Mrs. Beadnell were working in the Southern Desert from 1927 to 1929 exploring and supervising the digging of the wells at Bir el Sahra (so named by Mrs. Beadnell) and Bir el Messaha, or "Survey Well," (named by H. E. Sirrey Bey, the Surveyor-General). They had a fleet of four Ford "T"s and reached northwest from Bir Massaha to within sight of "the black hills beyond the plains."

So far, desert exploration had been planned and financed as a co-operative task involving the EGS, DSD, and the FDA. The Princes Kemal el Dine and Omar Tousoon, using respectively their Citroën and Renault vehicles, had gone as part of an overall plan with both Royal directives and the support of the Departments.

The officers of the Royal Engineers (RE), Signals (RCS), and Tanks (RTC) units of the British Garrison in Egypt lived together at Abbassia, then on the outskirts of Cairo. A Tank Corps officer who had served with the last Armoured Car unit at Sollum was Lieutenant Bather, he and a Signals officer, Lieutenant Holland, took two cars at Christmas 1924 for a week's cruise on the edge of the Western Desert. Bather taught Holland the old LCP desert techniques and survival rules—and then promprtly returned to England. Major Bagnold of the RCS arrived in October 1925 and met up with Holland. Finding that they had common interests, they soon had two Ford "T"s and started to explore the nearby deserts. Major Jarvis was by then the Governor of Sinai, and later enabled them to pass through there on their tour to Palestine.

It was from officers of these three Corps that Bagnold recruited his future desert companions for the 1927 expedition to Siwa and other sites, the 1929 expedition to Ain Dalla and other sites, the 1930 expedition across the Great Sea of Sand, Ammonite Hill and Uweinat, and the 1932 "6,000 Miles" expedition. Squadron Leader Penderel had persuaded the RAF (Royal Air Force) that the use of their Vickers Victoria troop carrier aircraft in unofficial support was in the interets of the Service, which established a long relationship with Bagnold's parties.

In 1929, the introduction of the "new" Ford—the Model "A"—meant that the desert could now be penetrated and explored much further. The DSD and Lieutenant Uniake of the FDA tested the early production models with considerable success, as did Bagnold. The change from a three-speed car gear-box to a four-speed lorry type gear box was found to be necessary. The next problem was the size of tyres available. Six-inch tyres were used to cross the Great Sea of Sand in 1930, but by the end of 1933 the nine-inch Dunlop tyre on 13-inch wheels had arrived, solving that problem.

Not until 1933 was there official British Army interest in the desert apart from the War Office Experimental Column, which tested a variety of vehicles from Cairo to the Ugandan frontier and back, a project in which Lieutenant Guy Prendergast took part.

Hungarian Count Ladislas Eduado Almasy, variously known as Lazlo or Teddy, was an aviator enthralled by the desert. He had driven Steyr vehicles from Mombasa to Cairo in 1929, and in 1931 he flew a Gipsy Moth light aircraft to Egypt, but it was damaged on the way out.

Sir Robert Clayton East Clayton, recently married and owner of a similar aircraft, was looking for adventure when he heard of the Zerzura Club in London, who put him in touch with Almasy in Hungary. They planned a joint expedition to find the "Lost Oasis of Zerzura" using Sir Robert Clayton's aircraft. In Cairo it was arranged for Major Patrick Clayton to guide them in a follow-up of his quick survey of the western side of the Gilf Kebir the previous year. They could explore

*Members of the Egyptian Geological Survey in 1925. From left to right, seated:*
*P. A. Clayton (second); J. Ball (fourth); L. Beadnell (sixth); and at the far right, Walpole.*

the top of the Gilf Kebir plateau from the air. Squadron Leader Penderel took leave in order to join them. In March and April 1932 the expedition named the "Peter and Paul Hills" and extended the exploration of the west side of the Gilf Kebir to the area where the pictures of giraffes dating from prehistoric times had been found earlier. They did not find Zerzura, but wooded wadis within the Gilf Kebir were seen from the air. Lady Dorothy Clayton, herself a pilot, did not go on this expedition and they returned to England, where Sir Robert died of a virus infection that September.

The planned DSD exploration of the Great Sea of Sand began at the end of 1932. Major Clayton's first task, with his crew of drivers Abu Fudail, Manufli, and Mohammed Eid and survey men Obaid, Hassan Eid, and Hassan Shahine (who had worked with him for ten years), was the first direct east-to-west traverse across the dunes of the Great Sea of Sand long the 27th North Latitude, to the Libyan Frontier. On the plain west of the Sands a survey cairn 5 feet high and visible for a great distance was built. This is Big Cairn on the map today. The second leg of this expedition was to go due south near the 24th meridian through the Sand Sea to locate the northern parts of the Gilf Kebir plateau. Again, a nearly straight line, but along the grain of the dunes this time. On 29th December, before reaching the Gilf, they discovered deposits of Silica Glass on the open streets between the dunes. They went on to locate the northern edge of the Gilf and into the wooded wadi seen from the air, now known as Wadi Abd el Malik, and to Wadi Hamra to its east.

At the same time as Lieutenant Orde Wingate was making his camel expedition west and north from Abu Mingar, where he found Major Clayton's motorised survey party in February 1933, Lady Dorothy Clayton flew her light aircraft out to Egypt with Lieutenant Commander Roundell as co-pilot. She "intended after her husband's death to finish the work of discovery we had begun." Sir Ahmed Hassanein, as he now was, took up her case and arranged that she and Roundell would join Clayton's on-going expedition to the northern and western part of the Gilf Kebir, but without the aircraft. She bought two Fords, one of them, "Big

Bertha," had belonged to Bagnold and had the earlier nine-inch balloon tyres. Their route was across the dunes to make a Base Camp on the west side of the Great Sea of Sand, down through the sand to the Silica Glass area, west to see the giraffe pictures, and the wooded wadi that had been seen from the air the year before. They visited Kufra, and returned direct to Siwa through the Great Sea of Sand. It had all been a splendid adventure, but they had not found Zerzura. Sadly, Lady Dorothy was killed in an accident with her aircraft at Brooklands in September of the same year.

Also in early 1933, Almasy organised an expedition directed to the east and south sides of the Gilf to look for Zerzura. Squadron Leader Penderel was his mentor this time on behalf of the authorities. Dr. Richard Bermann, a wealthy Austrian, funded the operation. Prince Kemal el Dine had hoped to join the party, but died earlier in the year. They went from Kharga to Abu Ballas and Regenfeld before heading for the Gilf Kebir, where, at its southern end, they placed a memorial to Prince Kemal. Penderel, on one of his earlier official flights, had spotted a possible route right through the Gilf south of the Gap [Aqaba]. This is now the Wadi Firaq, and it had saved them going round the southern outlier of the feature. They visited Kufra and returned to the old camp near the giraffe pictures. Not far away they discovered in the afternoon light the Swimmer's Cave and its now famous pictures, which had not been noticed in 1932. That is how the place got its name, *Wadi Sura*, the "Valley of Pictures." From here the expedition moved to Uweinat and later to Cairo. Almasy returned to the South West Desert with the German Frobenius' archaeology expedition.

In the spring of 1934, Almasy took von der Esch and others to examine a cache of pottery jars between Dakhla Oasis and the well at Abu Mingar that might have connections with the lost army of Cambyses. Later in that year he was back at Uweinat with a French group. Von der Esch accompanied Almasy on other expeditions, and like Almasy at that time, was strongly suspected of spying for Germay (Nazi ambitions at that time, if any, would have been on the Berlin-to-Bagdad plan, but "spy mania" was increasing).

The "Silica Glass Research Expedition" of November 1934 with Dr. Spencer from the British Museum and Tip Little were taken by Major Clayton through the Great Sea of Sand to the silica glass area for an extensive investigation.

In 1936 the Kennedy Shaw expedition through the Western and South Western Deserts and into the Sudan included Colonel and Mrs. Strutt, Mr. McEuen, Mr. Mason and Lieutenant Harding-Newman. Major Prendergast was at that time commanding a Motor Machine-Gun Battery of the Sudan Defence Force in El Fasher and fortunately had a private aircraft there to evacuate the seriously ill Colonel Strutt. Independently of all this, Lieutenant Mitford RTC had visited Kufra, on his honeymoon, at about this time.

Hans Otto Berent was the representative of a German chemical company and made small trips into the desert around Cairo and was known to the resident community of desert travellers. Also there was Vladimir Peniakov, a Belgian sugar planter who drove his car to out-of-the-way places. In 1936 Almasy was again in the Gilf Kebir and left a dump of sealed water cans above the Aqaba.

Bagnold had left the Army and was back in early February 1938 with four other scientists working around and on top of the Gilf Kebir. This time he was mainly doing his experiments with blown sand. They noted Almasy's dump, found rock paintings in Wadi Abd el Malik, and did useful archaeological work.

In late 1939, by chance, Major Bagnold, recalled to duty and en-route to India, was delayed in Cairo. After a meeting with General Wavell in June 1940 he was instructed to set up a mobile desert force. Captain Harding-Newman was in Cairo attached to the Egyptian Army, from whom the first desert-worthy vehicles were borrowed. Kennedy-Shaw was extracted from Trans-Jordan and Clayton traced and brought from Tangyanika. Together they set up the Long Range Desert Group. Major Mitford was located in his Tank Regiment and also joined the unit. Manufli and Mohammed Eid were borrowed from the DSD, where George Murray had become Director, to take a week's camel ride around Uweinat; and Abu Fudail joined Major Clayton to drive the two borrowed desert trucks and five New Zealanders across to the tracks north of Kufra in the blazing heat of July. The names of Hatton FDA, Tom Bather FDA in Siwa are mentioned in records as helping in their various ways.

On 5 September 1940, the Long Range Desert Group (LRDG) crossed the Great Sea of Sand from Ain Dalla to Big Cairn, where they set up a landing ground and a large supply dump before Mitford's Patrol with Lieutenant Kennedy Shaw headed for the Taizerbo area north of Kufra and Clayton's Patrol went south to Wadi Gubba to await the other two Patrols' return. Soon after this, Mitford attacked Uweinat while Clayton was attacking Aujila, 500 miles to the north. By the end of October, the Italian Forces in Southern Libya were having to have their supply lines guarded, taking resources away from the main battles on the Coast, and it was time for the LRDG to strike deeper into Libya. Murzuk in the Fezzan was to be the target. Bagnold, Clayton, and Kennedy-Shaw planned carefully and Major Clayton led the force of some 24 armed trucks from Cairo, Ain Dalla, around Taizerbo and Wau el Kebir, made contact with a French supply column from Chad before arriving to achieve total surprise at both the Ford and the Airfield at Murzuk. A distance of over 1,000 miles through enemy territory. Having completed that part of their mission, the force went south to Chad to joint the Free French attack on Kufra. On 31 January 1941, Clayton's Patrol was attacked by an Italian Auto-Saharan Company unit from Kufra supported by aircraft, as they reached Gebal Sherif. Clayton and his crew were captured after their truck had been crippled from the air.

By March 1941, the Free French had captured Kufra and it became the LRDG forward base. Bagnold was promoted and Lieutenant Colonel Prendergast took over command of the LRGD from August 1941 until the end of the Desert Campaign. Kennedy-Shaw remained as Intelligence Officer. Throughout the ebb and flow of war along the coast, the LRDG used the inner desert as their route behind enemy lines, secure that no Axis Forces could follow them. Their own survey section continued mapping ahead of Allied Forces to the end.

Berent was with Afrika Korps OKW as an Intelligence Staff Officer and was able to interview Clayton in the Tripoli prisoner-of-war compound after his capture. He also went with the Sonderkommando DORA to the Fezzan. Von der Esch has not been heard of. Peniakov became the Commander of "Popski's Private Army"—the PPA— which operated successfully in Tripolitania, Calabria, and even into Venice itself.

In May 1942, Almasy delivered Rommel's spies to the Nile Valley. He took four captured British vehicles through Jalo to the Gilf not far from Wadi Sura, where

*Major Bagnold's Ford "A". Prendergast is seated; standing are, from left to right, Newbold, Holland and Dwyer, during the 1930 expedition in the Great Sea of Sand.*

he carefully hid one with reserve supplies. In three vehicles the five men went on through the Aqaba, and used his 1936 water dump. He passed by Kharga, and near Asyut he dropped the two spies. He returned with three vehicles to where the first truck was hidden. He now had four vehicles but only three people to drive so that one truck was stripped and abandoned. They returned safely to Jalo and the German lines. This part of the "Operation Salam" was audacious and well-executed by Almasy. The two spies were arrested soon after, as the whole activity had been monitored by British Intelligence. In July 1942, Almasy visited Clayton in the Prisoner-of-War camp at Sulmona and told him his story.

**P. H. Clayton** – *January 2000*

# Bibliography

ALMASY, COUNT L.E. VON, *Récentes Explorations dans le désert Libyque, 1932-1936*, Cairo, 1936.

AMMOUN, DENISE, *Egypte, des mains magiques*, IFAO, Cairo, 1993.

ATIYA, AZIZ S., *Encyclopédie Coptique*, 2 vols., New York, 1991.

AUFRÈRE SYDNEY, GOLVIN JEAN-CLAUDE, GOYON JEAN-CLAUDE, *L'Egypte restituée*, vol. 2, *Sites et temples des déserts*, Paris, 1994.

BAGNOLD, R.A., "A Further Journey Through the Libyan Desert," *Geographical Journal* 82,3, 1933, pp. 103–129, 211–235.

BAGNOLD, R.A., *Libyan Sands, Travel in a Dead World*, London, 1993.

BALL, J., "Problems of the Libyan Desert," *Geographical Journal* 70, 1927, pp. 22–38, 105–128, 209–224.

BARGUET, PAUL, *Le Livre des morts des anciens Egyptiens*, Paris, 1967.

BARRAT, J.A., B.M. JAHN, J. AMOSSE, R. ROCCHIA, F. KELLER, G. POUPEAU, E. DIEMER, "Geochemistry and the Origin of Libyan Desert Glasses," *Geochim and Cosmochim Acta* 61,9: 1953–1959; 1997.

BAYAN G., ISRAËL TER, *Le Synaxaire arménien*, Patrologia Orientalis, vol. 6, Paris, 1911, pp. 185–277.

BEADNELL, L.J., "The Sand-dunes of the Libyan Desert," *Geographical Journal* 35, 1910, pp. 379–395.

BOURGUET (R. P. PIERRE DU), s.j., *Art paléochrétien*, Lausanne, 1970.

BOURNÉRIAS, MARCEL, CHRISTIAN BOCK, *Le Génie végétal*, Paris, 1992.

CAILLIAUD, FRÉDÉRIC, *Voyage à l'oasis de Thèbes et dans les déserts situés à l'orient et à l'occident de la Thébaïde, fait pendant les années 1815–18*, Paris, 1821.

CAILLIAUD, FRÉDÉRIC, *Voyage à Meroé, … à Syouah et dans les autres oasis, fait dans les années 1819–22*, Paris, 1826.

CAPUANI, MASSIMO, *L'Égypte copte*, Paris, 1999.

CARION, ALAIN, *Les Météorites et leurs impacts*, Paris, 1997.

CHARTON, E., *Voyageurs Anciens*, Paris, 1861.

CHEVALIER, JEAN, ALAIN GHEERBRANT, *Dictionnaire des symboles*, Paris, 1982.

CLAYTON, PETER. H., *Desert Explorer, A Biography of Colonel P.A. Clayton*, Cargreen, 1998.

DAUMAS, EUGÈNE, *Le Grand Désert*, in *Histoires de déserts*, Paris, 1998.

*Dictionnaire de l'Égypte ancienne*, Encyclopedia Universalis, Paris, 1998.

*Dictionnaire de l'Académie Française*, Paris, 1752.

DIEMER, E., "Observations concernant des fulgurites sahariennes et rappel des caractéristiques principales des fulgurites en général," *Colloque sur "Lightning and Mountains,"* Chamonix, June 6–8, 1994.

DUMONT, PIERRE, "Les Ford d'Henry Ford," *La vie de l'Auto*, Fontainebleau, 1984, p. 35.

DUNAND, FRANÇOISE, ROGERT LICHTENBERG, *Les Momies et la mort en Egypte*, Paris, 1998.

*Egypt*, Knopf Guides, New York, 1995.

FAKHRY, AHMED, "The Necropolis of El-Bagawat in Kharga Oasis," *Service des antiquités d'Egypte: The Egyptian Deserts*, Cairo, 1951, pp. 67–78.

FAKHRY, AHMED, *The Oases of Egypt*, vol. 1 : *Siwa Oasis*, vol. 2 : *Bahriya and Farafra*, Cairo, 1973f.

FAKHRY, AHMED, *The Egyptian Deserts*, vol. 1: *Bahriya Oasis*, Cairo, 1942.

FAYE DR BERNARD, *Guide de l'élevage du dromadaire*, Montpellier, 1997.

FRESNEL, F., "Mémoires de M. Fulgence Fresnel sur le Waday," *Bulletin de la Société de Géographie* 13, 1850, pp. 82f.

GAUTHIER, Y., G. NEGRO, "Magharat el-Kantara (Shaw's Cave) revisité: art rupestre du sud du Gilf Kébir (Egypte du sud-Ouest)," *Sahara* 9, 1997, pp. 124–133.

GAUTIER, P.A., *Le Roue et le Vert : sémiologie de la couleur en Égypte ancienne*, Egyptology thesis presented at the University of Paris IV-Sorbonne, 2 vols., Paris, 1995.

*Geopotential and Ecology. Analysis of a Desert Region*, Catena Supplement 2, Cremlingen-Destedt, 1993.

GOYON JEAN-CLAUDE, *Rituels de l'Ancien Empire*, Paris, 1972.

GRIMAL NICOLAS, *Histoire de l'Egypte ancienne*, Paris, 1988.

GUIDI IGNAZIO, *Le Synaxaire éthiopien*, Patrologia Orientalis, vol. 7, Paris, 1911, pp. 405–408.

HARDING KING, W.J., "Travels in the Libyan Desert," *Geographical Journal* 39, 1912, pp. 133–137.

HARDING KING, W.J., *Mysteries of the Libyan Desert*, London, 1925.

HAWAD, *Caravanes de la soif*, Aix-en-Provence, 1985.

HENEIN, NESSIM HENRY, *Poteries et potiers d'Al-Qasr*, Cairo, 1997.

HERODOTUS, *L'Enquête*, Paris, 1964; *The Egypt of Herodotus*, London, 1924; *Histories*, London, 1890.

*Holy Bible*, Oxford Revised Standard Version.

HORNEMANN, FRÉDÉRIC, *Voyages dans l'intérieur de l'Afrique pendant les années 1797, 1798*, Paris, 1802.

JUX, ULRICH, "Zusammensetzung und Ursprung von Wüstengläsern aus der Grossen Sandsee Ägyptens," *Zeit. dt. Geol. Ges.*, 134, 1983, pp. 521–553.

KEMAL EL DINE, HUSSEIN (PRINCE), "L'Exploration du désert de Libye III, expédition de 1925–1926," *Revue de Géographie* 50, 1928, pp. 171–183, 320–336.

KÉRISEL, JEAN, *Le Nil : l'Espoir et la Colère*, Paris, 1999.

KRÖPELIN, STEFAN, "The Gilf Kébir and Lower Wadi Howar: Contrasting Early and Mid-Holocene Environments in the Eastern Sahara," *Environmental Change and Human Culture in the Nile Basin and Northern Africa until the second Millennium B.C.*, Poznan, 1993, pp. 249–258.

KUPER, RUDOLPH, "Between the Oases and the Nile Djara: Rohlf's Cave in the Western Desert," *Interregional Contacts in the Later Prehistory of Northeastern Africa*, Poznan, 1996, pp. 81–91.

KUPER, RUDOLPH, "Sahel in Egypt : Environmental Change and Cultural Development in the Abu Ballas Area, Libyan Desert," *Environmental Change and Human Culture in the Nile Basin and Northern Africa until the second Millennium B.C.*, Poznan, 1993, pp. 213–223.

LACARRIÈRE, JACQUES, *La Poussière du monde*, Cairo, 1997.

LANGEWIESCHE, W., *Sahara Unveiled: A Journey Across the Desert*, New York, 1997.

LECLANT, JEAN, P. HUARD, *La Culture des chasseurs du Nil et du Sahara*, 2 vols., Mémoires du Centre de Récherches anthropologiques, préhistoriques et ethnographiques 29, Algiers, 1977.

LECLANT, JEAN, "Oasis, histoire d'un mot, à la croisée des études libyco-berbères," *Mélanges offerts à P. Galand-Pernet et L. Galand*, Paris, 1993.

LECLANT, JEAN, "Per Africae Sitientia. Témoignages des sources classiques sur les pistes menant à l'oasis d'Ammon," *Bull. Inst. Fr. Archéol.* 49, Cairo, 1950, pp. 193–253.

LECLANT, JEAN, *Dictionnaire des mythologies*, Paris, 1980.

LEOPOLDO, BETTINA, *Egypte, oasis d'Ammon-Siwa*, Geneva, 1986.

LHOTE, HENRI, *Chameau et dromadaire en Afrique du Nord et au Sahara*, Algiers, 1987.

LUCAS, A., *Ancient Egyptians' materials and industries*, ed. rev. by J.R. Harris, London, 1962.

MAUPASSANT, GUY DE, *Contes et nouvelles*, Paris, 1960.

MEEKS, DIMITRI, CHRISTINE FAVARD-MEEKS, *Les Dieux égyptiens*, Paris, 1995.

MICHAŁOWSKI K., J.-P. CORTEGGIANI, A. ROCCATI, *L'Art de l'Egypte*, Paris, 1968–1994.

MICHELE VINCENZO DE, « The "Libyan Desert Glass", Scarab in Tutankhamen's Pectoral », in *Sahara*, n° 10, Centro Studi Luigi Negro, Milan, 1998

MIDANT-REYNES, BÉATRIX, "La Taille des couteaux de silex du type Djebel el-Arak et la dénomination du silex en égyptien," *Origin and Early Development of Food-Producing Cultures in North-Eastern Africa*, Poznan, 1984, pp. 261–264.

MIDANT-REYNES, BÉATRIX, *Préhistoire de l'Égypte, des premiers hommes aux premiers pharaons*, Paris, 1992.

MILLS, A., "Research in Dakhla Oasis," *Origin and Early Development of Food-Producing Cultures in North-Eastern Africa*, Poznan, 1984, pp. 205–210.

MINUTOLI, HEINRICH VON, *Caravanenzug des Freyherrn, durch die libyschen Wüste*, Berlin, 1828.

MINUTOLI, HEINRICH VON, *Reise zum Tempel des Jupiter Ammon in der libyschen Wüste*, Berlin, 1824.

MONOD, THÉODORE, "Contribution à l'établissement d'une florule du Gilf Kébir S-O. Égypte.", *Bull. Mus. natl. Hist. natl.*, 17,4, section B, Adansonia, n° 3-4, 1995, pp. 259–269.

MONOD, THÉODORE, *Les Carnets de Théodore Monod*, Paris, 1997.

MONOD, THÉODORE, *Méharées*, Paris, 1989.

MONOD, THÉODORE, ET. AL., *Sahara: The Forbidding Sand*, New York, 2000.

MURRAY'S *Handbook for Travelers in Lower and Upper Egypt*, London, 1896.

MUNIER, ROGER, *Proverbes*, Paris, 1992.

NEUMANN, KATHARINA, "Holocene, Vegetation of Western Sahara," *Environmental Change and Human Culture in the Nile Basin and Northern Africa until the second Millennium B.C.*, Poznan, 1993, pp. 153–168.

PEEL, R.F., "The Tibu People and the Libyan Desert," *Geographical Journal* 100, 1942, pp. 73–87.

PLINY THE ELDER, *Naturalis Historia*, lat./engl., 6 vols., London, 1938–1962.

POSENER, G., S. SAUNERON, J. YOYOTTE, *Dictionnaire de la civilisation égyptienne*, Paris, 1992.

ROCCHIA, R., E. ROBIN, F. FRÖLICH, J. AMOSSÉ, H. MEON, L. FROGET, E. DIEMER, "L'Origine des verres du désert Libyque : un impact météoritique," *C.R. Académie des sciences*, Paris, 322, IIa, 1996, pp. 839–845.

ROHLFS, GERHARD, *Drei Monate in der libyschen Wüste*, Cassel, 1875.

ROWLEY-CONWY, PETER, "The Camel in the Nile Valley," *Journal of Egyptian Archeology* 74, London, 1988.

RUSSEL, D.A., B. GALEB, R. HOATH, "X-Raying the Gods : What Were the Mummified Horus Falcons of Egypt?" *American University in Cairo, Bull. B.O.C.* 117 (2), 1997.

SAÏD, RUSHDI, *The Geology of Egypt*, Rotterdam, 1990.

SAINT-EXUPÉRY, ANTOINE DE, *Terre des hommes*, Paris, 1950.

SAINT-EXUPÉRY, ANTOINE DE, *The Little Prince*, San Diego, 1968.

SCHLEGEL H., A.H. VERSTER DE WULVERHORST, *Traité de fauconnerie*, Paris, 1980.

SCHÖN, WERNER, *Ausgrabungen im Wadi el Akhdar, Gilf Kébir (SW-Ägypten)* vol. 1, Cologne, 1996.

SEGAL, H., *Introduction à l'oeuvre de Mélanie Klein*, Paris, 1969.

SERS, JEAN-FRANÇOIS, THÉODORE MONOD (eds.), *Le Désert Libyque*, Paris, 1994.

SHAW, I., P. NICHOLSON, *The Dictionary of Ancient Egypt*, New York, 1995.

STRZEPEK, K.M., J.B. SMITH (eds.), *As Climate Changes: Internaitonal Impacts and Implications*, Cambridge, 1995.

*Théo, l'encyclopédie catholique pour tous*, Paris, 1992.

THORNTON, J.F. (ed.), *The Desert Fathers: Translations from the Latin*, New York, 1998.

TISCHLER, WOLFGANG, *Ökologie der Lebensraüme*, Stuttgart, 1990.

TRAUNECKER, CLAUDE, *Les Dieux de l'Egypte, Que sais-je?*, Paris, 1996.

VERNE, JULES, *Cinq Semaines en ballon*, Paris, 1939.

VIAL, YVES ET MAURICETTE, *Sahara, milieu vivant*, Paris, 1974.

*Vie des saints et des bienheureux, selon l'ordre du calendrier, avec l'historique des fêtes*, by the RR.PP. Benedictine monks of Paris, vol. 9, Paris, 1950, pp. 477–482.

VIRGIL, *Georgics*, Oxford, 1999.

VIVANT DENON, D., *Voyages dans la Haute et la Basse Égypte pendant les campagnes de Bonaparte, en 1798 et 1799*, 2 vols., London, 1807.

VIVIEN, C., *Islands of the Blest, A Guide to the Oases and Western Desert of Egypt*, Cairo, 1992.

WAGNER, GUY, *Les Oasis d'Egypte*, Cairo, 1987.

WEEKS, R.A., J.D. UNDERWOOD, R. GIEGENGACK, "Libyan Desert Glass: A Review," *Journ. Non-Cryst. Solids* 67, 1984, pp. 593–619.

WELLARD, J.H., *Desert Pilgrimage: Journeys to the Egyptian and Sina Deserts, Completing the Third of the Trilogy of Saharan Explorations*, not yet published.

WENDORF, F., R. SCHILDE, "Les Débuts du pastoralisme," *La Recherche* 220, April 1990, pp. 436–445.

WENDORF, F., R. SCHILDE, A.E. CLOSE, *Egypt During the Last Interglacial: The Middle Paleolithic of Bir Tarfawi and Bir Sahara East*, New York, 1993.

ZIVIE, CHISTIANE M., "En Égypte les temples de l'Oasis méridionale témoins d'une intense vie religieuse," *Archéologia* 110, Sept. 1977, pp. 30–45.

# Acknowledgements

We are neither tourists nor explorers, but travelers, as Jean-François Deniau puts it. As desert enthusiasts we have had the chance to fulfil a dream: of returning often to discover and explore in an attempt to penetrate the mysteries of the Libyan Desert, while collecting some impressions to share with others.
We should like to thank the following from the bottom of our hearts:

Our guides, Samir and Wally Lama, without whom we would never have been able to explore this desert; thanks to them, we discovered and got to know places of unimaginable beauty, crossed huge dunes and vertiginous passes, visited the treasures preserved in the oases, experienced happy moments, shared great laughter and ... *mon Dieu!* ... what wonderful memories ...

Professor Jean Leclant, Permanent Secretary of the Académie des Inscriptions et Belles Lettres, for his exciting and well-researched publications, his wise advice, his stimulating enthusiasm and his help in writing and improving this book, as well as for his preface written in such glowing terms and with so much indulgence towards the authors.

Professor Nicolas Grimal, former director of the IFAO and holder of the chair of Egyptology at the Collège de France, who spared neither time nor effort in assisting us throughout the writing of this book, making its publication possible through his encouragement and his discerning knowledge of Egypt, and always concerned that the gods regained their thrones in all authenticity, and that history was presented in all verity. We are infinitely grateful to him for the help he gave in obtaining many specially researched bibliographical documents and introducing us to experts, for his constructive criticisms and all the advice he gave us at each difficult stage, and most importantly for a previously unpublished article on the gods of the desert and his conception of our far-off ancestors.

Georges Soukiassian, archeologist with the IFAO, director of the excavations in Balat, for his cordial welcome, his many explanations about the site, the story of these exceptional discoveries, and his contribution to our book.

Professor Théodore Monod, a great expert on the Sahara, for the interest he took in our expeditions, his contagious passion for the Libyan Desert, his work that is always spiced with diverting humor, his deep knowledge of books about the desert, and his illuminating advice on what research to undertake and pursue.

Edmond Diemer, geophysician, the close and loyal colleague of Professor Théodore Monod, for the precious help he gave us in the form of stimulating, spontaneous discussions held at the heart of the desert and for his precise and rigorous scientific information that has enriched our text thanks to his experience as a geologist and his unlimited curiosity. We should also like to thank him for the abundant documentation with which he has provided us, the access to an extremely extensive bibliography, and the fruitful contacts made through him. Our great thanks also go to the naturalist Monique Diemer, his wife, for her wide-ranging knowledge, her always pertinent comments and the attention she paid to correcting the text.

Professor Rushdi Saïd, renowned geologist, who has written numerous authoritative works and publications that have become basic reference material for Egypt. An indefatigable traveler, he has crossed the Eastern Sahara and acquired an unequalled knowledge of the Nile Valley. He helped us with all his legendary enthusiasm and gave us both his own views and a synthesis of those of others on the geology of the desert.

Dr. Didier Basset and Annie, his wife, whose passion for discovery is matched by their constant and stimulating curiosity. During many journeys they provided us with scientific and astronomic information as well as some wonderful photographs.

Dr. Rudolph Kuper, director of the Heinrich Barth Institute in Cologne for his scientific contribution and close collaboration, for providing us with the results of his work, and for his rapid response to our questions.

Major P.H. Clayton and his wife, Pamela, enthusiastic traveling companions, heirs to the memory of the first explorers of this desert, loyal friends always ready to provide us with old and precious documents and eyewitness accounts of this heroic epoch.

We should also like to thank the Egyptian Service of Antiquities, the personnel in the library of the Institut Français d'Archéologie Orientale [French Institute of Eastern Architecture] in Cairo, the Centre de Recherches d'Égyptologie [Center for Egyptological Research] at the Sorbonne in Paris, as well as:

Librarian of the Abbaye Sainte Maire
Jacques Amiard
Ass. Nationale des Fauconniers et Autourciers [National Association of Falconers and Hawkers]
Aly Barakat
Catherine Berger
Paul Berliet
Pierre Stéphane Berriot
Alain and Louis Carion
Sophie Casalis
Chamalières: the curé of Notre-Dame, the Tourist Office and Institution Sainte Thécle

Hervé Charbonneaux
Antoinette Charniot, Explorer
Nadine Cherpion
Frédéric Colin
Nathalie Dupin de Saint Cyr, Spot Image
Eyzies, SERPE
Yves Gauthier
Claude Geffré
Krystina Gritten
La Hulotte magazine
Sophie de Jocas
Jean Kérisel
Pierre and Isabelle Larbey
Nathalie Leenhard
Giovanni Leonardi
Antoinette Levèque
Ligue de Protection des Oiseaux [League for the Protection of Birds]
Sébastien Marignani
Sister Maylis
Jacques and Danièle de Minvielle
Bâtonnier Mollet Vieville
Giancarlo Negro
Marie-Georges Nida
Roberta Simonis
Jean-François Terrasse
Jean-Marc Thiollay
Jacques Vettier
Guy Wagner
Phox, rue de Laborde, Paris

## Photo credits

All the photographs in this book are the authors' except for the following pages:

Bibliothèque nationale de France, Paris, Cabinet des monnaies, médailles et antiques, p. 34
Musée Calvet, Avignon, p. 35
Gamma / Marc Deville, pp. 52, 53, 54, 55
Didier Basset, Farafra, White Desert, hematite pseudomorphs, p. 66
Didier Basset, Dakhla, portico of the Temple Deir el-Haggar, p. 78
Musée du Louvre, p. 97
Artephot / Oronoz / musée du Prado, p. 97
Didier Basset, Kharga, Temple of Nadura, view of the Temple of Hibis, p. 103
Stefan Kröpelin, Paleomonsoons Project, view of Siwa and the Great Sea of Sand, (Landsat 180-40) p. 118
Archive Rolls Royce, n° 1, p. 127
Archive P. H. Clayton, n° 2, p. 127
Archive Rolls Royce, n° 3, p. 127
Archive P. H. Clayton, Ford TT, n° 4 p. 127
Archive P. H. Clayton,, n° 5, p. 127
Stefan Kröpelin, overview of Gerhard Rohlfs' cave, p. 130
Stefan Kröpelin, entrance to the cave, p. 130
Edmond Diemer, grains of sand, p. 145
NASA, barkhanes on Mars, p. 148
Spot Images and Explorer, belt of dunes north of Gilf Kebir, p. 153
Spot Images and Explorer, western edge of the Gilf Kébir, p. 161
Edmond Diemer, green Wadi Hamra, p. 168
Edmond Diemer, flora : 1, 3, 4, 5, 6, 8, 9, p. 169
Dragesco-Joffé, fennec, p.173
Dragesco-Joffé, mouflon, p.173
Didier Basset, detail of fulgurite in the sand, p. 192
Giancarlo Negro, pectoral of Tutankhamun, p. 195
Annex: Archive P. H. Clayton, p. 234 and 235

## Graphic conception

Atelier Marc Rosenstiehl